"The bursting of residential housing price bubble and the subsequent systematic financial sector meltdown in the U.S. during 2006–2008 dealt a devastating blow and shocked the world economy into its worst downturn since the Great Depression. Many countries have been affected; Asia – the fastest growing region for decades – is no exception. Drawing upon a rich set of data and references, this book provides a timely account of the impact of the global downturn on Asian economies, the ways by which policy makers attempted to remedy the situation, and the daunting challenges that Asia is facing. The crisis is not over. Many analytical and policy issues that are brought to light by the severe downturn remain to be addressed, with a fresh look and in depth. The book offers a good start."

– Wei Ge, Professor of Economics, Bucknell University, USA

"There has been a proliferation of books on the anatomy of the global economic crisis (GEC) and, to a lesser extent, on the impact of the crisis on Asia. In contrast, much less has been written on the challenges that Asia faces moving ahead in a financially integrated world. With the faster than expected recovery of Asia from the GEC, a forward looking analysis has become necessary. This book by Dowling and Rana, who have many years of experience working for the Asian Development Bank, very ably fills this gap. The book will be of value to a wide spectrum of readers – academics, policy makers, students of economics, and the general reader."

– Professor Lim Chong Yah, Albert Winsemius Chair Professor of Economics, Director of Economic Growth Center, Nanyang Technological University, Singapore

"An important lesson from the Asian Financial Crisis was that in order to manage financial globalization, policy actions were required at the national, regional, and global levels. But the V-shaped recovery resulted in complacency and reform measures were quickly forgotten. This partially set the backdrop for the present global economic crisis. This book authored by two experts on Asia, in addition to providing an analysis of the crisis and its impact on Asia, takes stock of the policy actions implemented by countries to manage financial globalization and identifies the remaining agenda. Policy makers and students alike should benefit enormously from the careful analysis that the authors have offered in this timely book."

– Barry Desker, Dean, S. Rajaratnam School of International Studies, Nanyang Technological University, Singapore

Also by John Malcolm Dowling

CHRONIC POVERTY IN ASIA – CAUSES, CONSEQUENCES AND POLICIES
(co-authored)

CURRENT ISSUES IN ECONOMIC DEVELOPMENT: An Asian Perspective
(co-edited)

ECONOMIC DEVELOPMENT IN ASIA, 2ND EDITION
(co-authored)

FUTURE PERSPECTIVES ON THE ECONOMIC DEVELOPMENT OF ASIA
(ADVANCED RESEARCH IN ASIAN ECONOMIC STUDIES)

MODERN DEVELOPMENTS IN BEHAVIOURAL ECONOMICS
(co-authored)

SOUTH ASIA – RISING TO THE CHALLENGE OF GLOBALIZATION
(co-authored)

Also by Pradumna Bickram Rana

NATIONAL STRATEGIES FOR REGIONAL INTEGRATION: South and East Asian
Case Studies
(co-edited)

PAN-ASIAN INTEGRATION: Linking East and South Asia
(co-edited)

SOUTH ASIA – RISING TO THE CHALLENGE OF GLOBALIZATION
(co-authored)

Asia and the Global Economic Crisis

Challenges in a Financially Integrated World

John Malcolm Dowling

and

Pradumna Bickram Rana

palgrave
macmillan

First published 2010 by
PALGRAVE MACMILLAN

Palgrave Macmillan in the UK is an imprint of Macmillan Publishers Limited, registered in England, company number 785998, of Houndmills, Basingstoke, Hampshire RG21 6XS.

Palgrave Macmillan in the US is a division of St Martin's Press LLC, 175 Fifth Avenue, New York, NY 10010.

Palgrave Macmillan is the global academic imprint of the above companies and has companies and representatives throughout the world.

Palgrave® and Macmillan® are registered trademarks in the United States, the United Kingdom, Europe and other countries

ISBN 978-0-230-27363-4   hardback

This book is printed on paper suitable for recycling and made from fully managed and sustained forest sources. Logging, pulping and manufacturing processes are expected to conform to the environmental regulations of the country of origin.

A catalogue record for this book is available from the British Library.

Library of Congress Cataloging-in-Publication Data
Dowling, J. Malcolm (John Malcolm)
   Asia and the global economic crisis : challenges in a financially integrated world / John Malcolm Dowling and Pradumna Bickram Rana.
     p. cm.
   ISBN 978-0-230-27363-4
    1. Asia–Economic conditions–21st century. 2. Financial crises–Asia.
   3. Asia–Economic policy–21st century. I. Rana, Pradumna Bickram,
   1947– . II. Title.
   HC412.D695 2010
   330.95–dc22   2010023750

10   9   8   7   6   5   4   3   2   1
19 18 17 16 15 14 13 12 11 10

Printed and bound in Great Britain by
CPI Antony Rowe, Chippenham and Eastbourne

Contents

List of Tables

List of Charts and Boxes

Charts

Boxes

Foreword

This volume represents a valuable addition to the literature on the current global financial crisis. It briefly describes its origins in the US, a subject well hashed over by others, deals with the responses of the US and Europe, but then moves on quickly to focus on its spread to Asia and especially on Asia's reactions to it. It convincingly demonstrates what we have come to recognize, that the advanced and developing countries are indeed well connected, for better or worse, financially and via trade. But what makes this volume rather unique is its focus on the autonomous response of Asian countries, including larger stimulus packages than in most advanced countries. Tracing the differential impact of the shocks and the response to them in four groups of Asian countries, differentiated by size, extent of export dependency, and income level is especially useful. Chapter 6 is extremely illuminating by comparing Asia's response this time around to the events of the 1990s East Asian financial crisis when both IMF advice and Asia's responses were often misguided and served to deepen the crisis.

After tracing the impact of the current crisis on employment, poverty and growth the volume finally ventures into the implications of the current experience for possible changes in the international financial architecture, the need for collective action along with individual country reforms, North and South. All in all, this volume focuses on important issues in an innovative fashion, applies a nice mix of qualitative and quantitative analysis and makes a good read, of interest to an informed general public as well as development specialists.

Gustav Ranis, Yale University

Acknowledgements

The authors would like to thank Professor Gustav Ranis, Professor Lim Chong Yah, Dean Barry Desker, and Dr Wei Ge for their support and feedback. They would also like to thank Maria B. Boritzer for invaluable editorial suggestions and assistance and Yap Chin Fang for her efficient and untiring efforts to help assemble tables, charts and other materials as well as preparation of drafts for part of Chapter 9.

In addition, Dr Dowling would like to thank the Pacific Asian Management Institute of the University of Hawaii and participants in the seminar "Asia and the Global Economic Downturn" at the Shidler College of Business, University of Hawaii on June 2, 2009 and the United Nations Economic and Social for Asia and the Pacific, Social Science Research Council, Professor Peter Pauly, Dr J.P. Verbiest and the participants in the Project LINK meeting at the United Nations Conference Centre in Bangkok, Thailand, October 26–28, 2009 for their encouragement and support.

Dr Rana would like to thank the participants in a seminar organized by the National University of Singapore in February 2010 for the valuable comments and suggestions. He would also like to thank Neeru, Abhi, and Ayush for their inspiration.

List of Abbreviations

ABF	Asian Bond Fund
ABMI	Asian Bond Markets Initiative
ACU	Asian Currency Unit
ADB	Asian Development Bank
AFC	Asian Financial Crisis
AFSB	Asian Financial Stability Board
AFTA	ASEAN Free Trade Area
AIG	American International Group
APEC	Asia-Pacific Economic Cooperation
APTA	Asia-Pacific Trade Agreement
ARRA	American Recovery and Reinvestment Act of 2009
ARM	Adjustable rate mortgage
ASA	ASEAN Swap Arrangement
ASEAN	Association of Southeast Asian Nations
ASEAN+3	ASEAN plus China, Japan, and South Korea
ASEAN+6	ASEAN + 3 plus Australia, India, and New Zealand
ASEAN 5	Indonesia, Malaysia, the Philippines, Singapore and Thailand
ASEM	Asia-Europe Meeting
BIMSTEC	Bay of Bengal Initiative for Multi-sectoral Technical and Economic Cooperation
BIS	Bank for International Settlement
bps	basis points
BRIC	Brazil, Russia, India and China
BSA	Bilateral swap arrangement
CAC	collective action clause
CAT bonds	Financial catastrophic bonds
CBO	Congressional Budget Office
CCL	Contingent Credit Line
CCT	Conditional cash transfer
CDO	Collateralized debt obligations
CDS	Credit default swap
CECA	Comprehensive Economic Cooperation Agreement
CEPA	Comprehensive Economic Partnership Agreement
CEO	Chief Executive Officer
CGE	Computable general equilibrium
CGIM	Credit Guarantee and Investment mechanism
CLI	Composite leading indicator
CLSA	Credit Lyonnais Securities Asia

CMI	Chiang Mai Initiative
CMIM	CMI multilateralization
CNMOF	California, Nevada, Michigan, Ohio and Florida
CPF	Central Provident Fund (Singapore)
CPRC	Chronic Poverty Research Center
DFID	UK Department for International Development
DSBB	Dissemination Standards Bulletin Board
ECB	European Central Bank
EHP	Early Harvest Program
EIU	Economist Intelligence Unit
EMEAP	Executives' Meeting of East Asia Pacific Central Bankers
EMS	European Money System
EONIA	Euro OverNight Index Average
ERPD	Economic Review and Policy Dialogue
ETF	Exchange-traded bond funds
EURIBOR	Euro Interbank Offered Rate
Fannie Mae	Federal National Mortgage Association
FATA	Federally Administered Tribal Area
FCL	Flexible Credit Line
FDI	Foreign Direct Investment
FDIC	Federal Deposit Insurance Corporation
Fed	Federal Reserve
FHA	Federal Housing Administration
FNC	Florida, Nevada, California
FoBF	Fund of Bond Funds
Freddie Mac	Federal Home Loan Mortgage Corporation
FSAP	Financial Sector Assessment Program
FSB	Financial Stability Board
FSF	Financial Stability Forum
FTA	Free Trade Agreement
GATT	Global Agreement on Tariffs and Trade
GDDS	General Data Dissemination System
GDS	Gross Domestic Saving
Ginnie Mae	Government National Mortgage Association
GEC	Global Economic Crisis
GDP	Gross Domestic Product
GHI	Global Hunger Index
GTAP	Global Trade Analysis Project
HDI	Human Development Index
HIBOR	Hong Kong interbank lending rate
HLI	Highly leveraged institution
ICR	Interest Coverage Ratio
ICU	International Clearing Union
IFA	International financial architecture reform

IFI	International financial institutions
IFPRI	International Food Policy Research Institute
IIF	Institute of International Finance
ILO	International Labour Organization
IMF	International Monetary Fund
IOSCO	International Organization of Securities Commissions
ISM	Institute for Supply Management
KDI	Korea Development Institute
KSSK	Financial System Stability Committee
Lao PDR	Lao People's Democratic Republic
LIBOR	London Interbank Offer Rate
LTTE	Liberation Tigers of Tamil Eelam
MAS	Monetary Authority of Singapore
MBS	Mortgage-backed securities
MDG	Millennium Development Goal
MIER	Malaysian Institute of Economic Research
MSCI (Index)	Morgan Stanley Capital International
NAB	New Arrangements to Borrow
NAFTA	North American Free Trade Agreement
NBER	National Bureau of Economic Research
NIE	Newly Industrialized Economies
NPL	Nonperforming loan
NREGA	National Rural Employment Guarantee Act
NRI	Non resident Indian (remittances)
NSDP	National Summary Data Page
NTB	Non Tariff Barrier
OECD	Organisation for Economic Co-operation and Development
OTC	over-the-counter
PAIF	Pan-Asian Bond Index Fund
PC	personal computer
PMI	Purchasing Managers' Index
PPP	Purchasing Power Parity
PRC	People's Republic of China
PSI	private sector involvement
ROOS	Rules of origin
ROSC	Report on the Observance of Standards and Codes
S&P	Standard and Poor's
SAARC	South Asian Association for Regional Cooperation
SAFTA	South Asian Free Trade Area
SAPTA	South Asian Preferential Trading Arrangement
SASEC	South Asia Subregional Economic Cooperation
SDDS	Special Data Dissemination Standard
SDR	Special Drawing Rights

SDRM	Sovereign Debt Restructuring Mechanism
SEACEN	South East Asian Central Banks
SEANZA	South East Asia, New Zealand and Australia
SEC	Securities Exchange Commission
SIV	Structured investment vehicle
SLF	Short-term Liquidity Facility
SMC	Subprime Mortgage Crisis
SME	Small and medium enterprises
SOE	State owned enterprises
SPEXP	Social protection expenditure
SPI	Social Protection Index
SPIMP	per capita social protection expenditure as a percent of the poverty line
SNB	Syndicat National de La Banque et du Crédit
SRI	Special Risk Sharing Initiative
TALF	Term Asset-backed Securities Loan Facility
TARP	Troubled Asset Relief Program
TED	T-Bill and ED (the ticker symbol for the Eurodollar futures contract)
TFP	Total factor productivity
TNC	Transnational corporations
TPS-OIC	Trade Preferential System of the Organization of the Islamic Conference
UN	United Nations
UNCTAD	United Nations Conference of Trade and Development
UNDP	United Nations Development Program
UNESCAP	United Nations Economic and Social Commission for Asia and the Pacific
VA	Veterans Administration
VAT	Value-added tax
WAC	Weighted average coupon
WAM	Weighted average maturity
WAMU	Wells Fargo and Washington Mutual
WFO	World Financial Organization
WTO	World Trade Organization
WWII	World War II

1
Introduction

The Global Economic Crisis (GEC) of 2008 and 2009 which was brought to a head by the collapse of the brokerage firm Lehman Brothers in the United States in September 2008 sent shock waves around the world. Global economic growth stuttered, exports suffered, and poverty increased. This book looks at the GEC through the lens of the Asian region and highlights the challenges that the region faces in a financially integrated world. Slightly over a decade since the Asian Financial Crisis (AFC) of 1997–98, the countries in the region were once again hit by a financial crisis. The book examines in detail: (i) how Asian countries were affected by the GEC; (ii) how they responded to the crisis – what actions they took to manage and resolve the crisis and to prevent a similar crisis from occurring in the future; and (iii) what more remains to be done. Asian countries took actions at the national (country) level and also at the regional level. Asian countries have also been active in the reform of the international financial architecture. As the world emerges from the crisis toward the end of 2009 and early 2010, the book takes stock of what has been achieved so far and what more needs to be done in the future.

Financial globalization and capital account crisis

With financial globalization, the incidence of capital account crises, defined as crises associated with large inflows and sudden reversals of private capital flows as investor sentiment changes, has increased. In such a crisis, together with foreign investors, domestic investors also liquidate their assets. Since the 1990s, there have been ten episodes of capital account crises in Mexico (1994), Argentina (1995), Thailand (1997), South Korea (1997), Indonesia (1997), Russia (1998), Brazil (1999), Turkey (2000), Argentina (2002), and Uruguay (2002) (see Ghosh, 2006, for a discussion of capital account crisis).

Capital account crises tend to differ from each other according to the trigger or proximate cause and the root causes of vulnerability. Much like a bomb that requires both an explosive material and a detonator to cause an explosion, neither the balance sheet weakness nor the crisis trigger on its

1

own is likely to cause (as much) mischief. To a large extent, the Subprime Mortgage Crisis (SMC) in the US during 2007 also fits the pattern of such a crisis. The similarities and differences between the causes of the AFC and the SMC are discussed in Box 1.1, while a detailed discussion of the SMC and how it evolved into the GEC is presented in Chapter 2.

Traditional flow-based analysis of financial crisis, focuses on the gradual build up of unsustainable budget and current account deficits.[1] Capital account analysis on the other hand focuses on shocks to stocks of assets and liabilities in sectoral balance sheets and lead to large adjustments costs with significant contagion and high economic and social costs. Capital out-flows are accompanied by liquidity shortages and an appropriate response is temporary infusion of liquidity through expansionary macroeconomic policies and foreign assistance. International Monetary Fund (IMF) conditions seek to tighten monetary and fiscal policies and that is why they were not appropriate to resolve the AFC (see note 4 in Chapter 11)

Capital account crises – Prevention, management, and resolution

What are the lessons learned from the capital account crises that have occurred around the world so far in terms of managing and resolving and in trying to prevent a similar crisis from occurring in the future in Asia? Kawai and Rana (2009) and Kawai (2010) have focused on this issue and their findings are summarized in Table 1.1.

First, actions to prevent a crisis are required through: (i) establishment of effective financial regulation and supervision system that monitors and acts on economy-wide systemic risk; (ii) implementation of sound macroeco-nomic policies (monetary, fiscal, exchange rate, and public debt manage-ment policies); and (iii) maintenance of sustainable current account and capital account positions.

Second, once a financial crisis breaks out, the authorities must limit the magnitude and duration of the crisis. Crisis management tools include: (i) provision of timely and adequate liquidity in domestic and international currency; (ii) support of ailing financial firms through guarantees, stress tests, non-performing loan (NPL) removal, and recapitalization; and (iii) adoption of appropriate macroeconomic policies to mitigate the adverse feedback loop between the financial sector and the real economy. An important challenge is how to prevent such policy measures from creating moral hazard problems.

Third, if a currency crisis evolves into a full-blown economic crisis, with systemic damages to the banking and corporate sectors, it is vital to quickly resolve the problem. Crisis resolution measures should include: (i) use of mechanisms for resolving financial firms' impaired assets and corporate and household debt; (ii) use of well-functioning domestic insolvency pro-

Box 1.1   Similarities and differences between the causes of the AFC and the SMC

No two financial crises are the same. Hence there are similarities as well as differences between the AFC and the SMC. In the case of the AFC, there were two root causes of balance sheet vulnerability. The first was policy mistakes in the form of premature capital account liberalization and the choice of pegged exchange rates (Box Table 1.1). Indonesia defied the conventional wisdom of the time, and totally deregulated its capital account in the early 1970s even before deregulating its current account. Other countries such as Thailand and Malaysia deregulated their capital accounts in the early 1990s as part of their economic reform program. This led to a surge in short-term capital inflow or hot money into these countries leading to a buildup of vulnerability. Maintenance of pegged exchange rates also contributed to excessive amount of short-term capital inflows.

Box Table 1.1   Causes of the SMC and AFC

Causes	SMC	AFC
Proximate/trigger	Bursting of the housing bubble, subprime defaults and rising foreclosures	Large withdrawal of capital by private investors
Root causes	Policy mistakes – Fed's loose monetary policy – Repeal of the Glass-Steagall Act Weak regulation and supervision of the financial sector Large and growing payments imbalance	Policy mistakes – Premature capital account liberalization – Pegged exchange rates Weak regulation and supervision of financial and corporates

The second root cause of the AFC was weak regulation and supervision of banks (and corporates in mainly Indonesia). Commercial banks had intermediated large amounts of foreign capital for domestic investment and projects with doubtful quality leading to the so-called "double mismatch" problem, i.e., currency and maturity mismatches – short-term borrowing in foreign currency to finance long-term investment in domestic currency – and vulnerability in the balance sheets of debtors (banks and corporates), which exposed them to risks of sudden changes in currency values and interest rates. Rapid capital inflows had led to excess liquidity, overinvestment and asset market bubbles. Once markets started to lose confidence about the sustainability of exchange rate, however, there was a large withdrawal of capital by investors (the trigger) exerting large downward pressure on the currencies and putting sudden brake on the overextended economic activities.

The trigger of the SMC in the United States was different since there was no capital flight reflecting the safe-haven role of the US dollar. Domestic investors, however, quickly sold off their assets. US financial institutions deleveraged their activities abroad, after the onset of the crisis, and brought in capital to meet withdrawal needs at home. In broad terms, however, the root causes of the SMC and the AFC were similar – various policy mistakes and weak regulatory and supervisory framework of financial institutions.

The proximate cause or the trigger of the SMC was the bursting of the housing bubble in the US during the summer of 2007 when subprime lenders (people who did not meet credit quality requirements) began to default and foreclosures increased. It then spread to prime loans and other types of consumer credit. Various types of financial institutions, particularly those with large exposures to subprime-related structured products, became affected leading to a series of failures of several large financial institutions (e.g., Bear Stearns, American Insurance Group, and Lehman Brothers).

The root causes of the SMC were, however, policy mistakes in the US, and the weaknesses in the regulation and supervision of the financial sector in the country. A number of policy mistakes had been made during the past few decades. First, after the bursting of the dot.com bubble in 1999–2000, the US Fed ran a loose monetary policy for several years. The Federal Funds rate dropped from 5.98% in January 2001 to 1.73% two years later and stayed at about that level until 2005. This fueled a credit boom in the US.

Second, the repeal of the Glass-Steagall Act in 1999 during the Clinton Administration opened the gates for US banks to take on the full range of risky assets (securities, derivatives, and structured products) either directly on the balance sheets or indirectly through off-balance sheet conduits. This worked well in Germany and the other European countries, but not in the US where many of the activities of investment banks and other types of financial institutions were generally outside the preview of regulators. So commercial banks and investment banks and others went into complex derivative securities and also extensively leveraged their operations. The existing regulatory system was too weak to cover investment banks.

The weak financial and corporate sectors including the regulatory and supervisory systems in the US were also very seriously at fault. Alan Greenspan, the Chairman of the Federal Reserve Board for 18 years of the boom period, confessed that he had faith that financial institutions were prudent enough to make sure that they were not lending money cheaply to people who could not pay it back. But this is exactly what happened. This Anglo-Saxon belief on the "theory of efficient and rational markets" was shattered. Self-regulation meant an absence of regulation. Incentive compensation of CEOs of financial institutions was also very high. Much of this was possible because of the decision by the Securities and Exchange Commission in 2004 to permit these types of activities. The SEC also dismantled its supervisory unit during that year.

Banks and savings and loans provided money to home buyers through mortgage loans. In the bygone era, these financial institutions would have held on and collected interest and repayments. In the modern era, housing finance institutions repackaged mortgage loans into bundles of mortgage-backed securities (MBSs) with "triple A" ratings from credit rating agencies and sold them. Financial institutions did not hold on in this originate-and-distribute model. MBSs were further "sliced and diced" into derivative assets through the process of financial engineering and sold to investors all over the world. Major chunks of these assets were moved to the books of separate structured investment vehicles in order to make balance sheets of financial institutions look healthier than they actually were. Credit default swaps provided by large insurers such as the American Insurance Group were used to insure these assets against default risks. In hindsight, there was also excessive leveraging and irresponsible lending.

National financial regulators and supervisors failed to see the large buildup and concentration of systemic risks in the US (and the United Kingdom and several other European countries). The scope of regulation and supervision was narrowly focused on insured deposit-taking firms and did not adequately cover all financial activities that posed economy-wide risks. The "shadow banking" system – comprising investment banks, mortgage brokers and originators, special investment vehicles, insurance companies writing credit default swaps, and other private asset pools – grew, as it had long been lightly regulated by a patchwork of agencies and generally not supervised prudentially. The financial supervisors failed to recognize interconnections and links across firms, sectors, and markets due to the lack of a more comprehensive macro-prudential approach.

The US Federal Reserve underestimated the seriousness of financial imbalances created by excess liquidity, housing price bubbles, and the high-leverage and wholesale funding of, and interconnections between financial firms. There is a consensus that the Fed's tardiness in raising short-term rates fueled the bubble.

The SMC spread around the world especially after September/ October 2008, as banks holding "toxic" assets engineered in the US faced difficulties. In addition to this direct effect, there were the indirect effects due to the capital flows and the trade channels. Before the outbreak of the SMC many emerging markets were receiving abundant amounts of private capital and discussions focused on the possibility of such inflows undermining the macroeconomic and financial sector stability. After that, inflows dried up leading to huge asset price depreciations and collapse in demand. Capital was sucked back into the developed countries to restore damaged balance sheets, meet margin calls, and accommodate large withdrawals. The synchronized slowdown in the industrialized countries also had a negative impact on real economic activity of emerging markets through the trade channel as import demand in the industrial world collapsed. The SMC, therefore, became a GEC.

The large and growing global imbalances – the current account deficits in the US which reached the critical level of 5% of GDP or more over the past five years and surpluses in Asia – and the recycling of Asia surpluses through purchase of US Treasuries, added further fuel to the credit boom in the US. It is interesting to note that the often repeated warnings that the global imbalance could lead to a disorderly adjustment of the dollar (for example, made by the IMF staff) did not materialize. There were calls for a "shared approach" to address the problem, but little was done. The credit boom made possible by the imbalance led, however, to a build up of vulnerability in the US by fuelling the housing boom and extension of credit to subprime lenders.

cedures for non-viable financial firms; and (iii) use of international rules for the restructuring of external (sovereign) debt as well as the resolution of non-viable, internationally active financial firms, including clear burden-sharing mechanisms among private investors and debtors and among different countries' authorities, respectively.

Finally, given that contagion of a capital account crisis tends to be extensive and global in nature, crisis prevention, management, and resolution actions need to be taken at the national, regional, and global levels.

Table 1.1 Policy actions required to prevent, manage and resolve capital account crisis

Objective	National measures	Global measures	Regional measures
Preventing or reducing the risk of systemic crises	*Establish effective financial regulation & supervision to monitor and assess economy-wide systemic risk* • Establish a national systemic stability regulator or council in charge of containing systemic risk • Improve information transparency and disclosure in financial and corporate sectors • Strengthen macro-prudential supervision with focus on consolidated supervision of systemically important institutions • Improve monitoring of household and corporate sectors • Reduce procyclicality of regulation	• Strengthen capacity, resources and effectiveness of the Financial Stability Board (FSB) to promote global systemic stability • Support implementation of international standards and codes, and best-practice corporate governance • Agree on regulations over rating agencies, hedge funds, remuneration, etc	• Establish a regional systemic stability council, such as the proposed Asian Financial Stability Dialogue • Strengthen regional monitoring of financial markets • Develop regional early warning systems
	Adopt sound macroeconomic management (monetary, fiscal, exchange rate, and public debt) • Pursue non-inflationary monetary policy • Maintain sound fiscal policy and manage public debt prudently • Use monetary policy to head off excesses, booms and asset price bubbles • Avoid boom-and-bust business cycles	• Strengthen IMF surveillance and early earning systems, with focus on systemically important economies • Utilize private-sector monitoring	• Strengthen regional policy dialogue and monitoring • Develop regional early warning system • Promote regional exchange rate policy coordination

Table 1.1   Policy actions required to prevent, manage and resolve capital account crisis – *continued*

Objective	National measures	Global measures	Regional measures
	Maintain sustainable current account and capital account positions (rebalancing growth)		
	• Avoid excessive currency overvaluation • Avoid persistent current account deficits and heavy reliance on short-term capital inflows	• Coordinate policies to avoid unsustainable global payments imbalances	• Expand regional demand where savings rates are exceptionally high
Managing crises	*Provide timely liquidity of sufficient magnitude*		
	• Formulate consistent policy packages including liquidity support with a view to reducing moral hazard problems	• Strengthen IMF liquidity support, including the new Flexible Credit Line	• Strengthen a regional liquidity support facility to contain crises and contagion
	Support the financial sector within a consistent framework		
	• Extend guarantees of bank obligations • Conduct stress tests to identify losses and capital needs of financial institutions • Establish a consistent framework for NPL removal and recapitalization	• Establish a common international rule for public sector interventions in the distressed financial system • Avoid financial protectionism	• Harmonize national interventions in the financial system – such as bank deposit guarantees – at the regional level
	Adopt appropriate macroeconomic policies to mitigate the adverse feedback loop between financial and real sectors		
	• Adopt an appropriate monetary and fiscal policy mix contingent on the specific conditions of the economy • Be prepared for extraordinary policies	• Streamline IMF conditionality • Design international fiscal support programs for fiscally constrained economies	• Strengthen regional capacity to formulate conditionality • Create regional fiscal support systems

Table 1.1 Policy actions required to prevent, manage and resolve capital account crisis – *continued*

Objective	National measures	Global measures	Regional measures
Resolving systemic crises	*Create frameworks for resolving financial firms' impaired assets and corporate and household debt*		
	• Establish frameworks for resolving bad assets of financial institutions • Introduce legal and out-of-court procedures for corporate debt workouts	• Harmonize national frameworks for resolving bad assets of financial institutions • Provide international support	• Finance regional programs to help accelerate bank and corporate restructuring
	Introduce domestic rules for exit of non-viable financial firms		
	• Establish clear legal and formal procedures for exits of insolvent financial firms	• Harmonize national resolution regimes for non-viable financial firms	• Harmonize insolvency procedures by adopting good practices
	Establish international rules for sovereign debt restructuring and insolvent financial firm resolution		
	• Strengthen national procedures for debt workout and insolvencies of non-viable, internationally active financial firms	• Introduce international rules for cross-border debt workout and insolvencies	• Develop regional rules for cross-border debt workout and insolvencies
	Provide fiscal support to help emerging and developing economies resolve crises		
	• Maintain fiscal space to prepare for crisis response and resolution	• Provide fiscal support for crisis response and resolution	• Finance regional programs to assist crisis resolution

Source: Kawai, 2010

The next section of this chapter discusses national, global, and regional actions that are necessary for one important aspect of crisis prevention that has been highlighted by the GEC, namely to establish an effective financial regulation and supervision to monitor and assess economy-wide systemic risk.

Financial regulatory reforms

The GEC has highlighted that financial regulatory reforms are critically important and should be coordinated globally. First, the cross-border operation of many financial institutions and the strong contagion effects of the global economic crisis call for multilateral actions. Second, multilateral rules would provide a level playing field and prevent regulatory arbitrage – that is, businesses running away from tightly to lightly regulated jurisdictions. Third, international regulation would reduce the influence of politicians over regulators and give the latter a certain amount of independence. This means that regulatory reforms should be addressed at three levels – the national, regional, and the global level.

Reforms implemented by Asian countries after the AFC at the national level and lack of sophistication of Asian financial markets, had enhanced the region's resilience to the present shock. The GEC has, however, exposed gaps in global standards/codes which are now in the process of being revised. Asian countries should pro-actively implement them to pre-empt future financial crises (Table 1.1). As suggested by Kawai and Pomerleano (2009), countries should also establish "systemic stability regulator" similar to the Financial System Stability Committee (KSSK) in Indonesia headed by the Finance Minister with the central bank governor and other regulators as members.

At the global level, the Group of 20 (G20) appears to have reached a broad agreement on the need to tighten regulations, but partly reflecting the complexity of the issues views still appear to differ on several issues such as compensation packages and how to deal with institutions that are too-big-to-fail (See Chapter 12 for further discussions). It was easy to get a consensus on deregulation but difficult to get a consensus the other way around. The G20 Leaders have agreed to develop internationally agreed rules to improve quantity and quality of bank capital by end of 2010 and implement them by 2012. The various standard setting bodies are at work and revised standards are to evolve over the next few years.

In terms of institutions, at the present level of political will it is not possible to establish a supreme international body with full-fledged regulatory and supervisory power over all financial institutions. Political will to establish such an institution is absent as countries would like a certain amount of autonomy over regulations.

The G20's approach has, therefore, been to extend the mandates and improve the governance of existing bodies like the Financial Stability Board (FSB), the Basel Committee on Banking Supervision, the International Association of Insurance Supervisors, and the International Organization of Securities Commissions and encourage a voluntary process of closer coordination among national regulators based on agreed multilateral frameworks. The IMF and the World Bank through their Financial Sector Assessment Programs (FSAPs) and Report on the Observance of Standards and Codes (ROSCs) have been tasked to monitor the implementation of the new standards by countries. The G20's approach is, therefore, a network-based approach rather than a rules-based one with sanctions. This may not be enough. For example, the staffing and competencies at the FSB may not be adequate.

At some point in the near future, it may make sense to consider Barry Eichengreen's proposal (2009) to establish a World Financial Organization (WFO) because unless this is done gaps that have appeared in regulatory frameworks across the world may remain and so will the vulnerability to a new crisis. Eichengreen's proposal is to establish a WFO analogous to the already-existing World Trade Organization (WTO). In the same way that the WTO establishes principles for trade policy without specifying outcomes, the WFO would establish principles for prudential supervision (capital and liquidity requirements, limits on portfolio concentrations and connected lending, adequacy of risk measurement systems and internal controls) without attempting to prescribe the structure of regulation in detail. The WFO would define obligations for its members; the latter would be obliged to meet international standards for supervision and regulation for their financial markets. Membership would be mandatory for all countries seeking access to foreign markets. The WFO would appoint an independent panel of experts to determine whether countries were in compliance of those obligations failing which the authorities would be able to impose sanctions against countries that fail to comply. Eichengreen reiterates that the WFO would not dictate regulatory conditions on countries.

At the regional level, the global economic crisis has enhanced the case for establishing the Asian Financial Stability Board (AFSB) to work with the FSB and eventually the WFO when established (see Chapter 11 for further discussion). The AFSB would be responsible for both micro-prudential as well as macro-prudential supervision.[2] The AFSB could also: (i) promote financial stability in the region by developing and implementing early warning systems of banking crises; (ii) focus on long-term financial market development and integration issues in the region; (iii) work closely with the global standard-setting bodies in identifying best practices in financial regulation; and (iv) work closely with national regulators in providing training and capacity building to financial regulators in the region.

Outline of the book

The rest of the book is organized as follows. Chapters 2 to 10 focus on the anatomy of the crisis in the United States and how it spread to the other industrial countries and Asia. These chapters also analyze the impacts and policy responses taken at the individual country level. Chapter 11 focuses on ongoing regional actions and Chapter 12 on global efforts to prevent, manage and resolve capital account crisis.

Chapter 2 of the book analyzes the history of the GEC from several different perspectives. It considers how the crisis began in the United States and spread to the rest of the world. The bubble in the housing market and development of the subprime mortgage market are discussed. The role of leverage, the lack of appropriate supervision of mortgage lenders and the role of derivatives, particularly mortgage securities, are identified. The chapter then analyzes the spread of the crisis to other industrial countries. Particular reference is made to the inter-linkages between banks and other financial institutions in the United States and Europe that contributed to the contagion of the crisis.

In Chapter 3, the spread of the crisis to Asia is discussed. There were four major ways in which financial stress was transmitted. The first was investment by investors, banks and mortgage companies in what would come to be known as "toxic" assets that emanated from the subprime mortgage crisis in the United States and Great Britain. The riskiness of these assets increased and their prices fell when the mortgage bubble burst in the US and Great Britain. Banks made large losses and stock market values fell. Asians holding these assets were adversely affected. Second, foreign direct investment and portfolio investment flows into developing countries were also adversely affected. Third, as the global crisis deepened the demand for Asian exports also began to fall and there were impacts on foreign exchange markets. The fourth channel was through remittances flows from Asians working in industrial countries to their families back home. These remittance flows have an important impact on the well-being of developing countries in Asia.

Chapter 4 discusses the stimulus measures that were undertaken by the United States and other industrial countries. The size and timing of fiscal and monetary stimulus measures are discussed and reviewed. Conventional monetary easing including interest rates and reserve requirements as well as other quantitative easing measures are discussed. Fiscal stimulus including tax and spending measures are outlined including the size, time and scope of these measures in industrial countries is discussed.

The detailed impact on Asia and its responses to the crisis are discussed in Chapter 5 and Chapter 6. The former chapter develops a taxonomy for analyzing economic developments in the Asian region. Several country groups are developed based on country size, level of development and degree of globalization. The three large economies of China, India and Indonesia are in one group. Another group comprises the richer countries of Southeast Asia and East Asia. The poorer countries that are less integrated in the global economy are grouped together and a final group comprises three countries in Southeast Asia that are sandwiched between the other richer countries in East Asia and the poorer countries in South Asia. In Chapter 6, differences in responses for different countries are reviewed and the size of fiscal stimulus as a percentage of GDP is compared. Monetary stimulus measures are also reviewed as was additional details of forecasts for domestic demand, government budgets, current account, capital flows, unemployment and remittance flows.

A snapshot of the region as of early 2010 is provided in Chapter 7 including perspectives on the length of the recession, comparison with other recessions in Asia and the outlook for 2010. Loss of income resulting from the recession is estimated and these losses compared with losses sustained during the Asian financial crisis. Further analysis of poverty and unemployment are provided.

Suggestions for Asian and global initiatives to rebalance the global economy are discussed in Chapter 8. Ways to stimulate higher saving in industrial countries as well as ways to reduce saving in Asian developing countries, with special reference to China are identified. Some of these measures include wider safety nets, reduction in incentives to invest and exchange rate revaluation.

Chapter 9 examines the expected impact of the crisis on poverty in Asian economies. Reference is made to the Asian financial crisis and estimates of the impact on the Millennium Development Goals.

The analysis of poverty and growth in 2009 and 2010 is the subject of Chapter 10 where individual country experiences and measures are discussed in more depth. Poverty and unemployment are discussed within a framework of expected macroeconomic and international trade developments. Only the countries of the region which are expected to have significant poverty impacts are discussed. This leaves out the richer countries in East Asia.

The Asian financial crisis had ignited Asia's interest in promoting regional economic integration. Chapter 11 argues that the global economic crisis has further strengthened the case for Asian regionalism. It also discusses the various efforts that have been made and identifies the next steps in the region's economic integration.

The Asian financial crisis had also led to calls for the reform of the international financial architecture (institutions, policies, and practices to promote global financial stability). Progress was, however, limited because of the region's V-shaped recovery. Chapter 12 discusses renewed efforts that are being made for crisis prevention, resolution, and management. It cautions that failure to reform the international financial architecture could sow the seeds of the next crisis in the future.

2
The Crisis and How It Unfolded in the Industrial Countries

The run up in housing prices in the United States and Great Britain at the end of the 1990s that continued until 2006 culminated in what would come to be known as the worst global recession since the great depression on the 1930s. In response to slower activity in the economy during the recession of 2001 the United States had taken an accommodative monetary stance. The prime lending rate fell from around 9% in 2001 to 4% by 2004 as the federal funds rate came down from 6% in early 2001 to an all time low of 1% by mid-2003. While moderating somewhat in 2004 and 2005 the monetary base grew by over 6% in 2002 and 2003. Lower interest rates and aggressive lending fueled a housing boom that lasted for a decade beginning in 1997. Whereas housing prices had risen in line with the cost of living for more than a decade from the mid-1980s to 1997 they accelerated rapidly thereafter. The Case-Shiller index of housing prices (available at www.standardandpoors.com/home/en/us) had increased from 62.8 in January 1984 to 74.8 in January 1997, an annual rate of less than 2%. Between January 1997 and June, 2006 it went from 74.8 to 226.17, an annual rate of around 30%. This resulted in a tripling of average home values in less than a decade and an enormous windfall in wealth for home owners. A real estate and stock market boom of unprecedented strength and breadth ensued. Interest rates on risky assets also fell. One year adjustable rate US mortgage came down from 7.25% in late 2000 to 3.5% in mid-2004. Some home owners refinanced and used the proceeds to buy durable goods, vacations and other luxury items. The rapid increase in housing values prompted many households to enter the housing market and take out mortgages even though their incomes and savings were not strong enough to qualify for a conventional mortgage. They were lured by teaser rates and liberal down payment terms.

Average housing prices accelerated as the boom moved into the new millennium, more than doubling between 2000 and the beginning of 2006. Prices increased even more rapidly in prime markets of California, Nevada and Florida. The stock market peaked on October 9, 2007 (Dow Jones

Average of over 13,000), unemployment was a low 4.5% and GDP grew at a solid 3.2% in 2006 and 2007. Inflation was moderate although increasing toward the end of the period. The boom was accompanied by a rapid growth in what has come to be called the shadow banking sector, led by a group of powerful mortgage bankers known as the "big five" including Goldman Sachs, Merrill Lynch, Morgan Stanley, Lehman Brothers, and Bear Stearns.[1] While growth in the monetary base and the money supply were on a slight downward trend from 2001 to 2006 shadow banking grew by leaps and bounds. Capital flows to developing countries also increased and spreads on emerging market bonds narrowed sharply as perceived risks of these assets continued to fall. The boom was facilitated by financial innovations, particularly structured financial products. These included a wide range of derivatives such as collateralized debt obligations (mortgaged-backed securities) and credit default swaps which resulted in a sharp increase in leverage.

The bubble spreads in the United States

Towards the beginning of the crisis, Blanchard (2008) estimated that the global losses on subprime mortgage loans could total about $250 billion. He compared this with the accumulated expected loss of global GDP (based on forecasts made in October, 2008 by the IMF) of about $4.7 trillion during the period 2008 to 2015. The loss in global stock market capitalization from July 2007 to November 2008 was expected to be even higher at $26.4 trillion, about 100 times the initial subprime mortgage loss. How did this happen? As Blanchard questions "How could such a relatively limited and localized event (the subprime mortgage loan crisis in the United States) have effects of such magnitude on the world economy?"[2] Blanchard proceeded by first looking at the initial conditions that set the stage for the crisis. Then he considered mechanisms that amplified the impacts of the crisis. Let us follow Blanchard, who identifies several key features of the crisis.

Underestimation of risk contained in newly issued assets

This growth in credit featured a variety of new financial instruments issued by non-bank financial intermediaries, typically mortgage banks or investment banks. These institutions (the "big five" mentioned previously) could not take deposits and, therefore, were not part of the Federal Reserve System. They were not governed by the same regulations as commercial banks. As a result they were able to generate a very high level of financial leverage in terms of debt relative to liquid assets. They operated by borrowing funds from investors in short-term liquid markets such as the money market and commercial paper markets and lending to corporations and invested in a variety of longer-term instruments including mortgage-backed securities and other collateralized debt instruments. The time profile of assets and liabilities for these institutions is reminiscent of the financial boom in Asia preceding the financial crisis of 1997. In the Asian crisis financial institutions undertook short-term borrowing overseas either in dollars or yen and lent longer term at home. While spreads were relatively modest there were opportunities for lots of leverage.

In the current crisis the size of lending by the "big five" and other smaller investment banks in the shadow banking system was about the same size or slightly larger than the lending by commercial banks in 2007, about $10 trillion.[3] The economy was booming and there were a variety of profit opportunities for investment banks in this shadow banking system. Their success depended crucially on the continued liquidity and perceived safety of its stream of borrowing and lending.[4]

The mortgage market was a cornerstone underpinning the security of the shadow banking system. As housing prices increased the reputation of mortgage assets also strengthened. Default rates (or non-performing loans) on housing and commercial mortgages were low in the boom years following the 2001 recession, between 0.8% and 1.5% and lower than the default rate in the 1990s.[5] In assuming that the past is prologue both borrowers and lenders came to believe that housing prices would always continue to rise. Prices for houses had increased continually since 1991, even through the recession of 2001. The optimism and perceptions of low risk extended beyond the mortgage market to credit default swaps (CDS), a kind of complex insurance policy that offered cheap insurance against different kinds of risk, in this case default on a mortgage. Since default rates were low the cost of this insurance was also low.

The growth of securitization of mortgages

By the middle of 2008 more than 60% of all US mortgages were securitized. Securitization meant that mortgages were pooled or bundled by financial institutions to form mortgage-backed securities or (MBS). There was another variation called collateralized debt obligations (CDOs) or commercial paper (structured investment vehicles or SIVs). The income streams for these securities were separated or tranched to offer a menu of assets with different risk profiles to appeal to investors with a variety of appetite for risk. Bundles containing more questionable subprime mortgages had higher returns than less risky AAA mortgages. The entire process of bundling, securitizing, tranching and selling to investors became quite arcane and complicated. The underlying risk of the bundle of assets was difficult to ascertain. The fact that the initial pool of mortgages went through a series of stages made risk even more difficult to assess. These bundles of mortgage-backed securities were composed of individual securities with different yields and maturities and also different risks.

To get a picture of the bundle averages were calculated. For example, the weighted average maturity (WAM) of an MBS is the average of the maturities of the mortgages in the pool, weighted by their balances at the issue of the MBS. Similarly, the weighted average coupon (WAC) of an MBS is the average of the coupons of the mortgages in the pool, weighted by their original balances at the issuance of the MBS. For risk analysis, mortgages are listed in three categories.

First are Prime: comprised of conforming mortgages by prime borrowers with full documentation (such as verification of income and assets) and strong credit scores, etc.

Second are Alt-A: an ill-defined category comprised of generally prime borrowers but non-conforming in some way, with often lower document- ation (or in some other way: vacation home, etc.)

Finally there are Subprime mortgages: comprised of borrowers with weaker credit scores, no verification of income or assets, etc.[6]

The market for these asset-backed securities (MBS and SIVs) grew to about $1.2 trillion in the middle of 2007, double the level of early 2005.[7] These SIVs were sold to money market funds which were then purchased by a wide range of investors including schools, hospitals, pension funds and retail investors. The leverage could be very high, as much as $85 of mortgaged-backed securities for $1 investment. Fannie Mae and Freddie Mac[8] held about $5 trillion in mortgage-backed securities in 2007. Mortgage-backed securities and other similar products are described in Box 2.1.

At the end of 2007 the Center for Responsible Lending compiled an information sheet of the subprime market[9] which is listed in Table 2.1. The dollar amount of subprime loans outstanding was $1.3 trillion. The incidence of foreclosure was 20%, suggesting a financial hemor- rhage of epic proportion. Furthermore minorities were most adversely affected since they were the most likely to have taken out a subprime mortgage.

The adverse impact on minorities and those with lower educational attainment is also reflected by higher service charges on Federal Housing Authority (FHA) approved mortgage loans to small borrowers. African Americans paid additional average closing costs of $414 for their loans while Latino borrowers averaged an additional $365. The average closing costs for all borrowers was $313 on loans that averaged $105,000. Borrowers who lived in neighborhoods where no adults have a college education paid $1,160 more closing costs for loans than borrowers that lived in neighborhoods where all adults have a college education. (See R.H. Thaler and C.R. Sunstein, 2009; Susan Woodward, 2007).

These different types of collateralized debt obligations (CDOs) or commercial paper (structured investment vehicles or SIVs) and including mortgage-backed securities were sold all over the world and the under- lying uncertainty regarding their risk went with them. As long as risks were minimal there was no problem. However that would change as the subprime market hemorrhage unfolded.

Box 2.1   Mortgage-backed securities

Mortgage-backed securities (MBS) are debt obligations that represent claims on the cash flows of pools of mortgage loans, most commonly on residential property. Mortgage loans are purchased from banks, mortgage companies, and other originators and then assembled into pools by a governmental, quasi-governmental, or private entity. The entity then issues securities that represent claims on the principal and interest payments made by borrowers on the loans in the pool, a process known as securitization.

Most MBSs are issued by the Government National Mortgage Association (Ginnie Mae), a US government agency, or the Federal National Mortgage Association (Fannie Mae) and the Federal Home Loan Mortgage Corporation (Freddie Mac), US government-sponsored enterprises. Ginnie Mae, backed by the full faith and credit of the US government, guarantees that investors receive timely payments. Fannie Mae and Freddie Mac also provide certain guarantees and, while not backed by the full faith and credit of the US government, have special authority to borrow from the US Treasury. Some private institutions, such as brokerage firms, banks, and homebuilders, also securitize mortgages, known as "private-label" mortgage securities.

Mortgage-backed securities exhibit a variety of structures. The most basic types are pass-through participation certificates, which entitle the holder to a pro-rata share of all principal and interest payments made on the pool of loan assets. More complicated MBSs, known as collateralized mortgage obligations or mortgage derivatives, may be designed to protect investors from or expose investors to various types of risk. An important risk with regard to residential mortgages involves prepayments, typically because homeowners refinance when interest rates fall. Absent protection, such prepayments would return principal to investors precisely when their options for reinvesting those funds may be relatively unattractive.

Source: US Securities and Exchange Commission available at http://www.sec.gov/answers/mortgagesecurities.htm accessed on 10 April 2009.

Note that recently both Fannie Mae and Freddie Mac have been taken over by the US government and are backed as is Ginnie Mae by the full faith and credit of the US government.

Table 2.1   Subprime crisis index (as of November 28, 2007)

Number of families who hold a subprime mortgage	7.2 million
Proportion of subprime mortgages in default	14.44%
Debt amount of subprime loans outstanding in November 2007	$1.3 trillion
Dollar amount of subprime loans outstanding in 2003	$332 billion
Percentage increase from 2003	292%
Number of subprime mortgages made in 2005–2006 projected to end in forclosure	1 in 5
Proportion of subprime mortgages made from 2004 to 2006 that come from escalating adjustable interest rates	90%
Percentage increase of interest rates on a escalating adjustable rate mortgage to 12% from 7%.	70%
Proportion of subprime mortgages approved without fully documented income	43–50%
Proportion with no escrow for taxes and insurance	75%
Proportion of 2006 home loans to African American families that were subprime	52.44%
Proportion of 2006 home loans to Hispanic and Latino families that were subprime	40.66%
Proportion of 2006 home loans to white non-Hispanic families that were subprime	22.2%
Typical increase in monthly payments (third year)	30–50%
Proportion of completed foreclosures attributable to adjustable rate loans out of all loans made in 2006 and bundled in subprime mortgage-backed securities	70%
Estimated proportion of subprime loans made by independent mortgage lenders no affiliated with a federally insured bank in 2005	52%

Source: Center for Responsible Lending, 2007

The spread of securitization to the global stage

Securitization spread across global financial institutions and created a situation where almost any bank, in any country and their customers could be holding a CDO, and SIV or a MBS. Foreign claims by banks from the top five OECD countries (US, Japan, France, Germany, UK) increased from $6.3 trillion in 2000 to $22 trillion in June 2008, a few months before the collapse of Lehman Brothers.[10] When the perceived value of these assets began to fall, the asset holders started selling and the process of deleveraging began. This is what happened toward the end of 2008 and in Q1 2009 on a global scale.

The role of leverage

Commercial banks and other financial institutions as well as the general public make more money if they can leverage their initial investment. Banks like to lend as much as they can given their fiduciary obligations to hold a certain percentage of deposits with the Central Bank. Other financial institutions have less stringent regulations and holders of subprime mortgages might have infinite leverage if they put no money as a down payment. Of course with higher leverage comes higher risk. In the run up to the financial crisis banks and other financial institutions took as much risk as they could by exerting as much leverage as possible. There were loopholes in banking regulations that allowed them to reduce capital requirements by moving assets off their balance sheets into SIVs. In 2006, for example, Citigroup had more off balance assets than assets on their balance sheet ($2.1 trillion versus $1.8 trillion).[11] Insurance companies like American International Group (AIG) which offered insurance on mortgage-backed securities and municipals bonds had a small capital base insuring assets sometimes worth 100 times more than their capital backing. And with additional leverage came more risk.

The bubble bursts, uncertainty increases and the subprime mortgage crisis unfolds

The first signs of a potential unraveling of the boom started in the US housing market. The cycle of increasingly higher housing prices fed by buyers with low credit scores, limited down payment and higher levels of debt came to an end in 2006. In 2007 and 2008 as the US housing market softened, non-performing loan (NPL) ratios increased. Housing prices fell by nearly a third from their peak with bigger declines in the highly leveraged markets (California, Nevada, Michigan, Ohio and Florida – or the CNMOF). As house prices fell the NPL rate began to rise. The impact was strongest on the construction industry, the residential property market and somewhat smaller on the commercial property market. Default rates were considerably higher in parts of CNMOF than in the rest of the country. Research also demonstrates that the response of NPLs to housing price variations was much stronger in the 1990s than in the boom years of 2001 to 2007. As house prices fell default rates rose rapidly, as they did in the 1990s. The number of annual foreclosures nationwide doubled between Q3 2006 and Q2 2008 (1.3 million) compared with 0.66 million between Q2 1999 and Q2 2006[12] and 40% of subprime mortgages originating in 2006 were delinquent by the second half of 2008.[13] By the end of 2008, 700 billion of asset-based securities had been written off by financial institutions worldwide, 500 billion by commercial banks.[14]

The introduction of the adjustable rate mortgage and a relaxation in loan qualification requirements contributed to the run up in foreclosures and related mortgage difficulties. Adjustable rate mortgages (ARM) had been popular in Great Britain, Canada and Australia for some time and more recently have been more widely used as a means of lowering monthly payments and qualifying more potential home owners. The initial rate and payment of an ARM remain in effect for a limited period that can range from one month to five years or more. Even when the initial interest rate is fixed, it can change after some time and mortgage payments can also change depending on the terms of the loan. In this case the annual percentage rate would be higher than the initial rate. The interest rate of an ARM has two components, the index and the margin. The index is a measure of general interest rates and the margin is an amount added by the lender as its profit. When interest rates change mortgage payments adjust. The amount will depend on the terms of the contract.

By mid-2008 a third of subprime ARM were delinquent or in foreclosure while nearly 12% of subprime fixed rate mortgage holders were delinquent or in foreclosure.[15] Delinquency and foreclosure rates were much lower for prime fixed rate mortgages (3%) and also for FHA and Veterans Administration (VA) mortgages (5.8%). All categories were much higher in 2008 than they were in the boom years from 2002 to 2007 (see Chart 2.1). Subprime mortgages have accounted for more than half of all foreclosures since 2006. While ARMs may have been a contributing factor, clearly the major cause of the up tick in defaults was that many unqualified borrowers were enticed into mortgages they could not afford (see Box 2.2 for further details).

Box 2.2   Decline in capital base

As the housing boom accelerated in the early part of the new millennium, ARMs became more commonplace. Aggressive lenders such as Countrywide extended mortgages to borrowers that might not have qualified in a more rigorous environment and the default rate for so-called subprime borrowers increased. These borrowers could have been attracted by teaser rates and/or low or zero down payment terms. In the best of times these borrowers might have had difficulty meeting their monthly payments. Approximately 80% of US mortgages issued in recent years to subprime borrowers were adjustable-rate mortgages. When US house prices began to decline in 2006–07, refinancing became more difficult and as adjustable rate mortgages began to reset at higher rates, mortgage delinquencies soared. Securities backed by subprime mortgages, widely held by financial firms, lost most of their value. The result was a large decline in the capital of many banks and USA government sponsored enterprises and tightening credit around the world.

To protect themselves from the risk of default investors in MBS often purchased a kind of insurance called credit default swaps (CDS). Bondholders purchased insurance to offset risk. Bond investors face two risks. The bonds can fall in value or the bond issuer can default. In the case of a mortgage which is usually not traded, the only risk is default. A CDS is insurance against default. The seller of a CDS will pay off bonds held if the bond issuer goes bankrupt. A CDS can be sold in a "cascading" manner to many different institutions in successive transactions so that each institution promises to protect the previous institution (called retrocessionaires) against the default of the original bond issuer. If there is an increased risk of default this cascading system risks a chain reaction of default.[16] As the market evolved CDSs helped transform bond trading into a highly leveraged business and banks and hedge funds began buying and selling CDSs rather than the actual bonds. By the end of 2007 the CDS market had grown to roughly $60 trillion in global business.[17] This is slightly more than global GDP in 2007, which was estimated by the World Bank at $54 trillion.[18]

As the subprime housing crisis spread many of the mortgages that were packaged and sold around the world and insured with CDS were subject to increasing risk of default and eventual foreclosure. Many banks were involved on both sides of CDS transactions and so if there was a default they incurred few losses since they would buy CDS protection on the one hand and sell CDS protection to another bank with the other. However AIG was not so fortunate. They only sold CDS protection.

As the risk of default increased for the subprime mortgages which had been bundled and securitized the cost of CDS insurance escalated rapidly. AIG, which had covered more than $440 billion in bonds, began incurring steep redemption costs. Its stock value began to fall and it was forced to sell off assets like its aircraft-leasing division. As the outlook for AIG deteriorated further the US government came to their aid with a bailout package to keep AIG from going bankrupt. The government did this because such a bankruptcy would have had a devastating and cascading impact on the liquidity of the global banking system.

> Banks all over the world bought CDS protection from AIG. If AIG is not able to make good on that promise of payment, then every one of those banks has lost that protection. Overnight, the banks have to buy replacement coverage at much higher rates, because the risks now are much worse than they were when AIG sold most of these CDS contracts. In short, banks all over the world are instantly worth less money. The numbers seems to be quite huge, possibly in the hundreds of billions. To cover that instantaneous loss, banks will have to lend out less money. That means other banks can't borrow to pay

this new cost and weaker banks might not have enough: they'll collapse. This will further shrink the global pool of money.[19]

"The process of implosion would continue as a new round of CDS payouts caused more stress for the banking system."[20] As risks continued to increase the cost of agricultural crop insurance also increased, putting further strain on AIG and other insurers.

Importance of capital adequacy

As the risk of subprime mortgages increased banks and other financial institutions wanted to sell these assets and find something to invest in that was less risky. There was a flight to quality. To complicate matters the risk of these bundled mortgage-backed securities were difficult to assess. As a result, sellers were willing to sell at a lower price than the expected present value of payments on the mortgages. This amounted to a global bank run and resulted in a kind of panic syndrome because so many institutions were exposed to these so-called toxic assets. Capital to asset ratios will be adversely affected because of leverage and more institutions will be at risk because of the popularity of MBS and CDO, and SIVs.

For now we can follow the toxic asset syndrome to other parts of the US financial system, namely the mortgage giants Fannie Mae and Freddie Mac and the government insurer FHA. Both Fannie Mae and Freddie Mac issued bonds and provided capital for home mortgages. They also purchased mortgages from banks who had lent the money to households. FHA is an insurance agency of the federal government and was started in the Great Depression to guarantee mortgages and other loans. Its original purpose was to boost home sales in the Depression by guaranteeing loans to risky borrowers and inducing lenders to offer loans to people who might not otherwise qualify either because of a low income or a limited down payment. Guidelines for conventional loans are set out by Fannie Mae and Freddie Mac. Although Fannie Mae or Freddie Mac owned the mortgages, the originating bank collected payments and handled any customer service issues.

The portfolios of Freddie Mac and Fannie Mae started accumulating lower quality mortgages beginning in 2004. Subprime and Alt-A originations (the next most risky category after subprime) in the US rose from less than 8% of all mortgages in 2003 to over 20% in 2006. During this period the quality of subprime loans also declined. Fixed rate, long-term amortizing loans which comprised the bulk of loan portfolios in the early years of the decade gave way to loans with low down payments and low but adjustable initial rates. This suggests that banks originating the loans were scraping the bottom of the barrel to find product for buyers like Fannie Mae and Freddie Mac.[21]

Around 40% of home mortgages are financed by Fannie Mae and Freddie Mac. Countrywide Financial Corporation held another 20% of home mortgages with the balance being financed by others including savings and loans and other banks. As the financial crisis unfolded everyone dealing with mortgage-backed securities and involved in credit default swaps came under intense pressure as concern about their financial viability mounted. Institutions under pressure included the major investment banks as well as Fannie Mae, Freddie Mac and Countrywide. The investment banks became involved through their bond insurance business and underwriting.

The largest of the investment banks are referred to as "bulge bracket" banks, previously referred to as the "big five" investment banks. The term "bulge bracket" refers to the first group of investment banks listed on announcement of a financial transaction or deal. The bank responsible for organizing and controlling the allocation of securities to investors appears above the others in the announcement and this bank appears in larger letters than the others and so it may bulge out. Hence the name bulge bracket banks. The five American bulge bracket firms on Wall Street prior to late 2008 were, from largest to smallest: Goldman Sachs, Merrill Lynch, Morgan Stanley, Lehman Brothers, and Bear Stearns. In the face of huge losses and plunging stock prices all of these firms disappeared in the wake of the subprime mortgage crisis. Bear Stearns was purchased by J.P. Morgan Chase, Lehman Brothers filed for bankruptcy, Merrill Lynch was purchased by Bank of America, and Goldman Sachs and Morgan Stanley became bank holding companies in order to be able to take deposits like other commercial banks and also because there was pressure for them to become members of the Federal Reserve System. They joined other large commercial banks such as Barclays, HSBC, Citigroup, Credit Suisse, UBS and Deutche Bank which also have large investment banking departments as well as traditional commercial banking.

Faced with a decrease in the value of their assets and a lower capital base financial institutions had to attract funds from outside investors, increase deposits like commercial banks, or sell some of their assets as they deleverage. The sale of assets is complicated by the fact that their value is questionable and there are likely to be few buyers. The interaction of the mechanisms described in the previous sections has led to a downward spiral of asset prices, deleverage, rising illiquidity and insolvency. There are likely to be continuing waves of foreclosures as rate resets occur and more families suffer from layoffs and lower incomes as well as higher mortgage payments. While it is estimated that these resets peaked in 2008[22] the fallout for the rest of the financial system, stock markets and the real economy continued in 2009.

Stock markets effects

Stock market values of commercial banks and investment banks that held these toxic assets suffered huge losses as subprime difficulties spread. From the peak in 2007 United States stock markets lost approximately 50% of

Chart 2.1 Dow Jones composite index

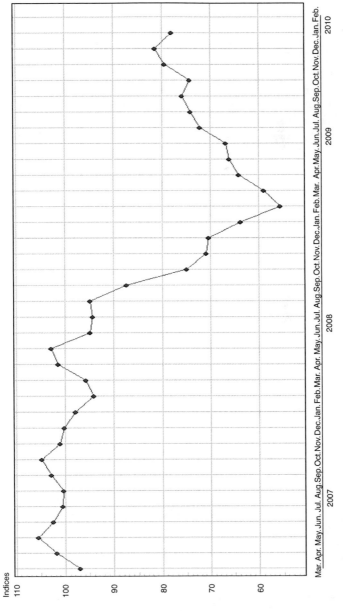

Source: Bloomberg database

its value at the bottom of the market in early 2009. The finance sector was hardest hit, losing close to 80% of value by Q1 of 2009. The automobile sector was also hard hit while other sectors suffered smaller losses. There was a stock market rally in the second half of 2009 in the US as the recession bottomed out in Q1 2009. At the end of 2009 US stocks had regained about 30% of their value from lows in early 2009 (see Chart 2.1).

TED spread

TED is an acronym formed from *T-Bill* (US treasury bill rate) and *ED*, the ticker symbol for the Eurodollar futures contract (LIBOR). The size of the spread is usually denominated in basis points (bps). For example, if the T-bill rate is 5.10% and ED trades at 5.50%, the TED spread is 40 bps. The TED spread fluctuates over time, and historically has often remained within the range of 10 and 50 bps or between 0.1% and 0.5%, until the financial crisis began in 2007. A rising TED spread indicates an increase in financial stress and credit risk and is loosely correlated with a bear market and reduced market liquidity. Since the treasury bill rate reflects a risk free return and LIBOR reflects the credit risk of lending to commercial banks, a rise in TED reflects lenders beliefs that the risk of default on interbank loans is increasing.

Chart 2.2   TED spread in hundred basis points

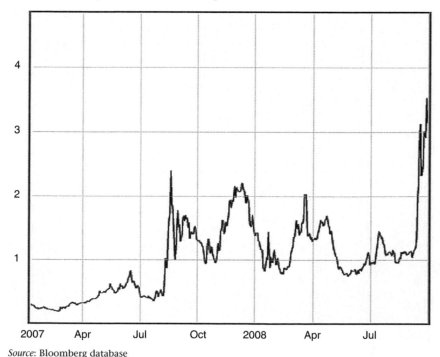

Source: Bloomberg database

As the subprime mortgage crisis unfolded in 2007 the TED spread increased. By mid-September (September 17, 2008) the TED spread exceeded 300 bps, breaking the previous record set after the Black Monday crash of 1987 and increased further to a new high of 465 bps on October 10, 2008. The TED spread in 2007 and 2008 through October 2008 is displayed in Chart 2.2.

As noted above the crisis began with the subprime markets and spread to financial institutions and money markets, then to lower risk mortgage markets and to corporate credit. It also spread to emerging markets with the fall of Lehman Brothers. With the demise of Lehman Brothers, default risk increased dramatically as the probability of large financial institutions failing rose and by the lack of government intervention to assure markets. As the crisis spread, the counterparty risk between banks also spread. This was reflected in the spiking of the TED spread. The increase in the counterparty risk also led to a sharp decrease in the maturity structure of bank to bank loans in an effort to increase asset liquidity. As the banks deleveraged, taking less risk and reducing their exposure to risky assets, they tightened lending standards for commercial and industrial loans as well as mortgages.

The subprime mortgage crisis gained momentum through the summer of 2008 and into the fall, exacerbating the political uncertainty surrounding the upcoming presidential and congressional elections in early November. In early September banks began building up excess reserves as uncertainty increased, perhaps spurred by new federal legislation (Emergency Economic Stabilization Act of 2008) that permitted the Federal Reserve to pay interest on excess reserves. The build up in liquidity in the form of excess reserves was more than ten times higher and sustained than a similar build up during the period following the September 11, 2001 attack on the World Trade Center. Excess reserve balances topped $870 billion by the end of the second week of January 2009 compared with $65 billion briefly after September 11, 2001.

After the collapse of Lehman Brothers in mid-September 2008 global financial markets seized up and economic activity took a sharp downward trend. This continued until the end of Q1 and early Q2 2009. As the crisis unfolded investors began a flight to quality that was reflected in increased interbank spread [the spread between London interbank rate and three-month US treasury bill rate (see Chart 2.3)], increased corporate spreads, falling interest rates tightening of credit by commercial banks and softening of equity markets. On Monday, September 29 it was announced that Wachovia, the fourth largest bank in the United States, would be acquired by Citigroup.

Stock market impact

On September 29, the Dow dropped 777 points (6.98%), the largest one-day point-drop in history. The Emergency Economic Stabilization Act of 2008 was voted down by the House of Representatives on Monday,

Chart 2.3   Spread between the US dollar London Interbank Offer Rate (LIBOR) and the overnight index swap rate

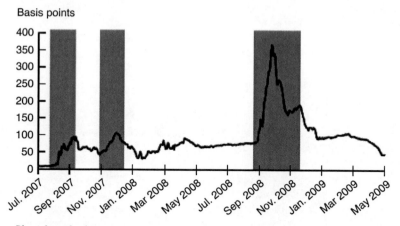

Source: Bloomberg database

September 29 and stock markets suffered further steep declines as a result. The bonds of the bankrupt Lehman Brothers were auctioned on Friday, October 10. They sold for a little over 8 cents on the dollar. Apprehension that credit default swap payouts would create large losses was unfounded as there were many countervailing claims. On October 11, the United States government announced a change in emphasis in its rescue efforts from buying illiquid assets to recapitalizing banks, including strong banks, in exchange for preferred equity; and purchase of mortgages by Fannie Mae and Freddie Mac. On Tuesday October 14, the United States announced a plan to take an equity interest of $250 billion in US banks with 25 billion going to each of the four largest banks. The nine largest banks in the US: Goldman Sachs, Morgan Stanley, J.P. Morgan, Bank of America, Merrill Lynch, Citigroup, Wells Fargo, Bank of New York Mellon and State Street were called in to a meeting on the morning of Monday 13 October. All eventually agreed to sign up. By Friday, November 13, stock losses in United States markets during 2008 as measured by the S&P 500 were equivalent to those suffered in 1931, over 50%. On November 20, the Dow Jones Industrial Average dropped 445 points in the last minutes of the trading session, closing at 7,552, the lowest point in six years. Shares in Citigroup plummeted another 26%, and shares of other major US financial institutions dropped by more than 10%. In March 2009, Blackstone Group CEO Stephen Schwarzman said that up to 45% of global wealth had been destroyed by the global financial crisis. By March 9, 2009, the Dow had fallen to 6,440, a percentage decline from its peak, exceeding the pace of the market's fall during the Great Depression and a level which the index had last seen in 1996. This was the bottom of the bear market. By April 14, financial stocks had rallied more than 90% in just over a month. Later in April, Federal Reserve Chairman Ben Bernanke said that the recession in the United States would recede and the recovery would begin later in the year. On April 20, the IMF released its World Economic Outlook. Its outlook for industrialized countries was much less optimistic than its earlier forecast in the fall of 2008.

Unemployment and manufacturing impacts

As of Thursday, November 20, 2009 new applications for unemployment benefits rose to a seasonally adjusted 542,000 per week; new applications had averaged over 500,000 a week for the last four weeks. The decline in non-farm payrolls for June 2009 (about 350,000) continued to moderate for the fifth month in a row, even as the unemployment rate continued to creep up. The Institute of Supply Management's (ISM) Purchasing Managers Index (PMI) has also risen every month since its low of 32.9 in December 2008. This index is a measure of the strength of the manufacturing sector and a score above 50 indicates that the economy is growing again. The June, 2009 ISM-PMI index rose to 44.8, the highest reading since August, 2008 but still far short of the level of 50 required to signify an expansion. The ISM was last above 50 in early 2008. The US unemployment rate in June rose to 9.2% and the pace of job losses increased compared with the previous month. On July 8, the IMF World Economic Outlook released in July, 2009 stated that "The global economy is beginning to pull out of a recession unprecedented in the post-World War II era." It revised its forecast for 2010 global economic growth up to 2.5% from 1.9% a few months earlier in April 2009. However its updated outlook for 2009 global growth was 0.1% less than its April forecast. Forecasts for advanced economies remained unchanged for 2009 and upgraded by 0.6% for 2010. On September 15, a year after the collapse of the investment bank Lehman Brothers, Federal Reserve Chairman Ben Bernanke made the cautiously optimistic statement that the US recession is probably over in a speech at the Brookings Institution. In July 2009 the Standard and Poor's/Case-Shiller housing price index increased for the fourth month in a row. Average housing prices had reached fall 2003 levels although they were still around 13% below the average a year earlier. Unemployment rate in the US rose to 9.8% in September 2009, a 26-year high. This prompted officials to begin discussing new ways to help those who continue to remain unemployed and to boost employment. These include giving employers a tax credit for each new hire, allowing businesses to deduct net operating losses for five years instead of two, continuation of tax credit for first-time home buyers, extension of unemployment and health benefits and food stamp programs that are due to expire at the end of 2009. On October 14, the Dow Jones average closed at over 10,000 for the first time in more than a year. As unemployment continued to rise so did the stock market. This highlights the different perspectives on the recession from the point of view of labor markets and financial markets.

What went wrong?

Before considering the spread of the crisis from the United States to Europe, Japan and the rest of the industrial world it is useful to take a step back and consider what went wrong in the US economy. What led to the brink of a devastating depression causing untold heartache and economic turmoil for millions of Americans? There are a number of new books and bloggers telling the story; we will be brief. For more detailed analysis and insights there are three books that we would recommend (see note 23). They look at the crisis from different perspectives and by reading them the reader can get a balanced account of what went wrong and some suggestions for moving forward.[23]

Animal spirits

We have discussed many aspects of the crisis which contributed to the bubble economy that emerged. We have not discussed the psychological and emotional motivation that led so many smart and well-educated people to buy such risky assets. Most investors failed to take a skeptical look at the underlying potential difficulties that could arise if the assumptions underlying their analysis were incorrect. The introduction of new financial regulations in the Reagan and Clinton administrations, including repeal of the Glass-Steagall Act made it much easier for banks and other financial intermediaries to repackage loans and to securitize them, thus creating new assets with more opaque risk profiles and increasing their financial leverage at the same time. They thought diversifying the components in these new repackaged securitized instruments would reduce risk. Reality turned out to be completely the opposite. Greater leverage meant greater risk and the quality of the underlying home mortgages and other assets in the portfolio was also compromised. As the housing market boom took off, investor concern in establishing the underlying riskiness of these new assets virtually evaporated and everyone wanted to get on the new gravy train. The perceived underlying safety and continued appreciation in the value of houses became a hallmark of promotion for housing investment. It had not always been so. A dispassionate look at history tells us that real home prices (adjusted for inflation) have gone up a negligible 0.2% per year from 1900 to 2000 (see Akerlof and Shiller, 2009, Chapter 12). The mistaken notion that real estate should go up because the stock of land is fixed has been disproved not only by the slow growth in real home prices but also by the fact that the US economy has not been an intensive user of land for many years. Agriculture now accounts for less than 1% of GDP compared with nearly 10% before WWII. Agricultural land price inflation was not part of the build up in real estate prices neither in this real estate bubble nor in other bubbles over the last hundred years.

Given this background, why were so many people were convinced that housing prices would never go down again? The build up in real estate values as well as stock market prices and markets for many other assets at particular moments in history are subject to what Keynes called "animal spirits". "*Our basis of knowledge for estimating the yield ten years hence of a railway, a copper mine, a textile factor, the goodwill of a patent medicine, an Atlantic liner, a building in the City of London amounts to little and sometimes to nothing.*" If people are so uncertain, how are decisions made? They can only be taken as a result of animal spirits. They are the result of "*a spontaneous urge to action*". They are not, as rational economic theory would dictate "*the outcome of a weighted average of quantitative benefits multiplied by quantitative probabilities*" (quoted in Akerlof and Shiller, 2009, p. 3)

The real estate bubble was the result of such *spontaneous urges to action* of millions of potential home buyers, many of them minorities that saw home ownership as the fulfillment of their American dream. As Ackeloff and Shiller note "*as home prices rose faster and faster, they reinforced the folk wisdom about increasing prices and imbued that folk wisdom with a sense of spectacular opportunity. This feedback interacted with the contagion of ideas and beliefs to reinforce the belief in an ever-upward trend of home prices*" (Akerlof and Shiller, 2009, p. 154). Furthermore anyone who questioned the inevitability of this upward movement was looked down on as either stupid, mentally deranged or both. When the bottom eventually fell out of the market the prices of low-priced homes fell faster (see the Case-Shiller home price indices at http://www.metroarea.standarandpoors.com)

Changes in regulations or no regulations

There were changes in banking regulations that contributed to the crisis. As noted above, foremost was the repeal of the Glass-Steagall Act which allowed commercial banks to enter the investment banking business and take more risks. The repeal of Glass-Steagall Act certainly allowed banks to get into the business of mortgage-backed securities and other new financial innovations. But an analysis of who was involved in the subprime lending boom does not feature commercial banks. Instead it was the unregulated investment banks that were the major players in the new markets for structured investment vehicles and other exotic financial products. As we noted above this "shadow banking system" grew quickly to rival the asset base of the commercial banking system. The assets of the top five investment banks rivaled in size the total assets of the top five bank holding companies. And these unregulated investment banks were the fundamental source of the crisis. They were never regulated and took more and more risks and exerted more leverage as the crisis bubble got bigger. As the shadow banking system grew creating a mountain on leveraged and risky debt there were no attempts to regulate or even begin to think of regulations that would rein it in. When it unraveled there were no federal protection systems in place for investors such as the protection of bank deposits through FDIC. *"The time profile of long-term risky and relatively illiquid assets financed by very short-term liabilities made many of the vehicles and institutions in this parallel financial system vulnerable to a classic type of run, but without the protections such as deposit insurance that the banking system has in place to reduce such risks"* (Talk by US Treasury Secretary Timothy Geithner quoted in Paul Krugman, 2009, p. 161).

The Long-Term Capital Management crisis of 1998 did not serve as a warning of what was to come. Did we not learn about the need for regulation from this crisis? Nor did we learn from the Savings and Loan crisis of the 1970s. What will we learn about the need for regulation from this crisis? This question is considered in more depth in Chapter 12.

Changes in structure of housing market

Traditionally the housing market had lenders who were either commercial banks or saving and loans. Buyers had to qualify with strict income requirements and make substantial down payments of 20% or more. The mortgage was held by the lending institutions. Most mortgages were conventional at fixed rates for a term of between 15 and 30 years. Some mortgages were FHA approved and funds lent by Freddie Mac or Fannie Mae. Down payments and qualifying income for these mortgages could be somewhat lower than for conventional mortgages. All of this changed as the housing boom of the late 1990s and early years of the new millennium unfolded. Variable rate mortgages became more common, down payment requirements fell, sometimes to zero and qualifying income requirements were ignored or fudged. These new loans, called "subprime" because they were riskier, got the biggest headlines since defaults were highest among the most risky buyers.

Why did lending practices change so quickly and dramatically? First, securitization of loans, which had been limited to prime borrowers who made substantial down payments in the past, became much more common with the spread of subprime mortgages. Furthermore lenders didn't exert due diligence when assessing the repayment potential and credentials of potential buyers. There was no perceived need to do so since these mortgages would soon be sold off as part of a bundled securitized package to other investors. As these new lending practices spread with the build up of the bubble, the quality of mortgages took a nose dive. More unqualified borrowers were granted mortgages and the actual rating of the securitized packages of collateralized debt obligations also fell. There was however a cover up or camouflage of the actual risk since the questionable mortgages were bundled with other less risky ones. And there was lax oversight by regulatory agencies charged with maintaining loan quality.

Misplaced belief in the riskiness of assets and the skill of rating agencies

As noted earlier buyers of mortgage-backed securities purchased insurance to protect themselves from the risk of default. This kind of insurance became known as credit default swaps (CDS). As the subprime housing crisis spread, CDSs were subject to increasing risk of default and eventual foreclosure. While banks were both buyers and sellers of CDSs, AIG only sold CDS protection. Because AIG believed that the insurance risk was very small they had a highly leveraged position and a small capital base insuring assets sometimes worth 100 times more than the capital backing. Rating agencies like Moody's and S&P's also believed that risks of mortgage failure were low and they gave many commercial banks and investment banks high ratings even as the quality of their portfolios deteriorated. However, as the crisis unfolded, the cost of CDS insurance increased, AIG's redemption costs rose and stock prices fell. Eventually AIG had to be bailed out by the US government. The downfall of AIG serves as a lesson for the financial community as a whole. There was too much leverage and too little appreciation of the need for risk coverage.

Spread of the crisis to the rest of the industrial world

As the financial crisis evolved in the United States there were developments in other industrial countries that created crisis conditions. It began with the nationalization of Northern Rock bank by the British government on February 22, 2008 after the bank experienced a liquidity crisis. Bids to take over the bank fell through following a run on the bank by depositors, falling stock prices and nervous institutional lenders. These lenders were reticent to lend to mortgage banks as the subprime mortgage crisis spread to Europe from the United States. The flight to quality described in the previous section also reflected the sentiment in Europe and Japan as the crisis spread. Financial institutions in major financial centers including US, UK, Canada, Australia, Germany, France and the Netherlands, reported large losses on US subprime assets which led to a downward spiraling of sales and depressed asset prices as margin calls were met and sales made to restore legal capital ratios. There was a flight to safety as investors flocked to buy US treasury securities and increased their cash positions. This further depressed equity prices and contributed to a collapse in the asset-backed commercial paper market and short-term money markets.

The size of market disruption globally is evident in the volatility of the spread between the London Interbank Offer Rate (LIBOR) and the overnight swap rate index. The difference in these indices reflects market risk as well as liquidity positions of the financial system and is a similar to the TED spread discussed earlier (see Chart 2.3). The peaks in Chart 2.3 reflect the initial realization of large losses on mortgage-backed securities, the suspension of redemptions by Bear Stearns and BNP Paribas and the UK rescue of Northern Rock in the summer of 2007, write offs by UBS and Lehman Brothers in December 2007, and finally the collapse of Lehman Brothers, take over of Fannie Mae and Freddie Mac by the US government and the bailout of AIG in the fall of 2008. Picking up the details of the story in September 2008 following the default of Lehman Brothers and the rescue of AIG, we highlight developments in the rest of the industrial countries.

On 30 September, 2008 the Dexia Group, a French Belgium lender incorporated in Luxembourg had exposure to the subprime mortgages of its affiliate Financial Security Assurance Inc and a large loan to a troubled German bank Depfa. Dexia had to write down losses of over $750 million. The governments of Belgium, France and Luxembourg agreed to inject $9 billion after its shares fell 30% and its credit rating was downgraded successively from AAA+ to Aa1 to Aa3 and the banks strength to C–. In Britain, the Financial Services Authority announced on Friday, October 3, 2008 that effective Tuesday, October 7, the amount of the guarantee of bank deposits would be raised to £50,000 from £35,000. Also on October 3, the government of the Netherlands took over the Dutch operations of Fortis, replacing the bailout plan of September 28, 2008. On October 6, 2008 BNP Paribas, the French bank, assumed control of the remaining assets of Fortis following Dutch nationalization of the operations of the bank in the Netherlands. Over the weekend and continuing on Monday, October 6, 2008 a major banking and financial crisis emerged in Iceland, where the exchange rate for the krona dropped by 30% against the euro. Emergency legislation was passed granting broad powers to the government to seize and regulate banks. Two banks were seized, while a third was subjected to a rescue plan and the trading of financial instruments issued by all Icelandic banks was suspended. On Monday, October 6 in response to the crises in Iceland and Holland several European countries including Denmark, Austria, Ireland and Greece assured depositors by guaranteeing bank deposits. This did not provide much support for markets as the FTSE100 index of leading British shares had its largest one-day point fall since it was established in 1984. On Sunday, October 19 the government of the Netherlands bailed out ING, the Dutch bank, with a €10 billion capital rescue plan. On Monday, October 20, 2008 the government of Belgium rescued the insurance company Ethias with a €1.5 billion capital injection. In Germany BayernLB has decided to apply for funds from the German €500 billion rescue program. Sweden announced the formation of a 1.5 trillion kronor fund to support inter-bank lending and a 15 billion kronor capital injection plan. Swedish banks were reported to be increasingly affected by the financial crisis. An IMF rescue plan for Iceland was reported to be near finalization while the Ukraine was reported to be in discussions with the IMF. Iceland was reported to have also received assistance from Denmark and

Norway while Britain has offered a loan to support compensation of British depositors in failed Icelandic bank Landsbanki. On Monday, October 20, 2008 France announced a €10.5 billion rescue plan for six of its largest banks, including Crédit Agricole, BNP and Société Générale. In Asia, Japan announced its second economic stimulus plan of $51 billion on Thursday, October 30, 2008. Hong Kong and Taiwan cut interest rates while an interest cut to 0.3% was announced by the Bank of Japan on Friday, October 31, 2008. Also on Thursday, October 30, 2008 the Federal Reserve established a $30 billion currency swap line with South Korea and Singapore as well as with Brazil and Mexico. In the UK car sales fell by 23% in October 2008 following a 21% decline in September 2008. The global economy continued to weaken through Q1 2009. On June 5, 2009 the OECD announced that its composite leading indicator series appeared to have reached a low point in February or March 2009 for many of the OECD economies and that since then markets have recovered somewhat. The TED spread has fallen steadily from 99 bps in Q1 2009 to 33 basis points in July 2009. On June 13, 2009 the Group of Eight industrialized nations acknowledged in a communiqué at the end of a two-day conference in Lecce, Italy that a strategy to reduce monetary and fiscal stimulus measures like tax cuts and lower interest rates was essential to promote a sustainable recovery over the long term. The communiqué tacitly assumed that the global economy has touched bottom and was on its way to recover from the worst recession in over 50 years. They agreed on the objectives of a strategy, dubbed the Lecce Framework to identify and fill regulatory gaps and foster the international consensus needed to rapidly implement new rules to govern the management of the global economy. In its twice yearly review of performance in industrial countries issued on June 20, 2009 the OECD revised its growth forecasts from its previous report in December 2008 and these forecasts were the most optimistic since early 2007. The latest prediction from the European Economic Network in February 2010 predicts a mild recovery in industrialized countries. In the Euro area, real GDP expanded for the first time in the Q3 2009 at 0.4% after contracting for five quarters. The upswing in domestic demand is temporary as the effect of government stimulus programs such as cash for clunkers is fading. There is some rebound in external demand. However the current concerns weighing on minds of government are soaring fiscal deficits and the timing to withdraw stimulus. Would industrialized countries move from financial crisis to sovereign debt and government failure? However, that is a new story altogether. We suspend the story here and move next to the transmission of the crisis to developing countries in Asia.

3
Transmission to Developing Countries in Asia

The short chronicle of financial developments in industrial countries during the crucial build up of the global recession and the spread of the crisis to the rest of the industrial world highlight the speed and ferocity of the financial meltdown as well as the timid response of central banks and governments. Regulators were initially fearful of choking off the economic boom while at the same time underestimating the power of leverage and the riskiness of many of the arcane financial instruments that were being marketed and sold so aggressively and widely by investment banks in the so called "shadow banking system". The degree of potential systemic risk was also underestimated. Investor panic and fear of default on subprime mortgages played a central role and this was compounded by the lack of risk transparency. In most cases it was a liquidity crisis not a solvency crisis. Since banks were unwilling to lend to each other even solvent banks were stressed because they were unable to meet withdrawal demands of jittery investors or to meet their short-term obligations that had been traditionally dealt with through short-term borrowing or trade credit. The crisis of confidence was widespread. The secondary impact of the subprime mortgage crisis was a crisis of trust and expectations which often morphed into depositor panic and sharp deterioration of equity markets. This perceived risk resulted in loss of capital and deposits and could only be stopped by sale to a more stable bank or by government or central bank intervention. By the fall of 2009 it became clear that the bottom of the recession has been reached while the process of rebuilding confidence and further growth began slowly and with substantial caution. The IMF downgraded its outlook several times beginning in September of 2008. In its report released in the spring of 2009 it speaks of the *"corrosive global feedback loop that has undermined policymakers' efforts to remedy the situation"* (IMF, 2009, Chapter 1, p. 4).

How fast did the recession in industrial countries move to emerging economies in Asia? In a recent paper Balakrishnan et al (2009) found that financial stress in late 2008 surpassed the peaks experienced in the 1997–98

Asian financial crisis and that the crisis spread to all segments of the financial system and spread to all major regions in emerging economies. Balakrishnan et al (2009) also found that 70% of the financial stress in advanced economies was transmitted to emerging economies and the transmission took only took one to two months. Of course the degree and magnitude of financial stress experienced depended on a number of factors including the strength of financial linkages and the strength of the emerging economy. There were four major ways in which financial stress was transmitted.

The first was investment by foreign investors, banks and mortgage companies in toxic assets that emanated from the subprime lending crisis in the United States and Great Britain. High risk mortgages were bundled and sold around the world. As the home loan mortgage bubble burst in the United States and the UK the riskiness of these assets increased and their prices fell. Banks and other investors holding these assets suffered large losses and confidence in financial systems around the world was shaken. Stock market values tumbled. Investments in these toxic assets are a specific example of developing countries portfolio investments in equity markets in industrial countries and it is an important linkage between the two markets.

The second way industrial and developing country markets are linked is through industrial country investments in Asian equity markets and foreign direct investment in Asian economies. As the global financial crisis unfolded US and European firms and banks withdrew their stock market positions in Asian markets as a strategy for reducing portfolio risk. As the crisis deepened these portfolio movements accelerated and contributed to further deterioration of equity prices in developing Asia. Foreign direct investment was less affected although the flow of fresh direct investment was also curtailed.

The third linkage was by a general decrease in import demand in industrial countries which translated into a decline in Asian exports. The strength and pattern of this relationship in individual countries depends on a variety of factors including the mix of exports and imports and the size of the export sector in each of the developing Asian economies. The pattern of trade also is related to demand for foreign exchange and exchange rates which create an additional linkage.

The fourth channel was through remittance flows from Asians working in industrial countries to their families back home. These remittance flows are affected by economic developments in industrial countries and have an important impact on the well being of developing countries in Asia.

Without going further than equity market indicators (Chart 3.1), interest rates (Chart 3.2) interest rate spreads (Chart 3.3) and private credit growth (Chart 3.4) it is obvious that Asia was hit hard by the global crisis and the impact was nearly immediate. Stock market indices throughout Asia fell beginning in 2007 and hit bottom in Q1 2009, losing between 40% and

Chart 3.1   Change in $ value of stock market index (% per annum)

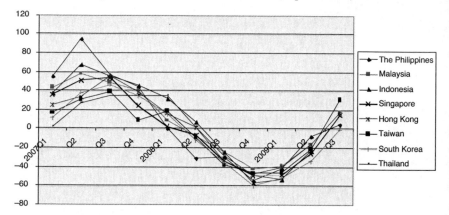

Source: EIU online database

Chart 3.2   Real interest rates

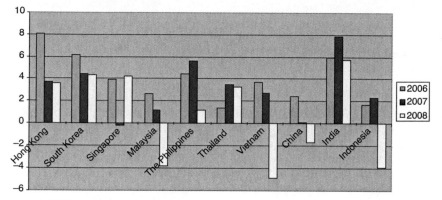

Source: World Development Indicators Online
Note: 2009 figures are EIU estimates

60% of their value compared with the Q2 2008. Real interest rates also fell in 2008 and to negative levels in Malaysia, Vietnam, China and Indonesia. Interest rate spreads widened in some countries in 2008 (Hong Kong, Singapore and Thailand) and narrowed in others before widening in 2009. Domestic credit growth in 2009 declined in most countries although it accelerated in Hong Kong and China as a result of the strong fiscal stimulus. Domestic credit growth was also up slightly in Vietnam.

Through further analysis of these four transmission mechanisms we can further our understanding of the strength, pattern and timing of global economic developments. The ability of economies to withstand further potential disruptions associated with subsequent shocks and weaknesses

Chart 3.3 Interest rate spread (lending rate minus deposit rate)

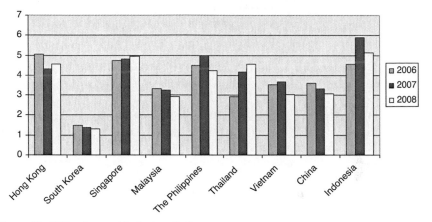

Source: World Development Indicators Online

Chart 3.4 Domestic credit growth (%)

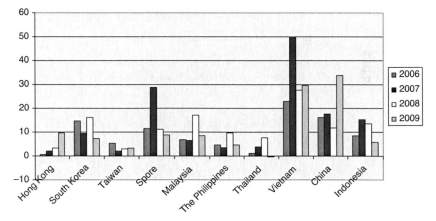

Source: EIU online database

is better understood by looking at individual countries' and financial institutions' resilience to potential stress points.

The spread of financial turbulence and investor panic in developing countries accelerated after the fall of Lehman Brothers in the fall of 2008. In hindsight many observers believe that the Lehman Brothers bankruptcy could have been avoided. It added significant risk to a global financial system already teetering on the brink of depression. Banks in industrial countries began to reduce their exposure in developing countries, closed credit lines and repatriated funds from stock markets and businesses. Those countries with greater sovereign risk as reflected by large current account deficits and volatile exchange rates were most adversely affected although there was also significant deleveraging in other economies as well. Countries which experienced exchange rate pressure placed further stress on their financial systems and some countries have had to go to the IMF for support. Pakistan was particularly vulnerable because of the political and social disruptions connected with the war against terror and the growing strength of Taliban dissidents.

Outcomes for 2010 are going to be affected by the transmission channels just described as well as specific developmental, institutional and historical factors particular to individual countries and regional subgroups. A general point to recognize is that Asian banks had limited exposure to the toxic mortgage assets that undermined confidence in industrial countries. Furthermore Asian financial systems were generally in good shape as a result of reforms undertaken following the Asian financial crisis of the late 1990s. However, slower growth in the USA and Europe is expected to take a toll on growth in developing economies of Asia primarily through the channels of portfolio investment and international trade. Slower growth of remittances and FDI will also have important negative impacts.

According to the IMF 2009 report export growth of emerging economies, including other economies in Latin America, Africa and Middle East as well as Asia was expected to falter to –0.8% in 2009 after growing at a rate of 9.6% in 2007 and 5.6% in 2008. This adverse impact is primarily a result of reduced import demand in industrial countries. The decline in exports is translating into slower growth in Asia in 2009 with a recovery anticipated in 2010.

Many observers and financial analysts initially believed the global recession would have a modest impact on Asia. Even the most pessimistic projections of global growth by the IMF in October 2008 (IMF, 2008) still showed expected global growth of 3% and a 70% confidence interval of growth between 2% and 4%. While this is not business as usual it does not reflect a serious downgrading of growth prospects in 2009. And it was reasoned that if growth was not going to be that much slower then other macroeconomic variables including unemployment, tax revenues and spending on poverty reduction would also not be seriously threatened. In its analysis of the unfolding crisis in October 2008 (IMF, 2008) did not believe that this slowdown in Asia would be as severe as the 2001/2002 recession and certainly not as severe as the Asian financial crisis of 1997/98 which took a much larger toll on economic growth.

Developments in the early part of 2009 suggested that the global recession was considerably more severe than previously believed. The recession deepened sharply in the United States toward the end of 2008 and in the first months of 2009. At the beginning of November 2008 the IMF further lowered its forecast for global economic growth from 3% to 2.2% (IMF, 2008a).

Further revisions were made in early 2009 and again later in the year. These revisions were reflected in the IMF forecasts in its World Economic Outlook in April 2009 (IMF, 2009) and in September 2009 (IMF, 2009a). The two 2009 forecasts are displayed in columns 3 and 4 of Table 3.1. Column 5 of Table 3.1 shows how dramatic the thinking of the IMF changed between the fall of 2008 and the spring of 2009. Growth was downgraded dramatically for all countries in the Asian region. However as 2009 unfolded, the forecasts were modified again and by October the forecasts were more optimistic. New forecasts for 2010 were also revised upward strengthening

Table 3.1   Projected macroeconomic GDP growth in selected Asian economies 2009 and 2010

Country	IMF October 2009 2009 forecast	IMF April 2009 2009 forecast	IMF October 2008 2009 forecast	Difference between columns 3 and 4	IMF October 2009 2010 forecast	EIU December 2009 2009 estimate	EIU December 2009 2010 forecast
China	8.5	6.5	9.3	–2.8	9.0	8.2	8.9
South Korea	–1.0 (1.0)	–4.0	3.5	–7.5	3.9 (5.5)	0.6	4.8
Taiwan	–4.1	–7.5	2.5	–10.0	3.7	–3.6	4.2
Hong Kong	–3.6	–4.5	3.5	–8.0	3.5	–3.3	3.3
Indonesia	4.0	2.5	5.5	–3.0	4.8	4.5	5.3
Malaysia	–3.6	–3.5	4.8	–8.3	2.5	–1.7	3.5
The Philippines	1.0	0.0	3.8	–3.8	3.2	1.6	3.7
Thailand	–3.5	–3.0	4.5	–7.5	3.7	–3.2	3.3
Singapore	–3.5	–10.0	3.5	–13.5	4.1	–2.7	3.9
India	5.4	4.5	6.9	–2.5	6.4	5.8	6.8
Vietnam	4.6	3.3	5.5	–2.2	5.3	4.7	6.0

Sources: IMF, 2009; IMF, 2009d values in parentheses are KDI forecasts for South Korea, November 21, 2009 and EIU Country Forecasts, December 2009

the conviction that the recession in Asia was sharply V-shaped. By the end of 2009 the EIU had increased the growth forecast for the region even further, by as much as 1.9% in Malaysia (from –3.6% to –1.7%), and from negative to positive growth in South Korea, with lesser amounts for other economies (compare column 2 and column 7 of Table 3.1).

Forecasts of international trade also predicted a dramatic decline, particularly for those used to seeing world trade increase more rapidly than global income. After increasing at a rate of 7.1% from 1991 to 2000 and even more rapidly between 2003 and 2007, the volume of world trade increased only 3.3% in 2008 and was projected to fall by 11.9% in 2009 (IMF, 2009). Clearly this dramatic decline in world trade is a major factor in dismal projected incomes and exports of the Asian economies. Columns 4

Table 3.2   **Growth in GDP per capita**

Year	South Korea	Taiwan	Hong Kong	Singapore	Indonesia	Malaysia
1973	12.0	11.0	11.1	7.0	7.1	9.0
1974	6.6	–0.4	0.9	4.3	5.7	5.7
1975	4.8	1.9	–2.5	6.4	3.7	–1.5
1976	11.9	11.4	14.9	4.2	3.4	9.0
1979	5.4	6.4	3.7	7.7	4.8	6.8
1980	–6.1	5.3	9.7	4.8	6.5	4.9
1981	4.4	3.8	6.9	7.9	6.0	4.3
1982	5.6	1.2	2.5	6.8	–0.8	3.3
1983	11.2	6.4	4.3	9.5	6.4	3.5
1984	6.8	10.0	7.6	9.8	5.2	4.9
1985	5.8	4.2	–6.5	–1.0	1.6	–3.8
1986	9.6	13.9	10.3	0.8	4.1	–1.7
1987	10.1	12.1	12.3	7.9	3.4	2.4

Year	China	India	The Philippines	Sri Lanka	Bangladesh	Pakistan
1973	5.5	1.0	5.9	5.2	0.8	3.7
1974	0.2	–1.1	0.7	2.3	6.9	0.3
1975	6.8	6.7	2.7	4.4	–6.4	1.0
1976	–3.1	–0.6	5.8	1.7	3.2	1.9
1979	6.2	–7.4	2.9	14.9	2.4	0.7
1980	6.5	4.4	2.5	–5.7	–1.6	7.1
1981	3.9	3.7	0.9	3.8	1.3	4.9
1982	7.5	1.2	1.1	2.9	–0.1	3.7
1983	9.3	5.0	–0.6	3.3	1.5	3.9
1984	13.7	1.7	–9.5	3.8	2.6	2.3
1985	12.0	3.1	–9.5	3.4	0.7	4.7
1986	7.2	2.5	1.0	2.5	1.8	2.7
1987	9.8	1.8	1.8	0.2	1.3	3.7

Sources: Chowdhury and Islam, 1993; World Bank, 2010 and Taiwan, 2008

and 5 in Table 3.5 contain the most recent ADB and EIU projections of export proceeds for 2009 in Asia. Except for India there are no positive numbers in this column and countries with less than double digit declines can count themselves lucky. The ADB simple average rate of projected decline is 14.2% in 2009 while for EIU it is slightly lower at 8.7%. The more recent forecast by EIU show some improvement for Indonesia, Vietnam and South Korea but less optimism for Taiwan, China and Hong Kong. These estimates of export growth have not been adjusted upward as dramatically as those for GDP growth. Export drag is a primary reason why 2009 was a recession year for most of the East Asian NIEs.

The severity of the economic downturn in Asia

While it now appears (early March, 2010) that the downturn has bottomed out additional insights can be gained by considering the relationship between labor market outcomes in the current downturn and previous recessions. Initial unemployment claims are displayed for the United States in Chart 3.5. The current downturn is following a similar pattern to the severe recession which began in July 1981. In that recession, it took more

Table 3.3   International reserves, government deficits and current account balances in Asian economies

Country	International reserves $ billion 2007 (Sept 2009)	Central government budget balance as % of GDP 2007 (2003)	Current account surplus/deficit as a % of GDP 2009 forecast	Short term debt as a % of reserves 2009 forecast*
China	1540 (2289)	0.7 (–2.2)	5.2 *	7
Hong Kong	153 (226)	7.2 (–3.2)	13.3*	
South Korea	262 (254)	–2.3 (–1.8)	3.8*	102
Taiwan	270 (332)	–0.2 (–2.7)	9.6*	26
Indonesia	57 (60)	–1.2 (–1.7)	1.2*	88
The Philippines	33 (38)	–0.2 (–4.6)	4.4	
Malaysia	101 (95)	–2.8 (–5.0)	13.6	15
Thailand	87 (129)	–1.7 (0.4)	5.8*	17
Singapore	163 (182)	12.2 (7.4)	16.0*	
India	306	–5.5 (–8.5)	–0.3*	9
Bangladesh	52	–3.2 (–3.4)	1.4	
Nepal	24	–2.0 (–1.4)	–0.1	
Pakistan	13	–5.8 (–3.6)	–1.5*	27
Sri Lanka	3	–7.7 (–7.8)	–4.2	
Cambodia	1	–3.2 (–6.7)	–7.8	
Laos PDR	0.5	–3.1 (–7.9)	–18.6	
Vietnam	20 (19)	–4.9 (–4.8)	–8.0	

Source: ADB, 2008 * Economist, November 28, 2009

Table 3.4   Share of exports by destination, 2007

	China	Japan	US	EU27
China		9.9	22.5	**23.7**
South Korea	**27.1**	7.1	12.3	14.8
Taiwan	**40.7**	6.5	13.0	10.9
Singapore	**20.1**	4.8	8.8	10.7
Malaysia	13.3	9.1	**15.6**	12.9
Thailand	**15.4**	11.9	12.6	13.9
Indonesia	10.0	**20.7**	10.2	11.3
The Philippines	**23.1**	14.3	16.8	16.9
Vietnam	8.1	12.5	**20.8**	19.7
India	10.3	2.2	13.8	**21.6**
Japan	**20.7**	–	20.1	14.8

Note: Exports from countries in first column to countries in first row. Highlights are largest destinations.
Source: Nomura Securities, 2009

Table 3.5   Export forecasts for 2009 and 2010

Country	CLSA in % 2009	Citibank in % 2009	ADB in % 2009	EIU in % 2009	EIU in % 2010
Thailand	−7.0	−15.4	−18.0	−13.8	6.6
Malaysia	−16.4	0.4	−13.3	−10.1	5.1
South Korea	−7.3	−16.5	−15.0	−0.6	7.5
Taiwan	−13.2	−9.3	−3.5	−11.6	9.6
China	−5.0	−8.1	−4.3	−9.0	4.8
India	0.9	−5.0	na	0.3	6.5
Singapore	−22.9 (non-oil)	−3.4	−16.0	−12.5	7.2
Indonesia	−8.5	1.0	−25.0	−10.4	13.3
Hong Kong	−7.3	−3.8	−6.2	−11.4	7.1
Vietnam	−7.4	−22.4	−31.8	−6.2	6.5
The Philippines	−13.6	−10.6	−8.4	−11.0	8.1

Source: Citibank, 2009; CLSA, 2009; Asian Development Bank, 2009 and EIU, 2009

than two years for payroll employment to return to its pre-recession level. Looking at the historical comparison of length of previous recessions a typical peak to trough real GDP contraction was 9.3% and lasted just under two years (See James et al, 2008 and IMF, 2009 for further discussion of these three transmission mechanisms and Hong et al, 2009 and Reinhart and Rogoff, 2008 for further analysis of US and Asian recessions.)

In Asia the developing economies of the region were most affected by a decline in demand for its exports as well as withdrawal of funds from equity markets, creating stress throughout the region. To appreciate the extent of this impact on Asia it is important to recognize that the Asian region is even more closely integrated with the global economy than it was a decade or two ago. Many countries now have export to GDP ratios of over 40% (China, South Korea, The Philippines, Thailand and Vietnam) and others over 100% (Hong Kong, Malaysia and Singapore). This increased export dependence means that a slowdown in demand from industrial countries will have a strong negative impact on economic growth throughout the Asian region. The ADB (2008) notes that the slowdown in the import demand of the US, Europe and Japan is particularly acute for clothing, footwear and computers.

The island states of Hong Kong and Singapore were hit particularly hard. Smaller countries with lower levels of per capita income and large trade exposure such as Malaysia, Thailand and Vietnam were also hard hit as were countries with already large budget deficits including India and the Philippines. South Asia was affected to a lesser degree since its export dependence were smaller and countries in this region are large enough to be able to compensate for a loss of export revenue by increasing consumption supplemented by fiscal stimulus.

An additional check on the likely impact of the global crisis on Asia can be obtained by looking at the historical record of income growth in Asia during the earlier United States recessions of the mid-1970s and early 1980s. There were years of negative growth in all of the newly industrialized countries of South Korea, Taiwan, Hong Kong and Singapore. Taiwan and Hong Kong registered negative growth in 1974 and 1975 respectively while only Hong Kong and Singapore experienced negative growth in the 1980s. There were also some years of negative growth in China and India in the mid-1970s and for the Philippines and Malaysia in the early 1980s. The Philippine episode of negative growth was largely a function of political problems as well as the US recession. However these years of negative or very low growth were usually followed by the resumption of strong growth after a year or two (see Table 3.2).

What pattern will the current recession follow in Asian countries and what will the evolution of growth be like in the next few years? Much will depend upon the shape and duration of the recession and recover in the United States. What is the likelihood of a strong rebound? Hong et al (2009) explore the pattern of previous crises in Asia and the United States. Using the Reinhart and Rogoff (2008) dating of average recession length in the US and using the NBER date of December 2007 as the start of the recession they suggest that the end of the recession in the US was somewhere around the end of 2009. Recent information and a recent paper by Gordon (2009) suggest an even earlier end to the recession. Gordon finds a very significant historical relationship between the cyclical peak in new claims for unemployment insurance measured as a four-month moving average and the subsequent NBER recession trough. New claims for unemployment insurance peaked in the week ending April 4. Gordon suggests that the lag between the NBER recession trough and new unemployment claims has been only a few weeks in the last five recessions. Gordon says

> it is tempting to conclude that the monthly trough on the US recession could come as early as the middle of May 2009, much sooner than most analysts.

Further discussion by Gordon supports the short lag, although there is a possibility that the April 4 peak could be exceeded in the future, which would put off the end of the recession beyond May. However analysis by Gordon and at http:bonddad.blogspot.com/2009/07/jobless-claims-comparing-corrent-data.html and the data in Chart 3.5 suggests that the April 4 peak has not and will not be exceeded. In many respects this pattern of new employment claims is similar to the 1975 recession, where jobless claims continued to be substantial many months after the recession ended. The Gordon analysis has been borne out as more data became available over the second half of 2009.

The IMF forecasts for Asia made in early 2009 (IMF, 2009) suggested that the Asian economies would experience a sharper fall in growth momentum

Chart 3.5   Initial unemployment claims as a percentage of peak value during recession, 1975–2009 (4-week Moving Average)

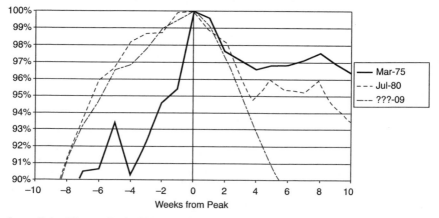

Source: Federal Reserve Bank of Minneapolis, 2010

than the US, on average. As the year progressed these observation were subject to further revision. Three of the Asian economies (China, India and Indonesia) have very large domestic economies which are serving to provide a consumption offset to the decline in exports. Nevertheless trade linkages between the smaller export dependent East Asian economies and the United States are strong and tended to drag down growth in Q4 2008 and Q1 2009. These observations are consistent with the Hong et al (2009) and the IMF analysis of Takatoshi Kata, Deputy Managing Director in a power point presentation on May 19 in Tokyo which stresses the importance of trade and financial linkages between the US and Asia as determinants of the severity of the downturn in Asia (see also Chart 3.6).

There are several other factors to consider. Although oil prices started back up in the spring and summer of 2009, it is still possible that relatively cheaper oil could add as much as 3% to GDP of Asian oil importers in 2009 and will also benefit the budgets of countries that have been offsetting higher prices by subsidies to consumers (Indonesia in particular). Furthermore countries with substantial exports of durable goods that have suffered from the lack of demand can be expected to rebound well when OECD economies begin to recover (see Chart 3.6).

The automobile industry as well as electrical goods and other machinery are highly cyclical in nature and should also recover quickly as the recovery takes hold in Asia. Housing markets were also weak in early 2009. In Q1 2009 housing prices continued to fall throughout the region although at a more subdued pace in some countries. Year-on-year declines of a few percent were recorded in China (3.9%), Thailand (1%) and the Philippines

Chart 3.6   Q4 GDP growth vs share of advanced manufactured in GDP

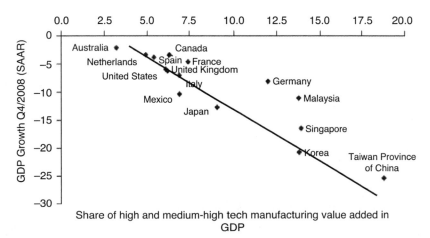

Sources: Haver Analytics; OECD; and IMF staff estimates

(1%) and more substantial declines in Hong Kong (15.7%) and Singapore (23.8%) (See Knight (2009)). The outlook changed rather dramatically as spring gave way to summer and autumn. This reflected the underlying financial strength of the region as well as the size and focus of the stimulus measures that where enacted in late 2008 and 2009. We suspend this discussion until after we have reviewed these policy responses and those of industrial countries and the Asian economies in the Chapters 4 and 5.

4
Policy Responses – Industrial Countries

In this chapter we review the policy measures industrial countries took in responses to the crisis.

United States

The United States adopted a number of policies to deal with the financial crisis and economic recession. In early 2008 a small stimulus package was enacted by the US Congress estimated at $168 billion, slightly more than 1% of GDP. It included tax incentives for businesses, income tax rebates for lower and middle-income families which were mailed out in May and June 2008. The bill also provided some help to the housing market by raising lending caps by the FHA and relaxed capital requirements for Fannie Mae and Freddie Mac as well as giving them permission to increase purchases of mortgage loans. As the subprime crisis unfolded the ventures of Freddie Mac and Fannie Mae into the mortgage-backed securities market created significant liquidity problems. Freddie Mac and Fannie Mae had been lending to prime borrowers in the past with excellent credit and large down payments. Because risks on these loans were low, leverage was quite high, as much as 70 to 1, whereas commercial banks would hold $10 of assets for every $1 of capital, a ratio of only ten to one. As the crisis deepened, in September 2008 the US Treasury put Freddie Mac and Fannie Mae in conservatorship, a fancy term for nationalization. Shareholders equity was wiped out. The fate of Lehman Brothers, also a large investor in subprime mortgages, was more or less sealed by the failure of Freddie Mac and Fannie Mae. Investors in Lehman Brothers began to sell and its stock price fell dramatically. Although the Federal Reserve and the Treasury tried to find a buyer to bail out Lehman Brothers, these efforts did not bear fruit – no one was interested. They allowed Lehman Brothers to go bankrupt, following in the footsteps of Bear Stearns a few months earlier. In hindsight that was a major blunder by the Treasury and the government. Lehman Brothers was bigger and its failure sent shockwaves through Wall Street and beyond. The FDIC insured limit of $100,000 was not high enough to keep high rollers from moving their funds out of banks that seemed shaky and a furious spate of mergers ensued. Merrill Lynch was sold to Bank of America; Wachovia was sold to Wells Fargo and Washington Mutual (WAMU), a giant saving and loan was absorbed by J.P. Morgan Chase. At the same time AIG, who had been writing insurance for mortgage-backed securities was under pressure because its credit default swap agreements were now riskier and were being downgraded by credit rating agencies. Those institutions that had bought credit default swaps demanded more collateral and this put AIG under extreme stress. With fears of another bankruptcy the Federal Reserve extended a large loan to AIG in exchange for majority ownership in AIG. In an attempt to stem the tide of rising default and escalating panic the Treasury and the Fed went before Congress with a plan to provide additional liquidity into the financial system called the Troubled Asset Relief Program – TARP for short. When the US Congress turned down the proposed $700 billion package which was short on details the stock market took another tumble. The imminent threat of another great depression caused Congress to do an about face and passed the bill a week later. In the interim the plan for TARP had changed and the Treasury now planned to buy equity in several big banks. At the same time the FDIC insurance limit was raised to $250,000 on the hopes that this would convince investors with deep pockets to keep their money in the banking system. With the election only a few weeks away there was a lull in financial activity on the hopes that the election would help bring clarity, new ideas and new leadership. However right after the election equity markets began to fall again with the news that the TARP was not going to buy up toxic mortgage-backed securities. Citigroup, one of the major investors in these securities came under pressure from its shareholders and the value of its stock plummeted. Again the Treasury had to step with a guarantee to keep Citigroup from bankruptcy.

Initially it seemed as if monetary policy would not play much of a role in combating the growing financial and economic crisis. Interest rates were already low and monetary policy was relaxed. What else could be done? The Federal Reserve began buying assets and thereby injecting money into the system. It bought securities and commercial paper either issued or guaranteed by Fannie Mae and Freddie Mac as well as a range of government bonds – the usual purchases of short-term securities that are a component of traditional open market operations and also longer-term bonds to help flatten out the yield curve and lower the cost of longer-term borrowing. Lowering rates of interest on residential mortgages was intended to put some spark back into the property market which had been continuing to add fuel to the recessionary fire particularly in a few key states (California, Michigan, Nevada, Florida and Arizona). In the spring of 2009 the Fed launched an investment facility to give private investors incentives to buy newly issued prime securities backed by residential and commercial mortgages, credit card debt and student, auto and small business loans. These were not toxic assets but a higher quality and lower risk bundle of assets that brought needed liquidity to the housing and commercial markets. It had the rather unwieldy title Term Asset-backed Securities Loan Facility (TALF for short). The Fed also took the unusual step of offering to guarantee troubled assets of struggling financial firms ranging from Bear Sterns (which ultimately failed despite the help from the Federal Government) to AIG and Citigroup. The Fed's policy of buying commercial paper was successful and interest rates began to fall and markets became more liquid. In Q1 2009 mortgage rates reached low levels and an active market in foreclosures emerged in some locations. However, the housing sector remained weak and was joined by increased weakness in the commercial property market. Several mall developers filed for bankruptcy. The TALF became operational in early 2009 and has financed $30 billion in lending, far short of its original projections of as much as $1 trillion as demand has been slow as a result of strict borrowing terms and the growing aversion of investors to finance debt. The program is scheduled to expire at the end of March 2010.

Additional fiscal stimulus was provided by the Obama administration not long after the inauguration on January 20, 2009. The American Recovery and Reinvestment Act include a potpourri of tax cuts and expenditures that were estimated at close to $800 billion, about 3% of GDP when spread out over two years. Tax cuts and spending shared about equally in the stimulus, although economists argue that spending provides more direct stimulus than tax cuts because of the balanced budget multiplier. The OECD estimates that the expenditure multiplier is about twice the size of the tax relief multiplier (See OECD, 2009 Box 3.1). Just under $300 billion of the funds from the Recovery and Reinvestment Act where scheduled to go to tax relief for individuals and businesses, $147.7 billion for healthcare, $90.9 billion for education, $82.5 billion for unemployment including food stamps, $80.9 billion for infrastructure, $61.3 billion for energy and the remainder for a variety of other programs including housing and science research. There are also provisions for tax breaks for first-time home buyers and a write off of state sales taxes and interest for purchase of new vehicles. The congressional budget office has analyzed the impact of the stimulus on GDP for the next few years. A simple schematic of the projected impact is displayed in Chart 4.1.

The Congressional Budget Office (CBO) analysis (see Chart 4.1) suggests that the depth of the recession will be substantially reduced, although the return to potential GDP will not be accelerated significantly. In the long term, the CBO expects the Recovery and Reinvestment Act to reduce output slightly by increasing the nation's debt and crowding out some private investment, but it notes that other factors, such as improvements to roads and highways and increased spending for basic research and education may

Chart 4.1   Difference between potential GDP in CBO's baseline and actual GDP without and with the impact of the American Recovery and Reinvestment Act of 2009

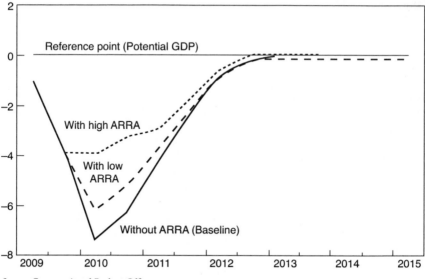

Source: Congressional Budget Office

offset the decrease in output and that crowding out was a not an issue in the short term because private investment was already decreasing in response to decreased demand.

While some argue the stimulus will burden future generations with a huge debt, others argue that the stimulus is really too small. The latter argument is based on the simple calculation of the fiscal requirement to fill a trillion-dollar shortfall in demand created by an economy that will grow much slower in 2009 and 2010 than it is capable of. OECD estimates an output gap for OECD countries of 6.5% in 2009 and 8.5% in 2010. Using the figure of 14 trillion for the estimated size of the US economy this amounts to over a $1 trillion a year in 2010 and slightly less than a trillion for 2009 (6.5% of $14 trillion and 8.5% of $14 trillion respectively in 2009 and 2010). The output gap could be lower for the US and the cost of the recession could be somewhat lower. Still, even a conservative estimate of the GDP shortfall for 2009 and 2010 would be in the range of $1.5 trillion to $2 trillion, around twice as much as the stimulus package and perhaps even more.

Potential GDP will also fall as a result of the recession. The Congressional Budget estimates a decline in potential output growth in the US of 2.3% on average per annum during the next ten years (2009–2018).[1]

The Obama administration also focused on mitigation of foreclosures by refinancing through Freddie Mac and Fannie Mae. Fannie Mae and Freddie Mac hold 25% of all outstanding mortgages in the country. Another plan is to encourage loan modifications and reduce foreclosures, although this is complicated by the fact that many mortgages are bundled as part of the collateral for mortgage-backed securities. Bankruptcy is also an option, particularly for those who are so deeply in debt that they cannot be helped by refinancing or loan modification. There could also be spillovers into the credit card business if the bankruptcy leads to default or negotiated pay down on these liabilities.

As part of the Treasury's agenda under Secretary Geithner a new plan has been proposed to further stabilize the financial sector by having the federal government finance the purchase of the bank's toxic assets, mostly mortgage-backed securities. Hand-picked private investors would bid for these assets that banks were willing to auction off. This would establish a fair price for these toxic assets (and the appropriate "haircut"), leading the way for the government to purchase these assets on a large scale. The FDIC, an experienced participant in the sale of assets of failed banks, would guarantee the debt financing for those purchasing the assets. The system has still to prove its success.

As the end of 2009 approached, the recovery from the recession appeared to have slowed down considerably, at least from the point of view of the labor market. The unemployment rate continued to increase, and by November was over 10%. The pace of job losses in June accelerated to 467,000 after four straight months of decreases and then declined slowly later in the year, finally declining to 11,000 in November, 2009. State budgets were in distress and cutbacks in spending required to balance budgets have dampened growth rather than energizing it.

Critics like Paul Krugman are lamenting the fact that the Obama stimulus package did not include more aid for the states (see Paul Krugman, 2009a).

Chart 4.2   Fiscal stimulus to GDP in the United States

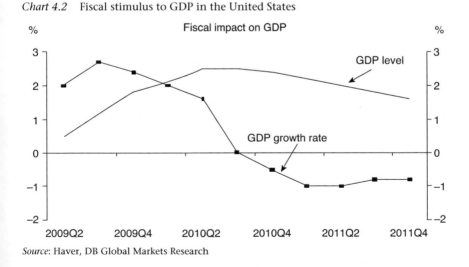

Source: Haver, DB Global Markets Research

Evidence for further weakening of the fiscal stimulus in the United States is provided by simulations by (Krugman, 2009b) and reported in Chart 4.2. While the impact on the level of GDP remains in the range of 1% to 2% the impact on the rate of change in GDP falls below zero beginning in Q3 2010 when the slope of the GDP growth curve turns negative.

It is true that history tells us that the unemployment peaks several months after the economy has reached a trough and there are some signs of business revival including the increase in the ISM index which has continued to rise since December 2008, reaching 52.9 in August 2009 and increasing further to 55.7 in October 2009. A level of 50 indicates the revival of economic growth. Nevertheless some economists were still calling for additional stimulus in 2H 2009.

European Union and Japan

With some adjustments for local conditions, the projections of economic activity in other industrial countries mirror the situation in the US. Growth collapsed at the end of 2008 and in early 2009, inflation receded, budget deficits increased and fiscal stimulus packages were put in place, unemployment rose and financial markets were slow to normalize. These developments are summarized in Tables 4.1–4.4. Growth was projected to be negative in 2009 with some recovery in 2010. House prices and financial markets have also softened and unemployment has increased and is expected to increase further in 2010. International trade is also expected to fall by double digits. Policy interest rates have been slashed to zero or very close to zero in all industrial countries and money market spreads have stabilized after spiking following the bankruptcy of Lehman Brothers. Germany and Japan have suffered because of their dependence of exports as a driver of economic growth combined with the large share of advanced

Table 4.1   Economic growth in OECD countries

	2008	2009	2010
Real GDP growth OECD	0.9	−4.3 (−3.5)	−0.1 (1.9)
US	1.1	−4.0 (−2.5)	0.0 (2.5)
Euro area	0.7	−4.1 (−4.0)	−0.3 (0.9)
Japan	−0.6	−6.6 (−5.3)	−0.5 (1.8)
Output gap in OECD	−0.4	−6.5	−8.5
Unemployment rate in OECD	6.0	8.4 (8.2)	9.9 (9.0)
Fiscal balance in OECD	−3.0	−7.2 (−8.2)	−8.7 (−8.3)
Global trade growth	2.5	−13.2 (−12.5)	1.5 (6.5)
Global GDP growth	2.2	−2.7	1.2

Source: OECD, June 2009 and November 2009 in parentheses

Table 4.2   Money market spreads

Q1 2007–Q2 2007	Spread virtually zero.
Q3 2007–Q3 2008	Spreads fluctuated between 0.5% and 1%.
Q3 2008–Q4 2008	Spreads shoot up to 1.5% and higher, peaking in the US at over 3.5% with Lehman Brothers bankruptcy. In Europe spreads remain at between 1.5% and 2%.
Q1 2009	Spreads fall to around 1%.
Q2 2009–Q3 2009	Spreads fall below 1% (between 0.2–0.8%).

Note: Spread between three-month EURIBOR and EONIA swap index for Euro area and spread between three-month LIBOR and overnight indexed swaps for the United States.
Source: OECD, 2009a, Figure 1.21 and OECD, 2009b, Figure 1.1

Table 4.3   Financial stimulus measures introduced since mid-2008

	Up deposit insurance	Guarantee or buy bank dept	Inject capital	Fund commercial paper	Fund asset-backed securities
United States	X	X	X	X	X
Japan		X	X	X	X
Euro area	X				
Germany	X	X	X		
France	X	X	X		
Italy	X		X		
UK	X	X	X	X	X
Canada		X		X	X
Australia	X	X			X

Note: All countries, with exception of Euro area, also introduced a ban or restrictions on short selling. The US nationalized Fannie Mae and Freddie Mac and the UK nationalized a few banks. The US, Germany and the UK also introduced legislation to purchase toxic assets or otherwise isolate toxic assets.

Table 4.4   Real house prices 2000–2009 (% change)

	2000–2006	2008	Q4 2008 or latest quarter	2009 latest figures
United States	5.4	–6.2 (–6.3)	–5.9	–3.1 (Q2 2009)
Japan	–4.3	–2.4 (–2.9)	–3.8	–3.3 (Q1)
Germany	–2.9	–2.7 (–2.7)	–1.8	–1.8 (Q4 2008)
France	9.5	–1.1 (–1.8)	–2.7	–9.1 Q2
Italy	6.1	–1.1 (–1.7)	–2.9	–4.7 Q1
United Kingdom	8.8	–4.3 (–4.3)	–12.1	–7.4 Q3
Canada	6.7	–3.4 (–3.4)	–11.5	1.5 Q2
Australia	7.1	0.4 (0.1)	–8.7	–5.3 Q3

Note: For Japan, France and Italy Q3 is the latest quarter.
Source: OECD, 2009a, November 2009 in parentheses

Table 4.5   Stock markets price indices 2000 and 2009

	Stock market index January 1, 2000	Stock market index March 23, 2009
United States	100	65
Euro area	100	60
Japan	100	50
United Kingdom	100	78

Source: OECD, 2009a, June

Table 4.6   Fiscal balance as a percent of GDP divided by potential GDP

	2009 spring 09 forecast	2009 fall 09 forecast	2010 spring 09 forecast	2010 fall 09 forecast
US	−10.0	−11.2	−11.9	−10.7
Japan	−6.8	−7.4	−8.4	−8.2
Euro Area	−5.4	−6.1	−7.0	−6.7
OECD	−7.2	−8.2	−8.7	−8.3

Source: OECD, 2009a Table 1.5 and www.oecd.org/dataoecd/18/26/2713584.xls

manufacturing in their export mix (see Chart 3.6). OECD has estimated that stimulus measures in Europe will rely more on automatic stabilizers than in Japan and the United States. Budget concerns will also constrain the extent of the stimulus throughout the industrial world.

The fiscal balance in the three major components of the OECD and the OECD in aggregate are displayed in Table 4.6. Deterioration in fiscal balances is anticipated in all three regions with the US experiencing the largest deficits measured as a share of GDP. The outlook has worsened somewhat between the spring and fall for 2009 with a modest improvement projected for 2010. As deficits increase there is a chance that higher risks will manifest in higher interest rates and the possibility of sovereign default. In late May 2009, Standard and Poor's issued a warning that the sovereign risk rating of the United Kingdom could be downgraded. It never was although there were fears that exchange rate pressures could strengthen as a result of such a downgrade. Iceland and Ireland have already been downgraded. As a result, higher fiscal deficits will constrain the extent of further fiscal stimulus going forward. This could attenuate the economic recovery in Europe and Japan. The OECD (2009a) says that the scope for further fiscal stimulus is limited in Japan, Italy, Greece, Iceland and Ireland while Germany, Canada, Australia, South Korea and a few other smaller countries have more room for further fiscal stimulus. As the crisis unfolded in Europe the stronger countries including France, Germany and other northern

European countries responded quickly and began to emerge with stronger growth in 2H 2009. Smaller countries that were not as well equipped to deal with the crisis including Portugal, Ireland, Greece, Spain and Eastern Europe have had a tougher time emerging from the crisis and could be faced with continued high unemployment and large budget deficits. Greece and Eastern European countries have not experienced as sharp a rebound in the OECD composite leading indicators as the stronger western European countries. In late February and early March 2010 fears of a sovereign default by Greece sent the cost of credit default swaps rising, a familiar echo of the sequence of events leading up to the default of Lehman Brothers and the global crisis in September 2008.

5
Impacts of the Global Crisis on Asia and Outlook

A variety of possible policy responses to the global recession were available to governments and central banks in Asia. For this chapter we developed a grouping mechanism to organize the discussion of developing Asian economies and review the outlook for countries within these categories. We then considered the background conditions in the developing Asian region, stimulus measures that were undertaken and analysis of future prospects and policies. We begin by dividing the Asian region into four country groups.

Group 1. Countries in this group are highly dependent on exports. Their export mix is composed of advanced manufacturing goods which have been heavily affected by the slowdown in industrial countries. This group includes South Korea, Malaysia, Singapore and Taiwan. All are higher income countries with sufficient resources including foreign exchange reserves and government revenue to provide strong fiscal stimulus. Their corporate sectors are not in a high risk category and poverty levels are low. We add Hong Kong, one of the richest countries in East Asia to this group even though its industrial capacity is small and is more service oriented. However, it is highly dependent on exports of goods and services and has been adversely affected by the decline in international trade.

Group 2. Countries in this group are in a middle income category that have high export to GDP ratios that are also susceptible to slower growth as export prospects are reduced. Countries in this group include the Philippines, Thailand and Vietnam. Growth shortfall is also high in these economies, though not as high as countries in Group 1. However poverty levels are also somewhat higher, particularly in the Philippines and Vietnam. Corporate risks to small-scale industries are also high. These countries tailor their stimulus packages to address needs of small-scale industries and the poor.

Group 3. Countries in this group consist of the three large economies of India, China and Indonesia. These countries have more modest expected average growth shortfalls in 2009 and 2010 without risk of experiencing negative growth in GDP. They are also more domestic demand oriented and have sufficient resources and enough flexibility to address aspects of regional poverty. The global recession is impacting different income groups in these economies. In China, workers in export-oriented industries have been laid off as a result of the global recession and some have migrated back to rural villages. In India workers involved in information technology and communications have been adversely affected. In Indonesia the impact has been more disperse and efforts to assist the poor in the eastern regions where the poverty incidence is high are being intensified.

Group 4. This group of countries comprises low-income economies with large poverty components that are not as highly integrated into the global economy as countries in the other groups. They are, however, still experiencing financial stress including large fiscal deficits and high levels of government debt. Countries in this group include Bangladesh, Cambodia, Lao PDR, Nepal, Pakistan, and Sri Lanka. With the exception of Cambodia and Sri Lanka, the export share of GDP for these countries averages just over 15% and the expected shortfall in growth as a result of the global recession is modest, ranging from zero for Nepal to 0.7% for Bangladesh, 1.3% for Sri Lanka, 1.7% for Lao PDR and 2.6% for Pakistan. The impact on Cambodia is expected to be larger, primarily because of the significant share of exports in GDP, a share that has increased dramatically in the last decade. The impact on Sri Lanka could also be larger depending on the cost of rehabilitation after the end of the conflict in the northern and western regions. Selectively, some export-oriented industries in countries in this group will also be affected including carpets in Nepal and apparel in Bangladesh and Sri Lanka. In these countries there is the risk that poverty reduction programs will be pared down as budgets are pared as a consequence of the crisis and related constraints.

We will now review the Asian response to the global crisis through the lens of these four groups of countries.

As a prelude to more detailed analysis of countries in these groups it is useful to consider the general nature of the adverse effect on Asian economies. There are several possible ways the global recession manifests in Asian economies

- GDP growth
- Export performance
- Currency depreciation and deteriorating terms of trade
- Fiscal stress as reflected by increasing government deficits and TED spreads
- Increasing current account deficit
- Lower level of international reserves
- Loss of remittance income

- Capital outflows in form of portfolio and FDI commitments. Some of this outflow is reflected in declines in stock market indices, which would also reflect sales by domestic investors.

Charts 5.1a, 5.1b, 5.1c, **5.1d**, 5.1e, 5.1f through Charts 5.4a, 5.4b, 5.4c, 5.4d, 5.4e and 5.4f summarize the position of the four economic groupings with regard to GDP growth, exports, fiscal stress, exchange rate, current account and level of international reserves from 2004 to 2008 and with projections for 2009 and 2010. Consistent forecasts of remittance flows and capital outflows as well as FDI commitments are not currently available and they are analyzed separately from an historical perspective. All analysis and projections are made against a background of economic performance since 2004.

The GDP forecasts for 2010 made by the EIU are compared with forecasts made by the IMF in their regional economic outlook assessment made in May and October 2009 along with the ADB Asian Development Update forecasts made in September 2009. Updates in data were available from IMF October 2009 and EIU for February 2010. These forecasts are displayed in Table 5.1. The IMF does not include forecasts for Group 4 countries.

Table 5.1 provides an interesting glimpse into the changes in forecasts for the selected Asian countries from spring 2009 at the onset of the crisis till the deepening of the recession within the year and subsequent signs of recovery for 2010. Initial IMF growth forecasts for 2009 made in April are somewhat higher than EIU for Southeast Asian economies and lower for China, India, Singapore and Taiwan while for 2010 they are generally

Table 5.1   EIU, IMF and ADB comparisons of GDP growth forecasts for Groups 1–3

	2009 IMF	2010 IMF	ADB 2009	ADB 2010	EIU 2009	EIU 2010
Hong Kong	−4.5 (−3.6)	0.5 (3.5)	−4.0	3.0	−6.0 (−3.5)	1.1 (4.6)
South Korea	−4.0 (−1.0)	1.5 (3.6)	−2.0	4.0	−5.0 (0.1)	0.6 (5.1)
Singapore	−10.0 (−3.3)	−0.1 (4.1)	−5.0	3.5	−8.6 (−2.1)	1.3 (4.9)
Taiwan	−7.5 (−4.1)	0.0 (3.7)	−4.9	2.4	−6.9 (−3.5)	0.5 (4.2)
Malaysia	−3.5 (−3.6)	1.3 (2.5)	−3.1	4.2	−5.2 (−2.4)	3.4 (3.7)
China	6.5 (8.5)	7.5 (9.0)	8.2	8.9	7.2 (8.7)	7.6 (9.6)
India	4.5 (5.4)	5.6 (6.4)	6.0	7.0	5.5 (6.5)	6.4 (7.3)
Indonesia	2.5 (4.0)	3.5 (4.8)	4.3	5.4	2.4 (4.6)	3.1 (5.5)
The Philippines	0.0 (1.0)	1.0 (3.2)	1.6	3.3	−1.8 (0.8)	3.0 (3.2)
Thailand	−3.0 (−3.5)	1.0 (3.7)	−3.2	3.0	−4.5 (−3.2)	1.9 (3.2)
Vietnam	3.3 (4.6)	4.0 (5.3)	4.7	6.5	2.1 (5.3)	4.9 (6.2)

Source: EIU, ADB, 2009a and IMF, 2009 and 2009a
IMF forecasts in brackets reflect the IMF World Economic Outlook forecasts made in October 2009. EIU forecasts in brackets reflect the EIU estimates made in February 2010.

lower than the EIU forecasts. On balance, however, the differences between the two forecasts are not significant, with the possible exception of the Philippines, where EIU shows more variation between 2009 and 2010 and in Malaysia where EIU shows a stronger revival. From September 2009 onwards, the ADB forecasts were generally more optimistic than either the IMF forecasts made in April or EIU for both 2009 and 2010. Projections for 2010 are generally a point or two (South Korea, Singapore) higher than either April 2009 IMF or EIU forecasts.

In the update for the World Economic Outlook, October 2009 the IMF was much more optimistic in its forecast. Forecasts for both 2009 and 2010 were significantly stronger than they were six months earlier and are close to the ADB forecasts made in September 2009. Upward revisions were particularly notable for Taiwan, South Korea and Singapore. We generally feature the EIU forecasts because the EIU has a comprehensive set of estimates for many variables going back to 2001 for all four groups and all relevant variables. EIU estimates as of February 2010 were even more sanguine with the revision of GDP growth rate further upwards for all countries. Only Hong Kong, Taiwan, Singapore, Malaysia and Thailand were suffering from a contraction of their economies in 2009 but all were expected to enjoy between 3%–5% growth in 2010.

Looking back, macroeconomic performance was expected to be generally weak in 2009 especially in export-oriented economies like Hong Kong, Taiwan, Malaysia and Singapore despite the significant upward revisions in expected performance made between the spring and the fall of 2009 and further upward revisions in early 2010. In 2009 GDP growth was initially expected to be negative for almost all countries in Group 1 in 2009 (Hong Kong, Malaysia, Singapore and Taiwan) as well as Thailand in Group 2 and Cambodia in Group 4. Along with GDP growth export, growth was projected to be strongly negative for all countries in all four groups with the exception of Pakistan and Bangladesh. There were, however, strong points in Asia's performance, notably China, India and Indonesia as well as Vietnam. As 2009 drew to a close the actual outturn for the year was generally much better than expected.

The sharp recession in industrial countries and the financial turmoil following the subprime mortgage crisis and subsequent events had a devastating impact on Asian trade in the short run. Trade finance dried up following the collapse of Lehman Brothers, reflected by spikes in the TED rate as well as the steep decline in ocean shipments as the volume of world trade fell. The strong linkages within Asia and with the rest of the world as well as the interwoven trade in parts and components as outsourcing has expanded serve to spread the pain of the recession throughout the region.

The growth of intraregional trade and the growing importance of China as the major assembler in the region reflect this pattern. While we will deal more with the composition of trade and who is most likely to be adversely affected when we turn to the four regions and country analysis, it is useful at this point to note that the electronics industry is bearing a large share of the impact on export performance. The income elasticity of demand for electronics is high and this is complemented by the strong pattern of intraregional trade in electronics within Asia. Preliminary data suggest that South Korea, Malaysia, the Philippines, Singapore and Taiwan were most affected which is reflected in the estimated declines in their export earnings. Labor intensive exports will be less affected since the income elasticity of demand for these products such as clothing and footwear and toys is lower than for electronics. Nevertheless countries like Bangladesh, Cambodia, Indonesia and Sri Lanka were adversely affected. The overall impact will also depend upon the relative shift in import demand by the US and Europe, reflecting not only differences in income elasticity but also the shift between consumption and investment. In a recession it is likely that the demand for low cost necessities will continue to rise, albeit slowly, while luxury goods demand will slacken further. Protectionist sentiments that have recently surfaced in industrial countries may also have a potential dampening impact on trade with Asian economies, particularly in the European Union.

Net capital outflows were also estimated to continue to be negative for 2009 as a whole, although there has been a revival of inflows in the second half. One indicator of these flows is the performance of local stock markets. While equity prices in these markets reflect the behavior of both domestic and foreign investors, the two tend to move in tandem, particularly as all investors try to unwind positions in response to the increase in risk in all global markets. Looking at peak to trough movements most Asian markets have moved together. From highs in the fall of 2007 all markets retreated anywhere from 46% to 60% through Q1 2009, an enormous destruction in asset value that has put stress on the banking community as well as business and households. There was a revival in stock markets during Q2 and Q3. However banks were showing reluctance to lend for new projects as many firms were losing business and unwilling to undertake new investment. Consumers were also less willing to spend, creating a secondary negative impact on demand. Furthermore, banks balance sheets are impacted to the extent that they have invested in stocks and the amount of leverage they are exposed to. However this channel is likely to be limited. Banks are generally more likely to be exposed to the inflated property market which has also crashed in most countries. Based on performance in 2008 fiscal stress on government as reflected by the size of the fiscal deficit are dangerously high in India (6.7% of GDP), Vietnam (4.7%) and Malaysia (4.7%). Fiscal deficits increased in 2009 as countries undertake stimulus measures to boost economic activity. Weak fiscal discipline can jeopardize the beneficial effects of such measures by putting pressure on the balance of payments and the exchange rate. Aside from balance sheet pressure resulting from the global crisis' impact on bank lending and asset quality, banks in the region have made substantial progress in building sound and sensible policies.

Non-performing loans were low as the crisis began. In 2008 Thailand's NPL ratio was highest in the region at 5.7% followed by the Philippines (3.5%) and Indonesia (3.2%). All the other countries in East and Southeast Asia had NPLs below 2.5%.[1] By comparison, the NPL rate in the United States was 5.1%. The Asian crisis of a decade ago has taught the region's bank to generally eschew reliance on foreign banks to finance loans. If the ratio of loans to domestic deposits is less than one then domestic deposits are large enough to cover loans. If the ratio is greater than one then the banking system has to borrow from both local and foreign sources. If foreign bank borrowings are large relative to the domestic market then there may be liquidity issues for Asian banks. A look at the data reveals that South Korea and possibly Malaysia were the only Asian economies in possible trouble on this score. However swap arrangement by the Bank of Korea with the US Federal Reserve and the central banks of China and Japan have provided additional security and stability.

Exchange rate movements have reinforced the perceived weakness in the Asian economies as growth has slowed and export revenue has fallen. There has been some currency devaluation as many economies have followed the weakening dollar down, particularly earlier in the year. Despite a fall in export revenue the current account balances for most of the Asian economies remain strong. Export revenue has fallen but import expenditure have also fallen as well. Because exports are still larger than imports in most countries this means that the current account remains robustly positive and foreign exchange reserves continue to accumulate. This war chest along with small fiscal deficits are important considerations to keep in mind as stimulative measures are undertaken.

Remittance income is an important factor for Group 2 and Group 4 countries. While remittances are difficult to predict, it is likely that domestic remittance from family members working in cities is likely to level off or fall, particularly where factory worker layoffs are large. International migration from adjacent Asian countries is also likely to be cut back as lower skilled workers are retrenched and sent home. Malaysia is sending Indonesian workers home and Hong Kong and Japan are also encouraging some temporary migrants to return home. International migration and remittances from other locations is more problematic although remittances from Hong Kong and Singapore are likely to fall. Remittances from the Middle East will depend upon local developments in that region, particularly oil revenue and political developments in Iran and Iraq. The OECD in 2009c says that the crisis was hitting immigrants harder than native-born workers in industrial countries. Temporary work visas were also getting harder to obtain and Japan is offering money for migrants to return home. Despite these developments it should be recalled that in past recessions remittances have remained robust. There is evidence that this pattern may repeat itself in this recession as reports come in for the second half of 2009.

We now look at individual performances within the four groups.

Group 1 Economies

Countries in Group 1 (Hong Kong, South Korea, Malaysia, Singapore and Taiwan) are highly dependent on exports, which comprise a substantial share of GDP. In these countries the export mix is composed primarily of advanced manufacturing goods and GDP growth rates have been adversely affected by the slowdown in industrial countries (see Chart 5.1a). According to initial estimates, GDP growth is projected to be strongly negative in all five of these countries in 2009, ranging from –5% in South Korea to –8.6% in Singapore with a strong rebound to slow positive growth foreseen for 2010. Recent IMF and EIU February 2010 estimates were more optimistic (See Table 5.1 and panel 2 in Chart 5.1a). The sharp V-shaped recovery is similar to the historical experience of these countries following the Asian financial crisis of a decade ago. Note that forecasts made in fall 2008 were optimistic and in spring 2009 were quite pessimistic. By spring 2010, optimism had generally returned.

Export growth (Chart 5.1b) is projected to follow a V-shaped pattern of recovery in 2010, although not to as high a level as 2007 or 2008. Competition from China and India as well as the emerging low cost economies in South Asia will continue to impinge on prospects for this group of countries which are continuing to adapt to competitive pressure from China and India on one hand and the lower cost producers of South Asia and the

Chart 5.1a   Group 1 Economies: Real GDP growth rate (annual %)

Panel 1: GDP growth rate, 2002–2010

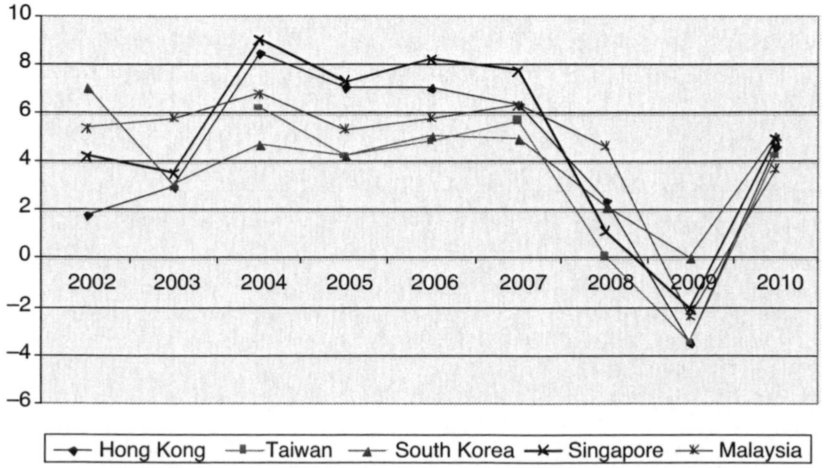

Panel 2: 2009 GDP growth forecasts

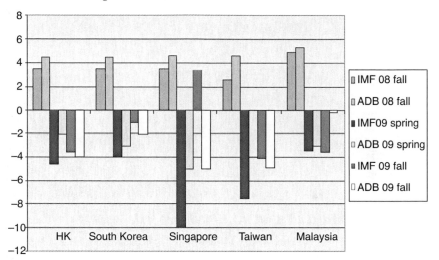

Source: World Development Indicators database, EIU, 2010, ADB, 2008, ADB, 2009, ADB, 2009a, IMF, 2009, IMF, 2009a and IMF, 2009d

Chart 5.1b   Group 1 Economies: Export of goods and services (% growth)

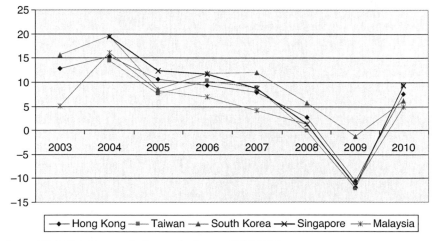

Source: World Development Indicators database and EIU, 2010

Mekong. Fiscal stimulus measures undertaken in late 2008 and through the first half of 2009 combined with softening of the tax base and tax revenues have led to deterioration in fiscal performance across the board in this

Chart 5.1c   Group 1 Economies: Fiscal balance (% of GDP)

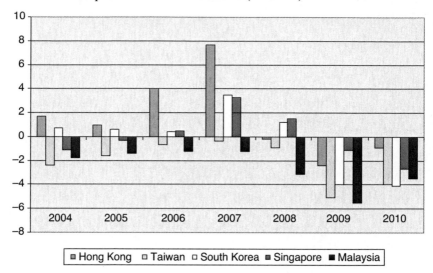

Source: EIU, 2010

group of countries (Chart 5.1c).This is not expected to abate in 2010 and these countries will have to work hard to develop new revenue sources and broaden the tax base if they are to avoid further fiscal difficulties including possible further currency depreciation and renewed inflation. Malaysia has the largest fiscal deficit of over 5% of GDP followed closely by Taiwan and Singapore. A positive development is that all of these countries have ample foreign reserves.

There have been minor exchange rate changes (Chart 5.1d) in this group of countries as a result of the global crisis. The most notable development is a rapid depreciation of the South Korea won between 2006 and 2008, though it had started a mild appreciation since then. The exchange rate in July 2009 was lower than the forecast for the entire year. Some observers suggest that this may be one reason why the South Korean economy has begun to recover so well in the second quarter of 2009. The trade balance was up 35.1% for the last 12 months ending in October 2009 and the current account balance was up 39.7% for the last 12 months ending in September 2009 (Chart 5.1e) (see Economist.com/indicators). The current account balances in the rest of this group of countries have remained robust.

Current account balances are up in Malaysia (36.7%), Singapore (21.4%) and Taiwan (38.6%) by comparable amounts to that reported by South Korea for a similar time period. Aside from a slight shrinking of Malaysian reserve position between 2007 and 2010, international reserves have held

Chart 5.1d Group 1 Economies: Exchange rate vis US$ (2004 = 100)

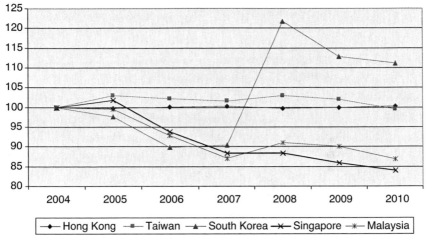

Source: EIU, 2010

Chart 5.1e Group 1 Economies: Current account (US$ billion)

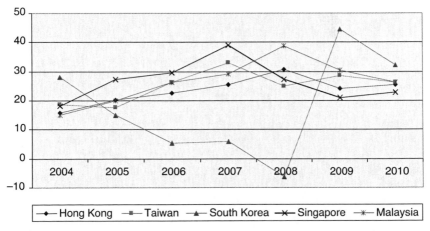

Source: EIU, 2010

steady through the crisis, showing little change between 2007 and projections for 2010 (see Chart 5.1f). This is quite remarkable give the gyrations in the global economic landscape in the past few years. Real estate markets have been very strong in Singapore, South Korea and Hong Kong raising some concerns of a potential speculative bubble not based on fundamentals.

Chart 5.1f   Group 1 Economies: International reserves (US$ billion)

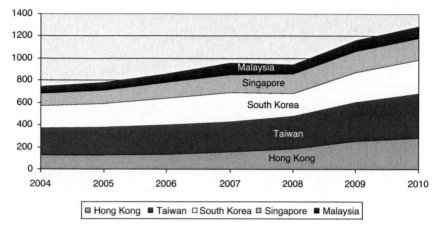

Source: EIU, 2010

Group 2 Economies

Countries in Group 2 are in a middle income category that has high export to GDP ratios that are also susceptible to slower growth as export prospects are reduced. Countries in this group include the Philippines, Thailand and Vietnam. Growth shortfall is also high in these economies, though not as high as countries in Group 1. However poverty levels are higher, particularly in the Philippines and Vietnam. GDP growth (Chart 5.2a) follows a similar pattern to the countries in Group 1 although the decline in 2009 is not as severe and the V-shaped pattern of forecasts over time is not as evident, except in the case of Vietnam. In both the Philippines and Thailand the forecasts continue to deteriorate over time. Despite this, late 2009 forecasts by ADB and the IMF (see Table 5.1 and the second panel of Chart 5.2a) show positive growth in the Philippines and Vietnam for 2009. Recent EIU February 2010 data confirm this. Growth is driven primarily by exports with some contribution from the local economy. Thailand, which has experienced political and social disruptions in 2008 and 2009, has the weakest outlook, followed by the Philippines and Vietnam. All three countries in this group are projected to recover further in 2010, although to levels at least a percentage point or more below trend rates between 2000 and 2007. Export growth is also projected to deteriorate for this group of countries, particularly for Vietnam, which had been experiencing export growth averaging nearly 19% per annum between 2002 and 2008.

Slower economic growth and a reduction in trade taxes is resulting in a further deterioration of fiscal balance in Group 2 economies (Chart 5.2c), particularly in Vietnam, where the fiscal deficit is projected to be more than 8% of GDP over the next two years. Smaller deficits in the range

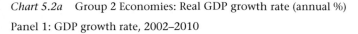

Chart 5.2a Group 2 Economies: Real GDP growth rate (annual %)

Panel 1: GDP growth rate, 2002–2010

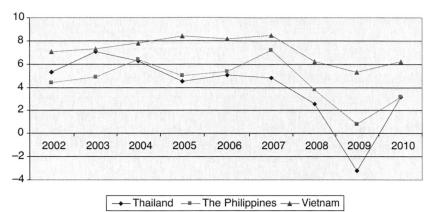

Panel 2: 2009 GDP growth forecasts

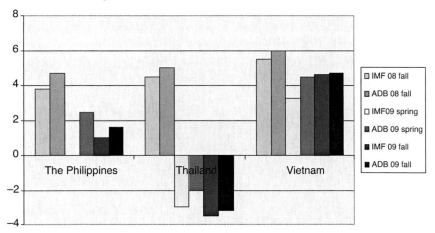

Source: World Development Indicators database, EIU, 2010, ADB, 2008, ADB, 2009, ADB 2009a, IMF, 2009, IMF, 2009a and IMF, 2009d

of 3% of GDP are envisioned in the Philippines and Thailand. All three countries in this group face challenges of maintaining poverty programs and fiscal stimulus given these fiscal constraints.

Despite higher fiscal deficits projections of exchange rates (Chart 5.2d) show few changes relative to 2008. Both the Thai baht and the Philippines peso are projected to either remain relatively stable or appreciate slightly in 2010 while the Vietnamese dong will continue depreciating, a trend that began in 2004. It seems that the exchange rate is more affected by trade, international reserves and current account developments (Chart 5.2e) than

Chart 5.2.b   Group 2 Economies: Exports of goods and services (annual % growth)

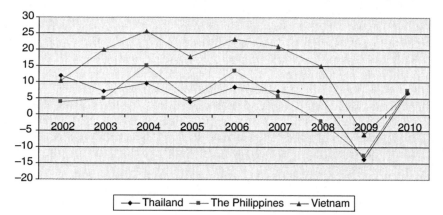

Source: World Development Indicators database and EIU, 2010

Chart 5.2c   Group 2 Economies: Fiscal balance (% of GDP)

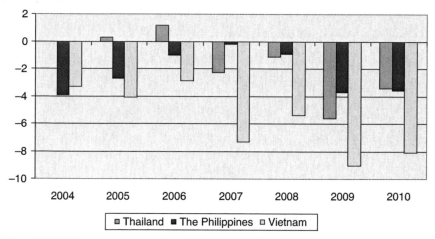

Source: EIU, 2010

the fiscal situation. Vietnam, the only country with a depreciating currency also has had a persistent current account deficit (since 2004) which has grown since 2006 and is projected to grow even further in 2010. Thailand and the Philippines, on the other hand have current account surpluses which are projected to reduce to some extent in 2010.

Thailand has by far the largest level of international reserves in this group of countries. However both the Philippines and Vietnam have a comfortable level of reserve (around $20 billion and $48 billion respectively) equivalent to

Chart 5.2d   Group 2 Economies: Exchange rate vis US$ (2004 = 100)

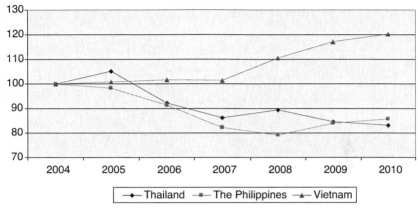

Source: EIU, 2010

Chart 5.2e   Group 2 Economies: Current account (US$ billion)

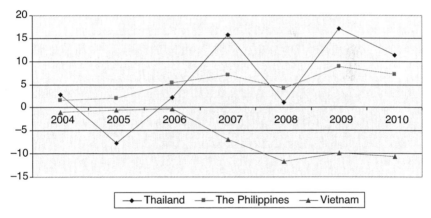

Source: EIU, 2010

several months of imports. The stock market and housing market in Vietnam has been buoyant and there is some concern that there might be a bubble in the making by 2010.

Group 3 Economies

The global crisis has not been as devastating for the three large economies of China, India and Indonesia as in some of the other country groups. GDP (Chart 5.3a) is projected to remain positive for all of the giant economies

Chart 5.2f   Group 2 Economies: International reserves (US$ billion)

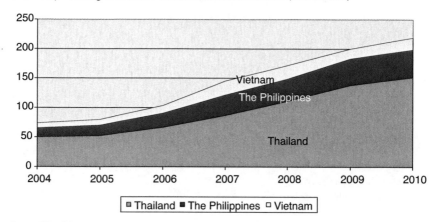

Source: EIU, 2010

although it will fall in 2009 before improving in 2010. China's growth has already rebounded in the latter part of 2009 and projections by the EIU February 2010 envision a rebound to 9.6% growth in 2010. Growth in India will be slower, 6.5% in 2009 and 7.3% in 2010. Indonesia will recover from projected slower growth to around 5.5% in 2010. As with Group 1 the pattern of growth forecasts over time follows a V-shaped pattern.

Export growth (Chart 5.3b) in China and Indonesia were estimated to be negative in 2009 before recovering to slow growth in 2010 as the global economy and import demand of industrial countries recover further. India's export performance was not as adversely affected for two reasons. First

Chart 5.3a   Group 3 Economies: Real GDP growth rate (annual %)

Panel 1: GDP growth rate, 2002–2010

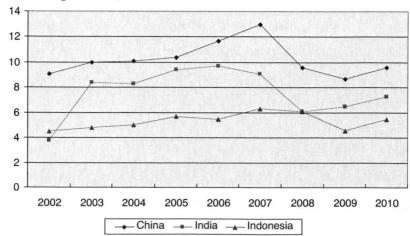

Panel 2: 2009 GDP growth forecasts

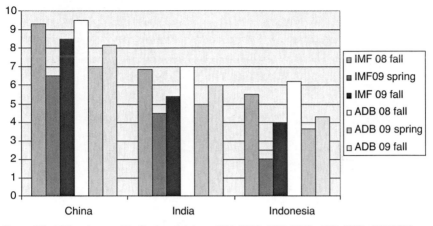

Source: World Development Indicators database, EIU, 2010, ADB, 2008, ADB, 2009, ADB 2009a, IMF, 2009, IMF, 2009a and IMF, 2009d

Chart 5.3b   Group 3 Economies: Exports of goods and services (annual % growth)

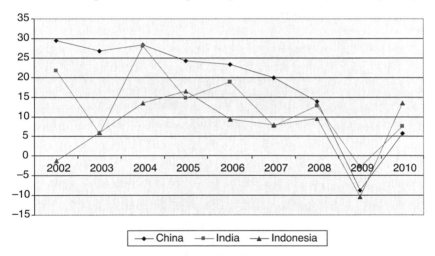

Source: World Development Indicators database and EIU, 2010

exports growth has been slowing since 2004 as the shift toward export of IT services continues. Secondly, exports are a small proportion of total income and domestic demand plays a bigger role in India than in economies in the other groups.

The fiscal balance of all three countries in this group (Chart 5.3c) will be in negative territory as a result of slower growth in tax revenue due to the economic slowdown and the cost of stimulus packages that were put in

Chart 5.3c   Group 3 Economies: Fiscal balance (% of GDP)

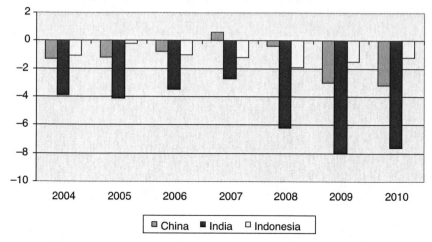

□ China   ■ India   □ Indonesia

Source: EIU, 2010

place in 2008 and 2009. India has by far the largest deficit which is pro-jected to grow to close to 8% of GDP in 2009 with some decrease in 2010. China and Indonesia will incur somewhat large deficits than in the past but still in the manageable range of 2% to 3% of GDP in 2010.

The exchange rates (Chart 5.3d) for India and Indonesia are expected to appreciate slightly in 2010, following mixed movements in 2009. The rate of depreciation in Indonesia is expected to moderate and even appreciate *vis-à-vis* 2008, when the rupiah lost close to 20% of its value compared to

Chart 5.3d   Group 3 Economies: Exchange rate vis US$ (2004 = 100)

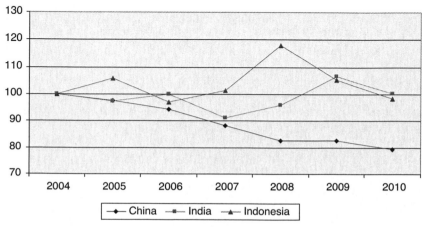

◆ China   ■ India   ▲ Indonesia

Source: EIU, 2010

Chart 5.3e Group 3 Economies: Current account (US$ billion)

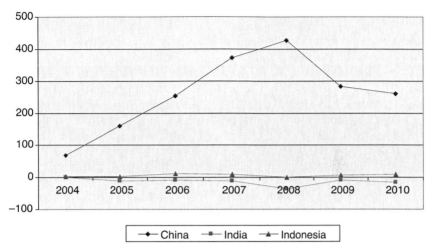

Source: EIU, 2010

2007. The economic and political climate in Indonesia has improved since the crisis began which has served to steady the value of the rupiah. In China the gradually phased slow and orchestrated appreciation of the yuan is expected to continue throughout the forecast period. By the end of 2010 it is forecast to have appreciated by around 20% compared with 2004.

Current account balances (Chart 5.3e) are projected to remain close to zero in Indonesia and slightly negative for India, while large balances

Chart 5.3f Group 3 Economies: International reserves (US$ billion)

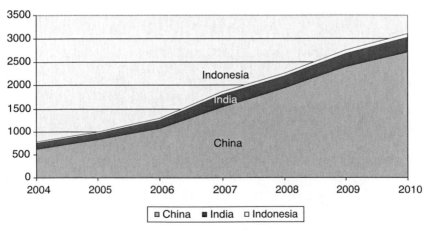

Source: EIU, 2010

accumulated between 2004 and 2008 in China are projected to moderate from high levels in 2007 but will remain in the range of $250 to $300 billion per year in 2009 and 2010. The slide in export revenue owing to an upsurge of trade disputes in 2009 will be balanced by lower import expenditures resulting in a positive trade balance.

International reserves (Chart 5.3f) are projected to continue to accumulate, with the bulk of the build up continuing to be in China. By the end of 2010 China will have over $2.7 trillion in reserves, over half the reserves of all emerging economies and almost as much as all industrial economies. The continued growth in these reserves and the imbalances in international trade and payments that they reflect is an issue that needs to be resolved. The trade imbalance is compounded by the continuation of the trend for investment to grow faster than other components of aggregate demand (forecast to grow at 14.8% in 2009 *vis-à-vis* consumption growth of 9.3%). To rebalance the Chinese economy investment must begin to take a back seat to consumption, which still remains less than 40% of GDP. Stock markets have been strong in all three economies raising some concern for a potential asset price bubble not based on fundamentals (see Chapter 8 for issues of rebalancing).

Group 4 Economies

Groups 4 economies (Bangladesh, Cambodia, Lao PDR, Nepal, Pakistan and Sri Lanka) are low-income countries with significant proportions of the population in poverty. Although not highly integrated into the global economy they are nevertheless experiencing financial stress including large

Chart 5.4a Group 4 Economies: Real GDP growth rate (annual %)

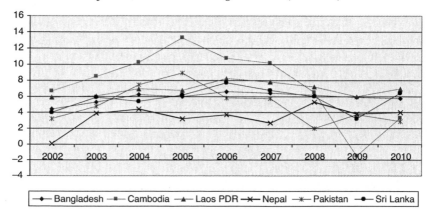

Source: World Development Indicators, ADB, 2009a update forecasts and EIU, 2010

fiscal deficits and high levels of government debt as they address the difficulties brought about by the global recession. Forecasts for Bangladesh and Cambodia suggest that growth in GDP (Chart 5.4a) will be adversely affected by the global recession, in particular Cambodia whose rate of export growth was dramatically reduced by the global crisis (Chart 5.4b). However Cambodia is expected to rebound in 2010 as both GDP and exports increase.

The fiscal balance (Chart 5.4c) in all countries in Group 4 were in deficit in 2009 and expected to remain similarly so in 2010. Sri Lanka will have the largest deficit followed by Pakistan and Cambodia. Only Lao PDR and

Chart 5.4b Group 4 Economies: Exports of goods and services (annual % growth)

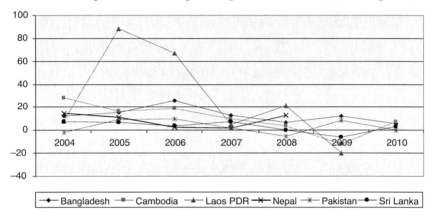

Source: ADB, 2009a update forecasts and EIU, 2010

Chart 5.4c Group 4 Economies: Fiscal balance (% of GDP)

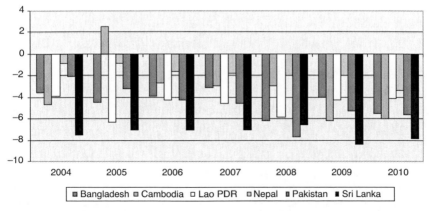

Sources: ADB, 2009; ADB, 2009b; EIU, 2009; EIU, 2010 and Business Monitor online database

Chart 5.4d   Group 4 Economies: Exchange rate vis US$ (2004 = 100)

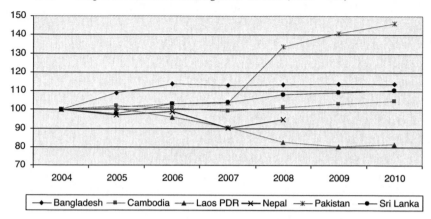

Sources: ADB, 2009; EIU, 2010 and Business Monitor online database

Chart 5.4e   Group 4 Economies: Current account (US$ billion)

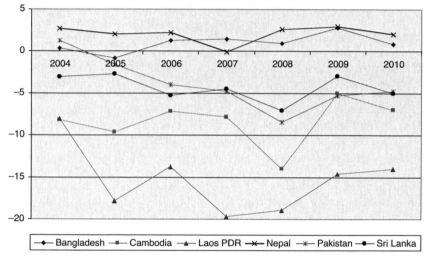

Source: ADB, 2009

Nepal are projected to have deficits less than 5% of GDP in 2009 and 2010. Aid from the international financial community will be needed to fill the financing gap and to help both countries deal with persistent poverty issues.

The exchange rate (Chart 5.4d) is projected to depreciate in all countries in Group 4. Pakistan will experience the largest depreciation of around 20% from 2008. Only a slight further depreciation is foreseen in 2010 for

Chart 5.4f　Group 4 Economies: International reserves (US$ billion)

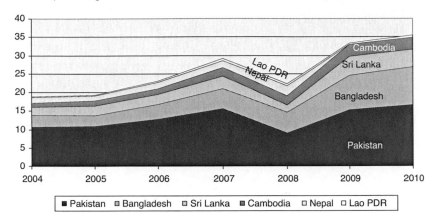

Sources: ADB, 2009; EIU, 2009; EIU, 2010 and Business Monitor online database

countries in this group with the exception of Lao PDR. All countries in Group 4 receive concessional assistance and this will continue.

The current account balance (Chart 5.4e) of Bangladesh is projected to remain positive through 2009 and 2010. The deficits in Cambodia, Lao PDR, Sri Lanka and Pakistan are projected to shrink slightly. International reserve positions (Chart 5.4f) will improve in Sri Lanka, Pakistan and Bangladesh while falling slightly in Lao PDR.

6
Policy Responses – Asia

Monetary and fiscal stimulus measures

Fiscal policy

The IMF has argued that

> fiscal policy can make a significant contribution to reducing the duration of recessions associated with financial crisis. In effect, governments can break the negative feedback between the real economy and financial conditions by acting as a 'spender of last resort'. But this presupposes that public stimulus can be delivered quickly.[1]

There are several factors to consider regarding how the stimulus can be best administered, including the size of the fiscal deficit, the likely impact of higher deficits on the exchange rate and investors' perceptions of risk and a downgrade of credit ratings making it more costly to borrow. There may also be implementation constraints both in the institutional capacity to ramp up spending quickly and in the delivery of the funds to appropriate subcontractors and implementing agencies. It is also important to consider the kinds of spending that are being undertaken and the probable size of the multipliers that result from additional public spending. Certainly more open economies are likely to have smaller fiscal multiplier than more closed economies because of their greater leakage through international trade and investment channels. Also multipliers will be larger the greater the complementarities between public and private goods. Multipliers will be larger if public goods are produced that are complementary with private goods and smaller if public goods are produced that are substitutes with private goods (see Graves, 2009).

Most countries put into motion some fiscal stimulus. Their size and projected impact on GDP are summarized in Table 6.1. The composition of the stimulus measures as calculated by Oxford Economics is outlined in Table 6.2. In China the simulations assume that only about 30% of the

Table 6.1   **Fiscal stimulus measures adopted in developing Asia**

Country	Group	Package as share of GDP in %	2009 impact on GDP (% change from baseline)	2010 impact on GDP (% change from baseline)	2011 impact on GDP (% change from baseline)	United Nations estimate of the size of the stimulus as a % of GDP
China	3	1.2	1.3	2.0	1.5	13.3
Hong Kong	1	1.4	1.1	0.5	0.3	5.2
India	3	1.6	0.5	0.3	0.3	3.2
Indonesia	3	1.3	1.3	0.8	0.4	1.4
South Korea	1	2.5	1.6	1.2	1.0	5.6
Malaysia	1	2.6	3.1	4.1	1.5	5.5
The Philippines	2	4.1	2.4	3.5	1.7	5.8
Singapore	1	5.9	3.6	2.8	0.4	5.9
Taiwan	1	2.1	1.4	1.2	0.7	3.9
Thailand	2	6.4	6.5	7.9	7.4	14.3

Source: Oxford Economics, 2009; United Nations, 2009 and authors' estimates

announced package of $850 billion is likely to be new spending, which accounts for the relatively small impact on GDP. There are, however, major differences between the estimates of the size of the stimulus, particularly in China. The United Nations calculates that the full package is equivalent to 13.3% of GDP (see Table 6.2 final column). If it is assumed that the 50% of the package is new funding then the impact would increase substantially to 2.2% in 2009 and 3.4% in 2010.

There is evidence that stimulus measures are beginning to have a positive effect. In China fixed investment has begun to grow at its fastest pace since 2006 and consumption has stabilized at a modest rate of growth. As noted in Chapter 5 there have been recent upgrades of forecasts for 2010 on the basis of these and other positive signs of recovery. The estimated impact of fiscal stimulus on the Thai economy is much higher than in the other countries, and even higher than China, because of the huge infrastructure component that is contemplated. If only half the package is implemented the GDP increase in 2009 would only be 3.7%. In the Philippines the projected stimulus package would raise GDP by 2.2%. If only half is implemented the impact on GDP would be a more moderate 1.4% in 2009 and 1.9% in 2010. Malaysia and South Korea and other countries have also announced stimulus packages and at the end of January 2009 Singapore announced a stimulus package equivalent to about 9% of GDP. This is somewhat higher than the 5.9% figure reported in Table 6.1. There have also been VAT rebates for exporters and some tax rebates and some efforts to boost both current and capital spending in Thailand's 2008 budget (see

Table 6.2   **Details of fiscal stimulus packages for Asian developing economies**

Country	Group	Fiscal stimulus measures
China	3	Package of around $583 billion (13.3% of GDP) for infrastructure, health and education, environmental protection, technology and housing. One-time payment to households in rural areas ($15) and urban areas ($22).
India	3	Stimulus of $38.4 billion (3.2% of GDP) in unspecified government spending, reduced VAT and excise duties, credit support for labor intensive industries and infrastructure financing.
Indonesia	3	Package of $7.1 billion (1.4% of GDP) for infrastructure, job creation and a variety of tax cuts.
South Korea	1	Package of $53.4 billion (5.6% of GDP) for infrastructure and tax relief for investment.
Malaysia	1	Two packages totalling $12.1 billion (5.5% of GDP) for roads, schools, hospitals, airport, investment guarantees and tax incentives.
The Philippines	2	Package of $10.6 billion (5.8% of GDP) for physical and social infrastructure spending and tax relief for consumers and businesses.
Singapore	1	Package of $13.6 billion (5.9% of GDP) for tax relief for consumers and business, temporary wage subsidies to employers who retain workers, support for small business.
Sri Lanka	4	Package of $ 0.1 (0.2% of GDP) for infrastructure projects.
Taiwan	1	Package of $15.3 billion (3.9% of GDP) for shopping vouchers, infrastructure, urban renewal and incentives for private investment and industrial upgrading.
Thailand	2	Package of $39 billion (14.3% of GDP) for infrastructure, supplements to low income earners, students and unemployed, healthcare, aid to rural communities and tourist development including airport.
Vietnam	2	Package of $8.4 billion (9.4% of GDP) for infrastructure.

Source: United Nations, 2009c

World Bank, 2009a). The ultimate impact of the packages will depend upon the timing and size of the actual expenditures. It will also depend on the mix of tax cuts and increased expenditure. The latter is more likely to have a strong multiplier effect on income since some portion of the income resulting from a tax cut is likely to be saved.

Prasad and Sorkin (2009) have developed an analysis of the fiscal stimulus packages in G20 countries using data compiled by the IMF, various news sources and their own calculations. They have analyzed only four Asian countries – China, India, Indonesia and South Korea. They find the stimulus measures, reported in Table 6.2, are somewhat higher than those compiled by Oxford Economics. This could be because Oxford Economics assumes that the stimulus is spread out over three years. It is interesting that in Asia, with the exception of Indonesia, most of the stimulus comes in the form of expenditures rather than tax cuts. Infrastructure plays a key role in most stimulus measures. In nine of the remaining 14 G20 countries surveyed tax cuts accounted for 30% or more of the stimulus. This could be a result of greater sensitivity to higher fiscal deficits combined with popularity of tax relief. The actual delivery of stimulus money will vary from country to country, depending on implementation and administrative capacity. Although efforts have been made to include only new expenditure and tax relief measures in some cases spending already allocated has been included as part of the stimulus packages.

As fiscal stimulus packages are developed it is important to understand that the poor are being adversely affected by the global slowdown, particularly those close to the poverty line. Any negative shock is likely to put them in a potentially desperate situation. Therefore, protecting the poor is a high priority and it also provides a larger multiplier effect since the propensity to consume is higher for the poorer groups in society. It also is important to consider measures that bring anticipated consumption forward to the present, perhaps by reducing taxes for a limited time only. A potential reduction in the need for high private savings would also be an additional benefit to the development of a more comprehensive safety net. This could result in a lower level of aggregate saving and higher consumption, a rebalancing that would contribute to the global effort to stimulate consumption and reduce inordinately high levels of saving and investment in Asia.

Because of the time bound nature of the stimulus, so-called "shovel ready" investment projects should be given priority over projects with a long gestation lag. Other things being equal projects with a large foreign exchange component should also be avoided. Because of the differential multiplier effects expenditure would have a greater impact on aggregate demand than an equal amount of tax relief. Under certain conditions credit guarantees of bank lending by the government may be appropriate methods to stimulate private lending, particularly in cases where the perceptions of credit risk have increased and are constraining lending to the private sector.[2]

Automatic stabilizers such as changes in tax revenue and expenditures that adjust to fluctuations in economic activity are more traditional ways of smoothing out business cycles and are also easily reversed. While automatic stabilizers provide a first line of fiscal defense against recession they are generally small in developing countries since excises and other taxes tend to dominate personal and corporate income taxes. Furthermore automatic increases in social security and other countercyclical measures also have limited traction in most developing countries. As a result most countries in Asia are relying on fiscal stimulus to provide support for aggregate demand in the current recession. In November 2009, the IMF estimated that the stimulus measures in the Asia-Pacific region added 1.75% to GDP growth in the first half of 2009 and that these measures are a linchpin in the recovery strategy. They have enabled the region to recover more rapidly than anyone anticipated a few months ago. We will discuss the details of these measures for each country when we turn to individual reports in Chapter 10.

Monetary policy

Most countries have implemented measures to relax monetary policy and encourage bank lending. These measures were designed to provide liquidity to the economy and also to stimulate investment. Many countries lowered interest rates in the last four months of 2008 and more relaxed monetary policy has continued in 2009. Falling energy and food prices that have resulted from the global slowdown should ameliorate any tendencies toward inflation and give more space for further monetary stimulus if needed.

A list of monetary policy actions for a group of Asian economies compiled by the World Bank are displayed in Table 6.3. Lower policy interest rates were employed by much of emerging Asia in order to stimulate investment. In cases where countries are committed to defending a fixed exchange rate (Hong Kong) interest rate easing will have to be coordinated with main-

Table 6.3 Monetary policy measures implemented in 2008 and 2009

Economy	Group	Lower policy rates	Higher deposit insurance coverage	Other debt guarantee provision	Bank recapitalization	Foreign exchange liquidity support	Domestic liquidity support	Capital controls
China	3	x				x	x	x
Hong Kong	1	x	x		x			
India	3	x			x	x	x	
Indonesia	3	x	x	x	x	x		x
South Korea	1	x	x	x		x	x	
Malaysia	1	x	x	x	x		x	
The Philippines	2	x	x			x	x	
Singapore	1	x	x			x		

x denotes policy adopted
Source: World Bank, 2009b, Table 1.4

taining the peg. Lowering reserve requirements can help to provide additional liquidity to the financial system. If interest rates are already at very low levels conventional monetary stimulus will be ineffective and other measures may be required. There are a variety of possibilities including debt guarantees, foreign exchange liquidity support and domestic liquidity support. The goal is to supply additional funds and reduce risk to improve the flow of funds to credit worthy borrowers. This can be done by central bank purchase of government securities or commercial paper to inject money into the system. Virtually all countries have adopted measures to provide liquidity support for the domestic banking system and several countries have also supplied foreign exchange liquidity support. Some countries have also recapitalized banks and in the case of Indonesia and China imposed capital controls to keep exchange rate fluctuations in check. In the absence of capital controls stabilizing the exchange rate requires sale of reserves in the foreign exchange market. There is reluctance to resort to such measures. During the Asian financial crisis of 1997 and 1998 Thailand, Indonesia and South Korea suffered reserve losses in trying to maintain their exchange rates against the dollar. There has been widespread devaluation against the US dollar with little intervention by the regions central banks. Lower oil prices should have a beneficial impact on the external balance of the regions oil importers – basically the entire region with the exception of Indonesia and Malaysia. So far there has been no need to supply liquidity to banks through currency swaps, although mechanisms are in place should the need arise. Further details are covered in the country reports in Chapter 10.

Is there room for further monetary and fiscal stimulus?

Inflation has come down in most Asian countries as a result of lower oil and commodity prices and this has muted the monetary stimulus resulting from a decrease in nominal interest rates. IMF analysis suggests that further loosening of monetary policy is warranted in some countries. Because inflation has also been falling real interest rates have remained relatively constant, albeit at levels close to zero or even negative. The IMF also suggests that other aspects of financial conditions in addition to policy rates need to be considered in the current global recession. The IMF has prepared a more detailed index that includes interest rates, credit growth, lending attitudes of banks, exchange rates and stock prices in order to determine the impact of financial conditions on income growth during the crisis period. The IMF analysis augments the general coverage discussed with regard to Table 6.3. Four countries are covered in depth – two developing Asian economies (China and South Korea) as well as Japan and Australia. In the case of South Korea, the IMF study found financial conditions were accommodative throughout the crisis period, perhaps primarily because of the depreciation of the won but also as a result of policy interest rate cuts as well as some decline in lending spreads. In the case of China monetary conditions have become more relaxed since Q4 2008, including interest rate cuts, support of lending to small and medium industry and relaxation of credit quotas and mortgage lending conditions. While real interest rates have increased somewhat as inflation has fallen faster than interest rates the monetary stance has supported economic growth.

The lesson from the IMF analysis of these two countries is that looking at policy rates, even real policy rates, is not enough to judge whether monetary policy has been supportive enough. The IMF argues that unnecessarily tight monetary conditions can restrict recovery while accommodative conditions such as adopted in South Korea can increase growth by as much as 0.5%. Further analysis of monetary measures should be carried out for individual countries to judge the appropriateness of monetary policy and whether further steps need to be taken. Adequate liquidity to accommodate borrowing needs of both large and small and medium sized industry as well as maintenance of appropriate spreads between borrowing and lending rates should be analyzed. Table 6.3 suggests that many measures have already been taken to ensure a flexible monetary policy response. Additional information is contained in the individual country reports in Chapter 10.

Asian economies have already provided fiscal stimulus measures. The size of these measures varies widely as we observed in the discussion of Table 6.1 and Table 6.2. Relying on the UN estimates presented above they vary from a little more than 1% of GDP to as much as 13% of GDP in the case of China and Thailand. The IMF reckons that the average stimulus is about 2.5% in 2009 and even higher for South Korea, Japan and China.[3] The IMF does not take into account the large Thai stimulus. The timing of the stimulus also varies as the implementation lags will change with the scope of projects. Are these stimulus measures appropriate given budget constraints and inflation and exchange rate considerations? Could more be done? The IMF believes there is generally scope for greater fiscal stimulus without risk of jeopardizing fiscal sustainability in countries with high external debt levels or exacerbating balance of payments and inflation difficulties. Looking at an index of fiscal space[4] and comparing it with output gaps in several countries they find generally there is some additional room for further fiscal stimulus. Although the region is recovering more rapidly than anyone anticipated even a few months ago it is still important to review the effectiveness of these stimulus measures. Such analysis is considered in the individual country reports.

Effectiveness of fiscal policy

The IMF 2009 has analyzed the effectiveness of fiscal policy in several countries. It concluded that the size of the fiscal multipliers varies with the analytical approach. Analysis of the fiscal stimulus in the US in the form of income tax rebates was successful in boosting domestic demand although the multiplier effect was well below 1. In Japan the 1995 stimulus was successful but its impact was short lived while the Finish automatic stabilizers were not because of the raised concerns about fiscal stability. Studies of industrial countries using econometric time series methodology (VAR) concluded that fiscal multipliers have declined over time and could even become negative. While the results varied significantly from country to country the IMF concluded that greater openness and therefore leakage through trade, liquidity constraints of households and greater focus on price stability could have been responsible for a weaker impact of fiscal policy. On the other hand estimates from macroeconomic models suggest that fiscal policy was effective in many cases. Putting all of the analysis together the IMF concluded that to be effective the fiscal policy had to be well timed, well targeted and worked better in an environment where there was macroeconomic stability and fiscal sustainability since this will reduce the possible offset from a buildup of precautionary savings. These results suggest that fiscal stimulus measures are likely to be more effective in Group 1 and Group 3 and less effective in Group 4 and some Group 2 countries. Additional research by Alesina and Ardagna (2009) conducted for OECD countries from 1970 to 2007 suggests that fiscal stimulus measures based on tax cuts are more likely to increase growth than those based on spending increases. Furthermore adjustments in spending rather than taxes are less likely to lead to recession and fiscal adjustments based on spending cuts and no tax increases are more likely to reduce deficits and debt to GDP ratios than those based on tax increases. While these findings are perhaps more relevant for industrial countries that are members of the OECD they may also be pertinent for Asian developing countries where deficit spending has been increasing to provide fiscal stimulus.

Current account and budget outlook

Generally, Asian economies have current account surpluses and most countries in the region have ample foreign exchange reserves (see Table 3.3). There are, however, several potential problem economies. South Korea and Indonesia have a high level of short-term debt as a percentage of reserves and Pakistan, Lao PDR, Cambodia and Vietnam have current account imbalances that need to be addressed. Several countries have central government budget balances that are negative and have either deteriorated or remain large. Using a cut-off of 4% of GDP in 2007 this group includes Pakistan, India, Sri Lanka and Vietnam. Cambodia, Lao PDR, Malaysia and the Philippines managed to contain or reduce their deficits by 2007. However as the revenue base shrinks with slower growth, deficits are projected to increase in these countries as the crisis continues to unfold.

A highly leveraged banking system and the weakness of the won, which has fallen 40% against the US dollar in the past year, creates a potential problem for South Korea in financing its foreign debt obligations. South

Korea does have a number of currency swap agreements that should help enable it to roll over nearly $200 billion debt which falls due in 2009 (see *The Economist*, 2009). Indonesia is less at risk because it has a current account surplus and its banking system has been conservative, having a low loan to deposit ratio. Pakistan, on the other hand has a very large current account deficit and also a high bank loan to deposit ratio. Its level of non-performing loans is 7.4%, and has increased slightly since 2006. This is higher than the other poor countries in Asia. For example in Q3 2008 the IMF estimated the NPL ratio of non-performing loans to gross loans among the poorest Asian economies was under 3% in Cambodia, India and Vietnam (Burki, 2009).

At the beginning of the 1997 financial crisis policymakers were faced with budget deficits that restrained their ability to provide fiscal stimulus and their foreign exchange reserves were depleted as a result of trying to maintain dollar exchange rates. However, while the region is now even more dependent on exports to industrial countries than it was a decade ago, it now finds itself in a more favorable position to address the current global slowdown. What is clear from the forecasts of economic growth discussed in Chapter 3 and the pattern of exports from the region is the growing importance of China and India as the star performers in Asia (see Table 3.4). As is evident from looking at column 1 in Table 3.4 China has emerged as the largest trading partner of most economies in Asia. While some of these exports to China may involve intermediate products, the emerging role of China cannot be underestimated.

India stands out for other reasons. It does not trade as much as the ASEAN and East Asian economies and to some extent it has been more insulated from the global downturn. Yet it continues to grow rapidly based on another growth model. India's economy is more driven by services than manufacturing and this further protects it from the business cycle. It is also benefiting from lower commodity prices and the impact of these adjustments on the balance of payments has allowed the central bank to cut interest rates without fear of deterioration in its external balance.

A more severe downturn

Early in 2009 there was speculation that the global downturn might be more severe than anticipated. The likely negative impact on international trade both intraregionally and on industrial countries would be much stronger than anticipated. As the recession gathered steam in Q4 2008 and Q1 2009 export and industrial production downturns made this seem increasingly likely. In Japan exports fell 35% in December 2008 from a year earlier and industrial production plunged a record 9.6%, month on month. Chinese exports declined for the third consecutive month in January 2009, falling 17.5% from a year earlier. Imports plunged even further in January, by 43.1%. More than 20 million Chinese migrant workers lost their jobs in

Q4 2008, Q1 2009 and in recent months. In India exports fell 24% in January and one million Indian workers in the export sector lost their jobs between September 2008 and January 2009. Experts were expecting another half a million workers to lose their jobs by March. New Delhi's public debt stood at 75% of its GDP in early 2009, compared to just 18.5% in China, leaving less room for a large stimulus package. South Korea's exports, the main driving force of the economy, plunged 32.8% in January 2009. Finance minister Yoon Jeung-hyun warned that the fourth largest economy in Asia would shrink by about 2% in 2009 while Credit Suisse projected as much as a 7% contraction. In Taiwan, the sixth largest Asian economy, exports fell by 44.1% in January from a year earlier – the biggest fall since records began in 1972. Imports plunged 56.5% in the same month. For an economy where exports account for 70% of GDP, the impact could be devastating (data in this paragraph reported by Market Oracle, 2009).

The depth of the downturn was also reflected in the IMF's Spring analysis in its World Economic Outlook (IMF, 2009). However as the year unfolded prospects for Asia improved dramatically. As noted in Chapter 5 forecasts for economic decline have been marked down dramatically from a few months ago and prospects marked up. This is evident from Table 3.1 and Table 7.3 in the next chapter where comparisons between forecasts made in the fall of 2008 and the spring 2009 World Economic Outlook are compared and analyzed. The difference is dramatic. For 2009 the average difference in anticipated growth for 2009 is 3% higher in South Korea and Taiwan (from –4% to –1% in South Korea and from –7.5% to –4.1% in Taiwan) and almost 7% in Singapore (from –10% to –3.3%). The revisions also highlight the uncertainty of short-term forecasting in a volatile environment which is also reflected in the sensitivity analysis carried out by the IMF. In any event there is no longer speculation of a double dip recession or a prolonged U-shaped recovery in Asia. Nevertheless export performance deteriorated throughout the region in 2009 (see Table 3.5). The ADB and EIU both predict a strong rebound in exports in 2010.

Another perspective on the impact of the recession in industrial countries in Asia comes from an analysis of growth in GDP and the share of advanced manufacturing in GDP. The latter figures have been compiled by a consulting firm and compared with Q4 2008 growth (refer to Chart 3.6). Countries in Asia with a high share of technical manufacturing in GDP, including machinery, automobiles, electrical machinery, pharmaceuticals, shipbuilding, etc., experienced much larger declines in growth than other industrial countries with a small share of advanced manufacturing in GDP.

Countries need to adopt appropriate countercyclical macroeconomic policies to compensate for the slowdown in exports. Governments also need to be ready to provide resources to protect the chronically poor from further deterioration in their living standards. In our view a deeper recession scenario becomes more probable every day the global crisis persists and the possibility of further contagion spreading to stock markets and banking systems in Asia increases.

Furthermore, developing Asia is now generally much better positioned to withstand this external shock than it was during the Asian financial crisis of a decade ago. International reserves have been built up, economic growth has accelerated in many countries, and financial systems have been restructured. However there are still large budgets deficits in several countries although they have come down in several countries including China, India and the Philippines. Current account deficits are still large, particularly in parts of South Asia and financial inflows from private sources are likely to dry up. The Institute of International Finance expects a 30% decline in global private capital flows to developing countries compared with 2007 (see *The Economist*, 2009). However recent strength in Asian stock markets suggests this may not hold true for this region. Despite potential weak spots, recent strong economic growth has been recorded in South Asia. In India export dependence is much lower than in China and Southeast Asia. However it has other difficulties in financing its investments because of weak local equity markets and lack of willing overseas lenders. It already has high debt to GDP ratio which constrains its options to provide further fiscal stimulus.

As the global crisis has intensified assistance is being offered by donors. The IMF has recently approved a loan of $7.6 billion to Pakistan to rebuild its economy and expand its safety net for the poor and it is not unlikely that similar requests will be made from other countries. In late October 2008 the IMF also created a Short-Term Liquidity Facility (SLF) that comes with no conditions attached and offers large upfront financing to help countries restore confidence and combat financial contagion.

Country size, domestic demand and the global recession

It is no coincidence that the largest economies in Asia have suffered the least as displayed in Table 5.1. To estimate the degree of "suffering" average yearly growth shortfall compares the IMF projections for 2009 and 2010 and the actual 2008 outturn with the actual 2007 growth rate. The sum of the differences between 2007 growth and the next three years are divided by three to find the average yearly growth shortfall which is a measure of the difference between potential and actual output for the years of the recession. These results are displayed in Table 6.4. GDP growth shortfall from 2008 to 2010 is considerably smaller for the three largest economies (China, India and Indonesia) than it is for the three of the smallest economies (Singapore, Hong Kong and Taiwan). In the three smaller economies the average yearly growth shortfall is 7.4%, 5.9% and 5.9% respectively for Taiwan, Hong Kong and Singapore respectively. This is an extraordinarily large shock to these small economies that have been used to growing in excess of 5% for many years. On the other hand the growth shortfall in the three large economies is less than half the rate for the smallest economies – 3.0%, 2.7% and 0.6% respectively for China, India and Indonesia.

There are several reasons for this. The larger economies have much larger domestic economies and considerably more consumers. They are also more diverse economies with large agricultural sectors as well as a manufacturing sector producing a variety of products both for export and domestic consumption. This allows them more flexibility in responding to the crisis by a menu of different stimulus measures to address different demand constraints. As they are more diversified, they are potentially more resilient than more narrowly based small economies. Large economies also generally depend less on exports than do smaller economies and so are less impacted when export demand falls off dramatically. Furthermore, since large economies are less reliant on trade, there is less leakage to other countries from fiscal stimulus than in economies that are more dependent on exports. This is aside from the fact that the decline in exports is in itself a cause of the recession in Asian economies. The resilience of the large Asian economies has been further assisted by fiscal stimulus, more so in the case of China than in Indonesia and India (see Table 6.1). This is also a reason why the large Asian economies are expected to recover from the recession more quickly than their smaller neighbors. India has turned to borrowing from the state banks rather than raising money on the stock market or borrowing overseas and its economy has been helped by other stimulus measures including work fare and debt relief for small farmers. In China state-owned enterprises have contributed to investment demand as investment from other enterprises tied more to foreign investors has dried up (see the India and China country reports below in Chapter 10).

Additional insight into the relationship between fiscal stimulus and the output gap can be gained by comparing the size of the fiscal stimulus with the average growth shortfall in the fourth column of Table 6.4. These comparisons are displayed in Table 6.5. Since the stimulus measures were generally adopted in 2009 a useful comparison would be to double the annual shortfall from Table 6.4 and compare it with the size of the stimulus measured as a percentage of GDP taken from Table 6.1.

The variation in the ratio of stimulus to GDP gap as displayed in the final column of Table 6.5 varies dramatically among the countries of the region. China, Indonesia, Vietnam and Thailand have adopted stimulus measures that exceed the shortfall gap although it should be noted that in the case of Thailand the fiscal measures are intended to extent beyond the end of 2010. For most of the other countries the ratio of spending to the gap is in the range of 0.33 to 0.75, suggesting that additional stimulus measures many be appropriate if budgets can accommodate the increase in spending.[5] For four countries stimulus measures were either not taken or not available to the United Nations when they made the survey. It should be recognized that these calculation are merely indicative of the extent of the stimulus

Table 6.4   Population, exports to GDP and shortfall in growth 2008–2011 compared with 2007

Country	Population in billion people	Export to GDP ratio (2007)	Average yearly growth shortfall 2008–2011 compared with 2007 in %
China	1.300	40.1	3.0
India	1.170	23.0	2.7
Indonesia	0.240	30.9	0.6
Pakistan	0.176	15.3	2.6
Bangladesh	0.156	19.0	0.4
The Philippines	0.098	46.4	2.9
Vietnam	0.087	73.5	2.2
Thailand	0.066	73.7	4.9
South Korea	0.049	43.2	2.9
Nepal	0.028	12.0	–1.2
Malaysia	0.026	117.0	4.1
Taiwan	0.023	61.3	5.9
Sri Lanka	0.020	39.0	1.1
Cambodia	0.014	45.0	7.7
Hong Kong	0.007	205.0	5.9
Lao PDR	0.007	19.0	1.0
Singapore	0.005	252.0	7.4

Numbers in the 4th column are based on five-year growth from 2003–2007 projected for 2008–2010 compared with actual 2008 growth and Asian Development Outlook (ADO) update for 2009 and 2010 published by the Asian Development Bank.
Source: ADB, 2009

measures and the actual impact of the fiscal stimulus will depend upon a number of additional factors including the effectiveness of implementation, leakage from international trade, graft and corruption in the executing agencies administering the stimulus.

Capital flows, exchange rates and terms of trade

In its report on Capital Flows to Emerging Market Economies in January 2009 the Institute of International Finance (IIF) noted that that the current international financial position of the countries in emerging Asia (China, India, Indonesia, Malaysia, the Philippines, South Korea and Thailand) was far stronger than in was in the 1997/1998 crisis. Foreign exchange reserves are substantial (Table 3.3) and there was limited exposure to toxic assets. Only South Korea had extensive short-term obligations which created some strain as noted above in the section on current account and budget outlook for Group 1 economies which have subsided after some swap arrangements made by the Bank of South Korea with the US Federal Reserve, Bank of

Table 6.5   **Fiscal stimulus as percent of shortfall in GDP**

Country	Average yearly shortfall from Table 6.4 times 2	Fiscal stimulus as a share of GDP taken from Table 6.1	Stimulus as % of shortfall
China	$3.0 \times 2 =$ 6.0	13.3	2.22
India	$2.7 \times 2 =$ 5.4	3.2	0.59
Indonesia	$0.6 \times 2 =$ 1.2	1.4	1.17
Pakistan	$2.6 \times 2 =$ 5.1	na	
Bangladesh	$0.4 \times 2 =$ 0.8	0.6	0.75
The Philippines	$2.9 \times 2 =$ 5.4	5.8	0.75
Vietnam	$2.2 \times 2 =$ 4.4	9.4	2.14
Thailand	$4.9 \times 2 =$ 9.8	14.3	1.45
South Korea	$2.9 \times 2 =$ 5.8	5.6	0.96
Malaysia	$4.1 \times 2 =$ 8.2	5.5	0.68
Taiwan	$5.9 \times 2 = 11.8$	3.9	0.33
Sri Lanka	$1.1 \times 2 =$ 2.2	0.2	0.10
Cambodia	$7.7 \times 2 = 15.4$	na	
Hong Kong	$5.9 \times 2 = 11.8$	5.2	0.44
Lao PDR	$1.0 \times 2 =$ 2.0	3.0	1.5
Singapore	$7.4 \times 2 = 14.8$	5.9	0.39

Source: Table 6.1 and Table 6.4

Japan and People's Bank of China. Current account balances are likely to remain strong, primarily as a result of falling oil prices in the first few months of the year which are unlikely to be reversed even as oil prices firmed up in the second half of 2009. This is evident for the group of emerging Asian economies reported in Table 3.4. IIF predicts that the current account balance for these countries would increase from $386.4 billion in 2008 to 474.5 in 2009 (IIF, 2009, Table 11) mainly on the strength of an increase of $50 billion in China, up to $450 billion from 400 billion in 2008. However net private capital flows are projected to fall further in 2009 from $96.2 billion in 2008 to $64.9 billion in 2009, a dramatic decline from net inflows of $314.8 billion in 2007. Equity investment, both portfolio and direct (FDI) are projected to fall while net private credit flows will be negative (refer to Table 6.6). Weakness in capital flows will have a negative impact on investment by multilateral firms as well as domestic businesses. The so-called flight to quality was one explanation for the negative capital flows to Asia in 2008 and the anticipated continuation of these outflows in 2009 as well as weak currencies in these countries. Anticipated slow or negative economic growth and export growth are plausible explanations for this view. However, since March there has been a resurgence in capital inflows into Asian markets and there has been currency appreciation as well. The MSCI Asia Pacific Index of regional stocks climbed 22% in Q2 2009 and Chinese stock prices have rise 45% since the beginning of 2009. There also appears to be little correlation between exchange rates

Table 6.6   Capital flows to emerging Asia (billion US dollars)

	2006	2007	2008	2009
Current account balance	289.5	420.2	386.4	474.5
Private flows net	258.9	314.8	96.2	64.9
Equity investment net	122.6	112.9	57.9	85.7
Direct investment net	87.2	148.6	112.7	79.3
Portfolio investment net	35.5	–35.7	–54.7	6.5
Private creditors	136.3	201.9	38.3	–20.8
Commercial banks net	90.5	155.7	29.8	–25.3
Non-banks net	45.8	46.2	8.4	4.5

Note: Emerging Asia includes China, India, Indonesia, Malaysia, the Philippines, South Korea and Thailand.
Source: Institute of International Finance, 2009

and projected strength of the Asian economies. The countries in Group 1 all experienced negative growth in 2009 as well as large growth shortfalls (Table 5.1). However as of the end of October 2009 all currencies in this group of countries and more generally throughout Asia have appreciated to some extent against the US$ since the beginning of 2009 – Thai baht by 10%, Indonesian rupiah by 18%, South Korean won by 6.8%, Indian rupee by 5%, new Taiwan dollar by 1.4% and the Philippines peso by 1.3%. Central bank policies have something to do with this and the stability of the Hong Kong dollar and the Chinese yuan are certainly a part of this pattern. Clearly fundaments are playing a smaller role in the adjustment mechanism that we would expect if only market forces were at work. Investor sentiment is also playing a role. Despite the poor expectations regarding growth in Group 1 countries Asia as a whole, buoyed by the outlook for China, Indonesia and India, is also playing a role in the resurgence of capital inflows through mid-year. The latest forecast of the IMF suggests that inflows to developing Asia will grow by almost 5% while the global economy contracts by 1.3%.

Corporate Asia and a possible negative feedback loop

The corporate sector in Asian economies has been hard hit by the recession. Lower demand, both domestically and from foreign customers has plummeted and many firms have had to borrow to keep afloat. Those that have been able to find finance through bond finance are the lucky ones and only since March 2009 have corporate bond markets begun to function smoothly. From the middle of 2008 until March 2009 the IMF notes (IMF, 2009c, Global Crisis: The Asian Context, III) that not a single emerging Asian company was able to issue an international bond, even a renewal of a maturing bond! While matters had improved somewhat by June 2009, both domestic and international sources of funding are difficult to obtain. The rate of economic decline has slowed and some countries and sectors are beginning to recover. Nevertheless it is possible that firms will begin to go bankrupt, putting additional pressure on the banking system and creating a toxic downward spiral of lower sales, rising unemployment, bank failures and further financial distress as the region sinks further into recession. The IMF has undertaken an analysis of corporate health in Asia at the end of Q1 2009 (IMF, 2009c, Chapter II). The IMF reached several conclusions which are similar to the analysis suggested above. There is a high risk of corporate default but it is lower than the default risk during the Asian financial crisis of a decade ago. While losses from default could be as high as 2% of GDP there would be fewer defaults and financial distress than a decade ago primarily because corporate Asia entered the crisis in robust health with low leverage and high profitability. Debt to equity ratios have fallen by half from their peak and the debt structure has improved with short-term debt falling as a share of total debt. The debt servicing burden has also declined has interest rates have fallen while profitability increased as companies became more efficient following the Asian financial crisis. In ASEAN 4 rates of return on assets went from 3% in 1997 to 14.5% in 2007.

The IMF analysis relies on a base case scenario which projects a V-shaped recovery beginning in the middle of 2009 and continuing through 2010. By exploring a slower and more tepid recovery scenario a series of inferences are drawn for possible policy actions if the base case turns out to be the most likely. As we have seen from our previous analysis the countries with the largest export exposure to industrial countries have been the worst hit (see Table 5.1 and Chart 3.6). Similarly those companies in the traded goods sector have been more affected than those companies specializing in the domestic market. Real estate companies have also been hit hard. The decline in industrial production relative to 1998 has been greater for the NIEs than for the ASEAN 4.

How bad is it and how bad will it get? One measure of corporate health is the Interest Coverage Ratio (ICR). ICR measures cash flow relative to interest payable on debt. If the ratio is less than 1 then a firm is technically bankrupt although survival can be extended by selling assets. However this cannot last for long. What are ICR levels in Asia? Complete data is not available for 2008. However using an estimated profit decline of 15% *vis-à-vis* 2007 it was estimated that 17% of firms with 10% of total corporate debt had ICR levels less than 1. However not all of these companies have declared bankruptcy. In fact there are few recorded by mid-2009. Partly this reflects the difficulty of legally declaring bankruptcy in Asia and also the hopes that things will get better and firms can stay in business. Nevertheless share prices fell quite dramatically from Q3 2008 to Q2 2009, from a 60 plus year-on-year percentage increase in March 2007 to a negative 60 plus percentage decline in February 2009. There has been a small subsequent rebound. The financial and industrial sectors as well as consumer durables have been the hardest hit. The fragile nature of the industrial sectors in Asia is also evident from spreads on investment grade bonds which literally doubled between September 2008 and November 2008 from 150 bps to 300 bps. The spread was even higher for riskier assets as reflected by the spread between safe assets and risky ones and also the cost of credit default swap insurance. Do these high costs of default risk insurance mean that many Asian companies are about to go under? Things may not be that bad because those buying default insurance are probably investing in very risky ventures. Furthermore the credit default swap market has fallen out of favor following all the problems created during the mortgage-backed securities bubble and the AIG difficulties.

The IMF suggests another method for looking at default risk based on share prices and default probabilities which is more arcane but has the advantage of covering many more firms. This analysis shows the default probability distribution has moved toward the risky end of the spectrum. However the risks are not nearly as high as they were during the Asian financial crisis. For example, for firms at the 75th percentile the risk of default was 8% in March 2009. Twenty-five percent of Asian firms had even higher default risk. This is less that half the level recorded in the Asian crisis where 19% of firms were at risk of default at the 75th percentile. This methodology of assessing default base on a probability distribution is based on a baseline scenario similar to our assumptions outlined earlier – trough in mid-2009 and gradual recovery thereafter.

What happens if the global economy recovers more slowly or deteriorates further? If profits fall further and corporate share prices also deteriorate the default probabilities increase as does the strength of a negative feedback loop between the corporate sector and the financial sector. Default increase and bankruptcy lead to further output declines, higher unemployment and further erosion of bank balance sheets. The IMF undertakes a stress test to explore the vulnerability of the financial and corporate sectors under such negative assumptions. The conclusions are that small firms will be hardest hit as lower earning would erode profitability and result in bankruptcy for many firms. Lower profits would also have an adverse impact on the electronics sector and the construction industry. As the region has made many adjustments since the Asian financial crisis the corporate sectors in Asia are not as sensitive to foreign interest rates or to exchange rates. It is the decline in earnings from exports and export sensitive related industries that is the key to potential bankruptcy.

What policy measures can be adopted in the case of such a negative scenario? Certainly increases in the capital base of the banking system would be warranted. Banks already have capital in excess of the Basle requirements. In view of the current uncertainties a further build up may be indicated. However, as the recovery gets underway and risks decline banks should begin to lend and lend vigorously to support the recovery. So a delicate balance between prudence and risk taking has to be maintained as the recovery unfolds. If things do get worse and even if they do not, bankruptcy in Asia is difficult, time consuming and a negative sum game for most parties. If the process can be streamlined it would enable the corporate and banking systems to write off losses and move forward quickly and efficiently without troubled assets weighing down balance sheets and reducing the flexibility of the economic system to recognize new opportunities for funding and investing. It is also important for governments to consider how a prolonged recession would impact the poor and what measures could be adopted to address poverty concerns. For the poorer countries this could require further development assistance from the ADB and World Bank. We consider these matters further in Chapter 8.

Remittances

Remittances are an important source of foreign exchange in the countries in Group 4 and selectively in Group 3 and Group 2. Countries in Group 1 are generally recipients of foreign migrants and serve to generate wage and salary income for these migrants, part of which is sent home as remittance income to families in Groups 2, 3 and 4. Aside from the impact on income generated domestically there will also be adverse impacts on poverty from a slowdown in remittances (see Table 6.7 for figures on remittance income in Asia). In Bangladesh, for example, remittances accounted for 8.8% of GDP in 2005 (Ahmed, 2006) and even more in 2007. Remittances are a vital part of the fabric of the social network support which the poor depend on. Remittances by Nepalese migrants in India and elsewhere to family households rose by four times to 12% of GDP by end of 2004 compared with a

Table 6.7   Remittance income in Asia

Country	Group	Workers remittances, compensations and migrant transfer ($ million) 2007	Remittances as share of GDP 2007 (in %)	Remittances as share of GDP 2008 (in %)
The Philippines	2	16291	11.6	
Vietnam	2	5500	7.9	
Indonesia	3	6174	1.5	
Bangladesh	4	6562	9.5 (9.0)	10.0
India	3	27000	2.4 (3.0)	
Nepal	4	1734	15.5 (18.0)	
Pakistan	4	5998	4.2 (4.0)	
Sri Lanka	4	na	(9.0)	
Cambodia	4	353	4.2	3.4

Source: World Bank reported in ADB, 2008 and World Bank, 2009a figures in parentheses and te Velde et al, 2009 (Table 7)

decade earlier (World Bank, 2006). Results of a recent study by M. Lokshin et al (2007) indicate that one-fifth of the poverty reduction in Nepal occurring between 1995 and 2004 was because of increased remittances. Adding to traditional remittance sources from India and Hong Kong recent Nepalese migration to the Middle East has also swelled to flow of remittances to close to 20% of GDP. In the Philippines, Capistrano and Sta. Maria (2007) show that remittances and the number of overseas workers both have a significant impact on overall poverty. They find that a 1% increase in the share of remittances in GDP leads to a 2.55% reduction in the incidence of poverty. Similarly, a 10% increase in the number of overseas workers as a share of the population results in a 0.73% decline in the level of poverty. In Cambodia, garment sector workers typically remit an average of 35% of their earnings back to rural families (Dahlberg, 2006). These remittances have enabled rural households to sustain current consumption and to invest in equipment, seeds, fertilizers and livestock. In Lao PDR, remittance rates are high both from family members working abroad and also domestically (World Bank, 2006). In Vietnam, over 9% of income of poor families comes from remittances (VASS, 2007, p. 59). As the global slowdown is reflected in slower economic activity globally, remittances are also expected to fall. Normally remittances are procyclical. Overseas workers send more remittances during tough times. While this motivation could help cushion the slowdown in remittances it is expected that the global nature of this crisis will result in significant return migration as adversely affected countries such as Hong Kong, Malaysia and countries in the Middle East undertake labor shedding and send some migrants home. This will have a significant impact on poverty, as the recipients are members of the poorest groups in society. On the other hand, the remittance impact on poverty is elastic as the studies cited above demonstrate. Efforts are also being made to make remittances transfers more efficient and governments are promoting migration to existing and possible new destinations with government missions.

Unemployment

The outlook for unemployment in Asia has been touched on earlier (see, for example, Chart 3.5 in Chapter 3 as it relates to the United States), particularly the long lag between the trough of the business cycle and the recovery in employment in industrial countries. In Q4 2009 the unemployment rate is still going up in most industrial and developing countries in Asia as forecasts for a slower economic recovery have become likely. Looking at three sub-regions in Asia (these correspond roughly to our Group 1, Groups 2 and 3 together and Group 4 (without India and including Cambodia and Lao PDR), ILO analyzes three possible scenarios, a middle road, a pessimistic and an optimistic scenario. Some aspects of the middle scenario are displayed in Table 6.8. Estimates of the unemployment

Table 6.8   Unemployment and the vulnerably employed – projections for 2009

Region	Unemployment rate	Number of unemployed (million)	Number of vulnerable now employed (millions)
East Asia	4.6	39.1	432.8
Southeast Asia (and Pacific)	6.0	18.0	176.5
South Asia	5.4	35.7	486.2

Source: ILO, 2009 May update

rate and the number of unemployed are based on labor markets that are organized and in the so-called "formal" sector. Estimates for the informal sector are difficult to arrive at. However the number of vulnerable employed relates to a wider reckoning of the size of the labor force and takes into account the chances of dropping into poverty. Over a billion people fall into this category in Asia. In East Asia and South Asia the estimated number of unemployed reflects an increase from 2008 of about three million people while in Southeast Asia the increase is 2.2 million. These rather modest increases in unemployment reflect the limited size of the formal sector. Estimates of the increase in the numbers of those employed in vulnerable jobs is also rather small – 3 million in East Asia, 6.6 in Southeast Asia and the Pacific and 16.3 million in South Asia. In this region the impact on poverty is more important than the modest changes in the formal sector employment picture. In Southeast Asia and the Pacific workers in export-oriented industries have been laid off. However, fiscal stimulus and trade surpluses are expected to help soften the blow on employment and to provide some offset to the contraction in private sector activities. In East Asia the large fiscal stimulus of China is expected to have a beneficial impact on the labor market by offsetting to some extent the loss in jobs in export industries.

Foreign direct investment

The outlook for Foreign Direct Investment (FDI) in 2009 and 2010 is being adversely affected by the ongoing global economic and financial crisis. A global survey of companies involved in international business by the United Nations Conference of Trade and Development (UNCTAD, 2009) suggests that companies expect a sharp decline in their FDI expenditure in 2009 with a revival in 2010 and 2011. Respondents to the survey listed three as especially threatening – a deepening of the global downturn, an increase in financial instability and a rise in protectionism as regulations regarding rules for FDI. Nearly 60% of respondents said they were likely to reduce FDI abroad in 2009 compared to 2008 and nearly a third were anticipating a large decrease of more than 30%. This having been said East, Southeast and South Asia are the most favored destinations of FDI among developing regions. In 2007 the region's share of FDI stock stood at 15.5%, nearly as high as North America at 17% and topped only by EU at 41.5% (see UNCTAD, 2009, Table 6). Latin America came in a poor second with 7.5% of global FDI among developing regions. Nine of the top 20 destinations are in Asia (China, India, Indonesia, Vietnam, Thailand, Singapore, Malaysia, the Philippines and South Korea). Over 50% of respondents listed China as the most attractive economy followed by India at 33% and Indonesia at 10%. The top 15 countries accounted for 74% of total responses, suggesting that only a few countries are likely to get any FDI. Among developing countries investors also remained focused on a few countries (ten countries accounting for 76% of responses).

The presence of suppliers and partners, availability of both cheap and skilled labor, size of the local market, access to international markets and growth in markets were listed as the most desirable factors favoring investment in these markets. The amount of FDI projected by participating Transnational Corporations (TNCs) in the World Investment Prospects Survey for 2009 is qualitatively only marginally lower for the Asian region than in 2008 (1.4 versus 1.9 where the scale runs from −4 to +4. −4 = decrease of more than 50%, 0 is no change and 4 = increase of 50%). This was the highest value of the index for any region, either developed or developing. In fact no other region had an index greater than 0.8 for 2009.

In China, FDI inflows fell by 43% to $43 billion in 1H 2009 from a year ago. FDI has been falling since October 2008. To combat the negative impact on FDI the Ministry of Commerce said that it would work to upgrade the investment environment and attract more investment to the western and central provinces. At the same time outward FDI nearly doubled in 2008 to $52.2 billion from 26.5 billion in 2007. All indications that this trend is continuing in 2009 as China works vigorously to secure foreign sources of raw materials and minerals, particularly in Australia (see Ken Davies, 2009).

In India, results from fiscal year 2008 (April 2008 to March 2009) showed FDI up 11% from the previous year. Investments in chemicals, telecommunications and automobiles were strong. Modifications in FDI regulations were partially responsible for the surge in FDI, overwhelming the negative impact of the outlook for the global economy. As a result the outlook for FDI for the rest of the calendar year is good.

Preliminary reports from the rest of the region are mixed.

7
Where We Stand at the Beginning of 2010

Output growth – globally and in Asia

The OECD compiles a composite series of leading indicators (CLI) for each of its member countries and also for some other developing countries. This series includes a number of different components and has served as a useful indicator of changes in aggregate economic activity in OECD countries and elsewhere. It is possible to get a snapshot of a significant component of the global economy by examining this index. We did this in mid-December

Table 7.1   Composite leading indicators – month of lowest and highest value May 2007–December 2009

Country	Month when index hit bottom	Value of index at the bottom	Value of index at peak	Value of index December 2009	Value of index Oct 2009	Growth cycle outlook
Indonesia*	February 2009	93.6	106.5	98.8	99.5	recovery
India	January 2009	94.0	102.6	99.2	99.3	recovery
China	January 2009	91.9	102.7	103.1	103.2	expansion
Major Asian 5	January 2009	92.6	102.6	102.5	101.0	expansion
OECD total	February 2009	92.6	103.0	103.1	101.3	expansion
OECD Europe*	January 2009	94.0	103.4	100.5	103.0	recovery
G7	February 2009	92.2	103.0	103.1	101.1	expansion
Big 4 Europe*	January 2009	94.2	103.2	103.3	104.7	recovery
US	February 2009	91.0	103.4	101.5	99.6	expansion
UK	January 2009	95.9	103.2	105.8	103.8	expansion
South Korea*	October 2008	90.0	102.4	100.3	100.9	possible expansion
Japan	May 2009	89.2	101.8	102.1	99.6	expansion
Germany	February 2009	90.5	104.5	104.6	102.1	expansion
France	December 2008	95.8	102.3	106.7	104.7	expansion
Canada	February 2009	93.0	101.7	104.3	102.1	expansion
Australia*	April 2009	96.5	101.3	98.8	99.7	recovery

*Value of Index is November not December 2009.
Major Asian 5 include China, India, Indonesia, Japan and South Korea.
Source: OECD, downloaded August 7, 2009, September 11, 2009 and January 3, 2010

2009. The relative size of these indicators month by month gives a good indication of the possible trough of the recession. The lowest value of the CLI for a variety of countries and country groups is displayed in Table 7.1 as well as the value for October 2009 and December 2009.

If these composite leading indicators are accurate the evidence from Table 7.1 is overwhelming. For countries in Asia and the industrial world, the global recession has reached a trough in income growth (decline) either in Q4 2008 or Q1 2009. There is chance that some countries could experience a retrenchment in progress leading to a so-called W-shaped recovery. However, by December 2009 all indications were for a continued rebound of the global economy and most countries had indices over 100 and many were in the expansion phase of the recovery. Some had index values higher than their previous peaks (Canada, China, Japan, France, G7 and OECD). Of course there is no guarantee that this index of leading indicators is infallible. However, when put together with evidence from other countries and international sources there is growing conviction that the global economy began to recover in Q2 2009 and that the recovery is continuing at the time this chapter was drafted in early 2010. Comparing the size of the trough with the value of the index in June 2007, the experience of the US, South Korea, Germany and Japan is notable. All had high index values in June 2007 and all had relatively low values at the bottom of the recession. Aside from the US which had the subprime collapse to deal with South Korea, Germany and Japan are all export-dependent manufacturing economies and suffered substantial losses. It is all the more remarkable that South Korea was able to break out of the recession at such an early date. Further analysis is required to determine the reasons for this. A strong stimulus and support of industry by the government are probably main contributing factors. An additional encouraging sign is that the index for France, OECD and OECD Europe have broken into triple digits, suggesting that economic expansion is under way (OECD is conservative with regard to OECD Europe despite the November index of 100.5).

How does this analysis of the OECD relate to predictions of Hasan et al (2009) and the congressional Budget Office estimates of the recession profile for the US presented in Chart 4.1?

The results for Q4 2009 are quite encouraging. Growth in China and Indonesia accelerated and Singapore has recovered rather dramatically from a projected –10% negative growth a few months ago to relatively robust growth in Q4 (Table 7.2). Hong Kong, Malaysia Taiwan and Thailand all recorded growth in Q4 compared with negative growth in the previous two quarters. Also notice that growth in China, Taiwan and South Korea was quite robust.

Putting this evidence together a picture emerges of dramatic declines in growth in Q4 2008 and Q1 2009 in Asia and the OECD followed by a gradual recovery through the rest of 2009 and in the early months of 2010. This pattern of recovery is also consistent with the projections reported in

Table 7.2   GDP growth in Q4 2009 – various Asian countries

Country	Fourth quarter growth 2009 year on year except South Korea which is quarter on quarter in %
China	10.7
South Korea	6.0
Hong Kong	2.6
Singapore	3.5
Taiwan	9.2
Indonesia	5.4
Malaysia	4.5
Thailand	5.8
India	7.9

Sources: Various country reports and *The Economist*, July 18, 2009; February 2010

Table 5.1. Stock prices in the US rose as much as 15% in Q2 erasing losses in Q1 and the panic that had accumulated in Q4 2008 and the early part of 2009 and stock prices in Asia also recovered in the latter part of the year

Chart 7.1   Selected indexes, 2000–2009

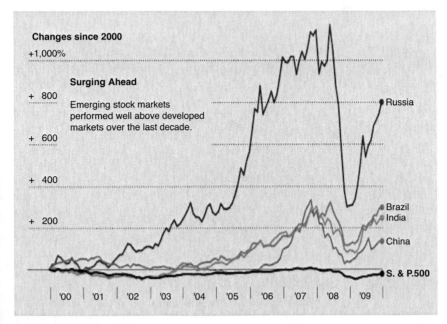

Source: Bloomberg, December 29, 2009

(see Chart 7.1). There was some concern that another stock market bubble is arising in emerging markets, particularly the BRICs of Brazil, Russia, India and China (see Chart 7.1). Stock markets in Russia (800%), Brazil (300%), India (250%) and China (125%) are up dramatically since 2000 compared with the US S&P index which is down slightly.

It is also consistent with the IMF World Economic Outlook Update dated July 8, 2009. The October 2009 IMF and January 2010 revisions of forecasts made in April 2009 are reported in Table 7.3. Positive numbers in columns 4 and 5 reflect an improvement in growth prospects. With a few exceptions (UK and Japan) for most countries the recent forecasts in January 2010 represent a significant upward revision from the forecasts made in October 2009. There is a divide between the giant economies of China and India and the rest of Asia that is further reinforced by the revision in forecasts which show China and India projected to grow faster (1.0% and 1.3% respectively) in 2010. The latest forecast displayed in Table 7.3 also predict the ASEAN 5 to grow, but at a slower rate than the two giant economies in 2010. These forecasts are further buttressed by rebounding equity markets throughout Asia. Stocks in Shanghai are up 85% in the first half of 2009 and also in Jakarta by 83%, 61% in Mumbai, 51% in Taiwan and 43% in Singapore. Gains were also recorded in Manila (41%), Bangkok (40%), Hong Kong (39%) and Seoul (35%).

Furthermore, anecdotal evidence from financial centers in Asia (Hong Kong and Singapore) suggests that firms have begun to rehire as business is picking up. According to a *New York Times* report (Bettina Wassener, 2009) Standard Chartered, HSBC, Bank of New York Mellon and ANZ Australia are all hiring new staff. On top of this, unemployment rates in these financial centers never ballooned as they did in the US and parts of Europe. Unemployment is 5.4% in Hong Kong and 3.3% in Singapore, despite sharp declines in GDP growth in the first half of the year.

The revisions for industrial countries are mixed for 2009; more optimistic for the US and Japan and more pessimistic for the Euro area countries and the UK. For 2010 the forecasts for all countries, both advanced and emerging, are more optimistic than they were a few months ago. The IMF forecasts are consistent with forecasts of the OECD and the US Conference Board. On June 10 the OECD also issued a statement that OECD composite leading indicators for May 2009 point to tangible signs of improvement in the outlook for most OECD countries.[1] Furthermore, the US Conference Board Index of Leading Indicators increased by 1.2% in May following a 1.1% increase in April. These were the largest back to back increases in this index in more than eight years. On Monday, July 13, Goldman Sachs announced a $3.4 billion quarterly profit for Q2 2009 and on Thursday, July 16, J.P. Morgan Chase announced a $2.7 billion second quarter profit from trading and investment banking transactions. These results buoyed stock markets and prompted a statement form Treasury Secretary Geithner saying that financial markets were sending "important signs of recovery". He also noted that European stimulus packages were "quite substantial ..." and that signals from China, where the economy grew by 7.9% in Q2 "offers reason to be cautiously optimistic about the global outlook." In July the IMF made a prediction that the economies of the Euro area (18 economies) will contract by 4.8% in 2009 and also in 2010 by 0.3%. These forecasts were revised upward in October. For the Euro area the contraction will be a more modest 4.2% in 2009 followed by a recovery to slow growth of 0.3% in 2010. For the US, the revised forecast is for a 2.7% decline compared with a 2.8% decline in 2009 forecast in July (see Table 7.3).

Marco Annuziata of UniCredit Group and some other forecasters believe that the potential GDP grow in Europe is lower than in the US. The argument for a higher potential in the US revolves around higher investment risk in Europe combined with a more regulated economic environment. On the other hand, unemployment in both regions is now about the same: around 10% in both regions, even though the US rate rose more rapidly from a 4.4% low compared with 7.2% in Europe. In both the US and the Euro area forecasters are suggesting that unemployment will peak at over 10%. The probability of a quick turnaround in the Euro area is also being discounted by most observers although a recent forecast (early January quoted by Jack Ewing (2010)) of the European Central Bank (ECB) staff cited by Jean-Claude Trichet, the president of the ECB, suggested that the

Table 7.3   Revision of IMF forecasts for 2009 and 2010 – selection of countries and regions

	January 2010 projections		Difference from October 2009	
	2009	2010	2009	2010
Advanced economies	−3.2	2.1	0.2 (0.6)	0.8 (1.5)
US	−2.5	2.7	0.2 (0.1)	1.2 (1.9)
Euro	−3.9	1.0	0.3 (0.9)	0.7 (1.3)
Japan	−5.3	1.7	0.1 (0.7)	0.0
UK	−4.8	1.3	−0.4 (−0.2)	0.4 (1.1)
Other advanced economies	−1.3	3.3	0.8 (2.6)	0.7 (2.3)
Developing Asia	6.5	8.4	0.3 (1.0)	1.1 (1.4)
China	8.7	10.0	0.2 (1.2)	1.0 (1.5)
India	5.6	7.7	0.2 (0.2)	1.3 (1.2)
ASEAN 5*	1.3	4.7	0.6 (1.6)	0.7 (1.0)
World trade volume**	−12.3	5.8	0.3	3.3

* Indonesia, Malaysia, the Philippines, Thailand and Vietnam.
** World trade is October 2009 estimate.
Figures in brackets are differences between July 2009 and January 2010 forecasts.
Source: International Monetary Fund, 2009a and 2009b

Euro zone growth would be 1.5% in 2010. This is much higher than an earlier forecast of close to zero growth.

Further indications that the recession has bottomed out come from the Institute for Supply Management's (ISM) Purchasing Managers' Index (PMI) which has been mentioned earlier in the time line for the US. *The Economist* (February 6, 2010) reports January 2009 and January 2010 indices for a number of OECD countries. The index is based on a survey of purchasing executives and a reading above/below 50 indicates the manufacturing economy is generally expanding/contracting. The good news is that the indices was over 50 in most countries at the beginning of 2010 after being far below 50 a year earlier. Only Greece and Spain were still below 50 in January of 2010 (see Table 7.4). Also notice that India and China did not suffer as much as OECD countries since their indices were significantly higher in January 2009.

Additional evidence of recovery comes in the form of a coordinated statement by central banks in late September 2009. On September 24 the Federal Reserve announced it was scaling back its Term Auction Facility which was introduced to lend cash on 28- and 84-day terms. The announcement was made in conjunction with the European Central Bank, Bank of England and SNB. This action was prompted by limited demand and improved conditions in funding markets. Finally, the Q3 result for US GDP growth showed a substantial recovery of 3.5%.

Volatile oil prices also have to be factored into the recovery equation and have created additional uncertainty as to the strength and durability of the recovery in industrial countries. The sharp reduction in global energy demand and oil prices in Q4 2008 and Q1 2009 crisis resulted in an estimated over $100 billion in planned oil investment being curtailed or postponed, primarily in Canadian oil sands and other projects dependent on sustained higher oil prices. At the end of Q2 oil prices began to retreat again after rising for most of Q1. As the global economy recovers there is a risk of another spike in oil prices if the growth in demand meets limited

Table 7.4 Purchasing Managers' Index – January 2009 and January 2010

	January 2009	January 2010
China	42.0	57.0
India	46.5	57.2
Britain	36.0	56.5
United States	35.5	58.4
France	38.0	55.5
Spain	32.0	45.5
Germany	32.5	53.5
Greece	40.0	47.0

Source: *The Economist* February 6, 2010 figures interpolated from chart

Chart 7.2   US average retail gasoline price, regular grade (per gallon)

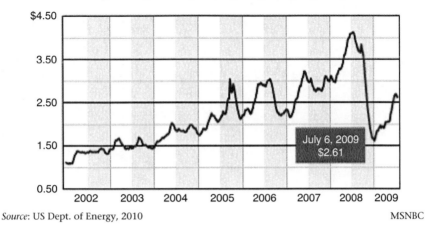

Source: US Dept. of Energy, 2010   MSNBC

supply, particularly if there is no spare capacity available to moderate price movements if demand grows more quickly than anticipated.

After plummeting from a peak of over $4.00 per gallon in July, 2008 to $1.60 in early 2009, the average US retail gasoline prices rebounded to $2.61 a gallon in early July 2009 where it has remained at a reasonably steady level through August (see Chart 7.2).

Industrial countries growth performance through Q2 and Q3 show some improvements relative to the previous quarter but are still significantly lower than a year ago (see Table 7.5). Although there is some improvement in Q3 compared with Q2, the Euro area as a whole is down 4.1% from Q3 a year ago. Some countries have also improved in Q3, most notably the US, France and Germany although most countries are at least 4% lower. Changes from Q2 to Q3 are a bit more optimistic, a sign that the recession has bottomed out and economies are recovering. The Euro area is only 0.2% lower and only the UK, Netherlands and Spain recorded negative growth between 0.5% and 1%. All the rest of the OECD countries shown in the table recorded positive growth or slight negative growth of less than 0.5%.

For Q4, OECD is projecting some more growth acceleration in Germany and the US, which is consistent with the outcomes presented in Table 7.5. The US was projected to grow at an annualized rate of 2.4% in Q4 relative to Q3 and preliminary estimates made at the end of January 2010 showed that at an annual rate of 5.7% the US economy grew at its fastest pace in over six years. Prospects are less rosy for other OECD countries. Combining Q3 and Q4 no growth in Japan is expected in Q3 and Q4 and over-all growth is expected to be –5.6 lowest among the major OECD countries. GDP in the Euro area is still expected to decline by 3.9% although

Table 7.5   GDP growth – % change from previous quarter and from the same quarter in 2008

	Q2 GDP % change from Q1 (annual rate)	Q2 GDP % change from Q2 2008	Q3 GDP % change from Q2 (annual rate)	Q3 GDP % change from Q3 2008
Greece	1.0	–0.3	–1.7	–1.7
France	1.4	–2.6	1.0	–2.3
Germany	1.3	–5.9	2.9	–4.8
Euro area	–0.5	–4.7	1.5	–4.1
US	–1.0	–3.9	2.2 (5.7)*	–2.6
Belgium	–1.1	–3.7	2.0	–3.4
Austria	–0.4	–4.4	2.1	–3.7
Italy	–1.9	–6.0	2.3	–4.6
UK	–0.75	–5.6	–1.2 (0.4)*	–3.2**
Netherlands	–3.4	–5.1	1.7	–3.7
Spain	–4.2	–4.2	–1.2	–4.0

* Q4 GDP at annual rate.
** Q4 2009 change from Q4 2008
Source: *The Economist* September 19, 2009, p. 109 and January 2, 2010, p. 69

prospects for Q4 relative to Q3 are for positive growth of 2%. Prospects for Britain, Italy and Canada will not improve much in the second half of 2009.

German and Japanese exports are also showing a sign of recovery as destocking seems to have come to an end. This is being reflected in new import orders both within Asia and from Europe and North America. While growth in the UK, Greece and Spain is still anemic there are signs of a turn-around in the housing market in the UK. However, consumer demand remains weak in the US, where the number of houses placed under contract fell sharply in November 2009, and in Japan. Therefore the outlook, though more upbeat is still tinged with fears of a relapse to slower growth.

As evidence of a more optimistic outlook a Swedish bank (September 1, 2009) revised upward its forecast for 2009 and 2010 for some countries. In the US, the forecast went from 0.8% to 1.8 % in 2010 and in Europe from –0.3% to 1.2%. The ISM/PMI index in the US for August also broke the 50 barrier to 52.9, signifying a shift from contraction to expansion, the first such reading since January 2008. The index moved up further in the next three months, reaching 55.9 in December 2009. The German job-less rate fell in August, signifying a strong response to government stimulus as well as subsidies to encourage companies to keep workers on payrolls. However the unemployment rate remained stuck at 8.1 % the rest of the year through December 2009. Unemployment in the US continued to rise through the summer and fall, reaching a peak of 10.3% in October 2009 before falling slightly in November as new unemployment claims fell significantly.

The forecasts reported at the beginning of this Chapter displayed in Table 7.2 and Table 7.3 and also Table 5.1, suggest that more recent forecasts for GDP growth and general economic activity in Asia are more optimistic than forecasts made even a few months earlier. This adds credibility to thinking that the recession in Asia is – V shaped and that recovery is gaining strength faster than forecasts can track it.

Further evidence of this rebound is that job growth was positive in Q2 in South Korea, Taiwan and Singapore while real effective exchange rates depreciated against the US dollar in South Korea won (24%)) New Taiwan dollar (12%) and Singapore dollar (9%) between September 2008 and September 2009. This adjustment in exchange rates facilitated a rebound in exports of 37% in Singapore, 59% in Taiwan, 46% in South Korea and 45% in China over the same period. Being tied to the US dollar, Hong Kong experienced a real exchange appreciation of 11% and deterioration in employment growth in Q3 2009.

The fall OECD Economic Outlook for 2009 (OECD, 2009b) was released in November, 2009. Some of the analysis and forecasts were reported above in Table 5.1. Comparisons of these forecasts with those of the June 2009 OECD Economic Outlook suggest that OECD, like the IMF and the ADB have further revised their forecasts to reflect a more optimistic macro-economic outlook for 2009 and 2010. While fiscal balances in OECD are forecast to widen further than anticipated six months earlier output forecasts suggest slower decline in 2009 and more rapid growth in 2010 (from –4.3% to –3.5% in 2009 and from –0.1% in 2010 to 1.9% in 2010). Unemployment is also forecast to decrease, but only slightly and is still forecast to continue rising in 2010. In early January 2010 the head of the European Union suggested that growth in the EU would be only 1% in 2010 while growth in the US and developing Asia would be higher. Such a low growth rate was unsatisfactory and would need to be raised to 2% for the EU to achieve a satisfactory economic recovery. Further indications of a weak recovery were reflected in concern that Greece, Portugal and Spain were having trouble financing large fiscal deficits. Debt has also increased generally in industrial countries as fiscal stimulus measures have continued. The IMF estimates that the debt of G20 countries will increase to 118% of GDP by 2014, up from 80% of GDP before the crisis (see *The New York Times*, February 6, 2010). However the outlook for the US brightened somewhat as the unemployment rate fell to 9.6% in January 2010 and manufacturing added 11,000 jobs, the first monthly increase since November 2007. A further indication of the health of the United States financial sector is the February 19 announcement by the Federal Reserve that it would raise the discount rate on loans made directly to banks by 0.25%, raising the rate to 0.75% from 0.50%. This move was considered by observers to be a "baby step" toward reestablishing a more normal monetary policy stance that would eventually ease the extraordinarily loose monetary policy that was put in place to stimulate the economy and help it to recover from the recession.

While the Asian economies have also had an increase in external debt as a result of greater fiscal stimulus none of the countries in this region are in as much peril as the weaker countries in the European Union. Pakistan and Sri Lanka have large levels of external debt and they have turned to the IMF for assistance. India's fiscal deficit has increased dramatically to 8% of GDP in 2009, a significant increase from 3.3% in 2008. While this growing fiscal deficit could make it harder and more expensive for firms to borrow, most of its debt is owed to local creditors and thus presents no risk of default to external creditors.

Further evidence of a stronger, yet still tepid economic recovery is an improvement in global trade growth and stronger housing and stock markets. These global and industrial country outlooks are further reflected in OECD forecasts for developing countries in Asia as displayed in Table 7.6 Even in the space of two months the outlook for the four major Asian economies for which both the OECD and IMF have made forecasts has improved by as much as 2% or more in the case of South Korea and smaller amounts for the other countries. (Note that the China forecast is lower in the OECD forecast for 2009.) The OECD further notes that the modest recovery in OECD countries will result in continued high unemployment rates while the major stimulus for growth in the global economy will fall on the larger developing economies including Brazil, Russia, India and China – the so called BRICs. The OECD notes that the BRICs are expected to grow at over 6% in 2009–2011 while OECD growth is a much lower 2% on average. As the global economy recovers structural imbalances that grew during the previous decade are expected to fall. Current account surpluses as a percentage of global GDP are forecast to fall in China, Germany and the oil exporters to about 1.5% of GDP while the US current account deficit will shrink, accordingly to less than 1%

Table 7.6   IMF and OECD forecasts for major Asian economies – September 2009 and November 2009

Country	IMF GDP growth 2009 (September 2009 forecast)	OECD GDP growth 2009 (October 2009 forecast)	IMF GDP growth 2010 (September 2009 forecast)	OECD GDP growth 2010 (October 2009 forecast)
China	8.5	8.3	9.0	10.2
India	5.4	6.1	6.4	7.3
Indonesia	4.0	4.5	4.8	5.3
South Korea	−1.0	0.1	1.5	4.4

Source: IMF, 2009b and OECD, 2009b

of global GDP (see OECD Economic Outlook database). At its peak the US current account deficit was upwards of 2% of global GDP.

Analysis of these trends and developments in the Asian region will be discussed in Chapter 10 where we look more closely at individual country experiences.

Poverty and unemployment

Analysis of previous business cycles and the current global recession suggests that unemployment and poverty are lagging indicators. In the United States, for example, the level of unemployment is not expected to peak until sometime near the end of 2009 or in early 2010. New jobless claims have fallen back from their peak in the Q1 2009, when they reached 674,000 per week at the end of March 2009. In early January 2010 claims were just over 400,000, a level at which economists predict a transition from job shedding to new job creation. Nevertheless the level of unemployment in the United States reached a high in October 2009 of over 10% and fell slightly in November, 2009. However in December the US economy shed an additional 85,000 jobs causing economists to revise their forecasts for the speed of recovery in the labor market. The US has lost 7.2 million jobs since the recession began. One of the difficulties in lowering unemployment is that many jobs will never return. Compared with previous recessions new employment gains will have to come from the creation of new jobs, not from those laid off being rehired. Similar patterns are being observed in other industrial countries. In Europe, the Euro zone unemployment rate rose to 10% in November, the highest level since the introduction of a single currency ten years ago. There are 15.7 million unemployed in the Euro zone where more than 4 million jobs have been lost since the start of the recession. Unemployment is expected to rise further until mid-2010.

In any case if past recessions are any guide, the unemployment is a lagging indicator, perhaps as much as six months (see Chart 7.3). The peak in unemployment is always a few months after the trough of the recession which is indicated by the shaded area in the Chart 7.3. It is interesting is that the unemployment rate has lagged more and more in the past two recessions in the United States. The National Bureau of Economic Research (NBER) notes that the US unemployment rate peaked 15 months after the NBER trough month in the 1990–91 recession and 19 months after that NBER trough month in the 2001 recession. If the current recession follows the 1990–91 recession pattern and assuming that the trough of the current recession is March 2009, we should not expect the unemployment to start to drop until mid-2010 in the United States. If the recession follows the 2001 pattern it would be the fall of 2010 before unemployment begins to retreat. Employers are more likely to hold on to key employees in the

Chart 7.3   Unemployment and cycles of GDP in the United States

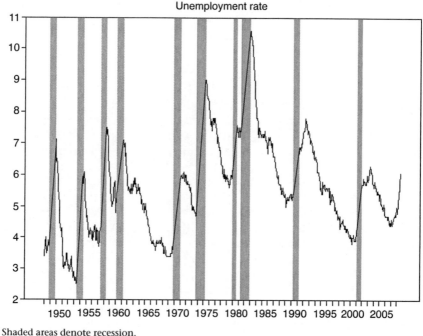

Shaded areas denote recession.
Source: US Bureau of Labor Statistics

recession, making do with a skeleton crew. As the recovery proceeds they have become more reluctant to rehire until they are sure that the worst is over and they can look forward to fatter order books. Notice that in the downturn of the early 1980s the unemployment rate peaked at close to 11%. At that time there was no talk of the recession being tantamount to a mini great depression. It is useful too keep these thoughts in mind when evaluating the state of the economy and the labor market in mid-2009. It is also interesting to note that the current recession bears a marked similarity to the 1975 recession (see Chart 7.3). In both recessions the decline in new jobless claims was very slow.

What factors might explain this slow recovery in employment? In the current recession, employers are showing a persistent reluctance to rehire workers that have been fired or laid off for fear that the recovery will be slow and they will lose competitive advantage to other employers who are benefiting from lower labor costs. In the 1975 recession there was ambivalence regarding the effectiveness of fiscal policy. The recession was characterized by the presence of inflation alongside recession – so called stagflation – as a result of the oil shock which was largely responsible for the onset of the recession. For example, fiscal policy was tightened in 1974 and the budget deficit decreased. However shortly afterwards fiscal policy became explicitly expansionary in 1975 as the Tax Reduction Act was passed and federal revenues fell by about 1.4% of GDP as a tax rebate was sent out in Q2 1975. Expenditures were increased and the budget deficit increased. These measures eventually resulted in a resumption of growth and a reduction in unemployment. However hesitation in providing a fiscal stimulus in a timely manner resulted in a longer lag in the response of unemployment to stronger growth prospects. Fear of inflation could have also prompted employers to adopt conservative hiring policies as the recession ended and the recovery began. The oil shock also had a strong impact on other industrial countries as many oil importing countries also suffered recessions, including Western European countries and Japan. The result was an overall decline in growth in industrial countries which was partially offset by more rapid growth in oil exporters as they invested petro dollars in their economies and elsewhere (see M. Labonte and G. Makinen, 2002). In one sense the oil shock played a similar role as a shock to the global economy in the 1970s as the subprime loan bubble of 2008, the difference being that some oil exporters benefited in the 1970s. No country or group of countries seems to have benefited from the current toxic asset meltdown.

The pattern of unemployment is more difficult to ascertain in developing countries since the size of the informal sector, with its lack of reliable unemployment information, is so large. However it is probably safe to say that both unemployment and poverty react more slowly to revival of aggregate demand than the standard macroeconomic indicators such as consumption and investment. There are some aggregate estimates of poverty and unemployment available for Asia from the World Bank, ILO and the Asian Development Bank. The ILO estimates that the number of unemployment in Asia would rise by around 30 million and that 85% of families in South Asia would fall below a $2 per day poverty line. This is nearly twice the poverty line we have been using so the absolute figure is not comparable. However poverty levels using a lower threshold would also be increasing. The proportion of workers in vulnerable employment, which ILO defines as those workers less likely to benefit from safety nets that guard against loss of income during economic hardship, would rise to 77% in South Asia. The widespread level of these deprivations estimates is startling and governments need to be able to provide stopgap measures to protect minimal living standards. Poverty levels are expected to increase as well.

Length of recession

Although the results are still preliminary, we can make some rough comparisons with previous recessions. If we assume that the current recession is delineated by the peaks and troughs of the OECD composite leading indi-

Table 7.7   Length of recessions from peak to trough in selected OECD countries – 1975 to 2003

Length of recession in quarters	Number of recessions in selected OECD economies
2 quarters	7
3	5
4	3
5	3
6	3
7	1
8	1
9	–
10	1

Countries sampled: Australia, Canada, France, Germany, Italy, Japan, UK, US. Germany had the longest recorded recession of 10 quarters: Q1 1980–Q3 1982.
Source: Authors' estimate based on data from National Bureau of Economic Research

cators we can estimate the length of this recession compared with previous recessions in OECD countries. Looking at the larger OECD member countries the length of recession from peak to trough in quarters is displayed in Table 7.7.

For most OECD countries the current recession began with a peak in Q2 2007 and ended with a trough in Q1 2009, duration of seven quarters. For some countries the recession may be a quarter more or less. But seven quarters seems to be the strong average for most countries. This makes the present recession longest down cycle in the last 35 years for most countries in the sample. Only the UK with an eight-quarter recession from Q2 1990 to Q2 1992 and Germany with a ten-quarter recession from Q1 1980 to Q3 1982 experienced a longer recession in the past. Of course these rough comparisons tell us nothing about the severity of the recession either in terms of loss of income or employment. It also tells us nothing about the length of recovery to the next peak. Nevertheless it does provide useful information on the length of the recession.

From another perspective, that of the Great Depression of 1929, two well known economists Eichengreen and O'Rourke (available on a ongoing basis at the website http://www.voxeu.org/index.php?q=note/3421) argue that world industrial production is tracking closely the fall in the early days of the Great Depression beginning in 1930. They also track world stock markets and industrial output in developing countries. They concluded that stock markets have rebounded since March and world trade has stabilized. However both variables are far below the ones they followed in the Great Depression. They also note that industrial output for North America, Germany and Britain are closely following the rate of fall in the early 1930s while France and Italy are doing much worse. Japan's industrial output was

25% lower than at an equivalent stage in the Great Depression although there was a sharp rebound in March. For the nine months since this recession began, say April 2008, the decline in global industrial production has been just as steep as it was for the nine months beginning in June 1929. Furthermore global stock markets are falling even faster than in the Great Depression. The same is true for the volume of world trade. Eichengreen and O'Rourke conclude

> "To sum up, globally we are tracking or doing worse than the Great Depression, whether the metric is industrial production, exports or equity valuations. Focusing on the US causes one to minimize this alarming fact. The 'Great Recession' label may turn out to be too optimistic. This is a Depression-sized event."

Eichengreen and O'Rourke go on to say that these are still early days. We are only about a year into the crisis/recession and as we have indicated earlier there are good signs that a turnaround is near. The Great Depression continued on for three more years before it reached a trough and never did recover completely until World War II. They also argue that looking at the US only gives a distorted picture of the depth of the global slump. Global stock markets are falling faster than the US market as is global industrial production and the volume of world trade. World trade volume is now only about 85% of what it was nine months ago. At a similar time in the Great Depression world trade had only fallen by 5%. Global stock markets have lost half their value compared with only 10% at a comparable stage in the Great Depression. Eventually stocks fell to around 30% of their initial value in the Great Depression but it took three years. All of these trend comparisons are disturbing and the destruction of world trade is a key factor in the historical analysis of the persistence and depth of the Great Depression. Are events likely to be different this time around? Central banks have responded by lowering discount rates more sharply than in the Great Depression. However they started from a lower base and there was also a lag of about five or six months before discount rates responded to the passing of the peak in economic activity. This is about the same time lag as in the Great Depression. Monetary supply has continued to increase throughout this recession while there was leveling and then severe contraction in the Great Depression. Governments have also loosened their purse strings more quickly and more vigorously than in the Great Depression. Budget deficits are now averaging between 4% and 5% of GDP whereas global deficits were only around 1% of GDP at the same time in the cycle during the Great Depression. Current budget deficits are being used to provide stimulus to aggregate demand by working to boost consumption and investment whereas as in the early days of the Great Depression there was very little recognition of the power of compensatory finance. The power of fiscal policy and Keynesian analysis was not widely recognized until after World War II.

Which view of the business cycle is likely to prevail is now being played out in the global economic theater. Forecasts from the OECD and the IMF were circulated at the end of June 2009 and are compared with more recent forecasts in Table 7.6. As noted above the recent forecasts are more optimistic. Nevertheless the tendency for private saving rates in the US and to a lesser extent in Europe, to increase may also result in a slower recovery in aggregate demand and an attenuation of the cycle, resulting in a U-shaped or even a "bathtub"-shaped recovery. One of the potential downside risks is the continuing problems in the US housing market, centered mostly in Florida, Nevada and California (FNC), combined with recent weakness in the commercial property market. The focus lies in the resetting of interest only mortgages that were taken out during the boom years between 2001 and 2007.

An analysis for *The New York Times* by the real estate information company First American CoreLogic (see David Streitfeld, 2009) shows there are 2.8 million active interest-only home loans worth $908 billion. The interest only periods, which put off the principal for five, seven or ten years are now beginning to expire. In the next 12 months, $71 billion of interest only loans will reset. The year after, another $100 billion will reset. After mid-2011 another $400 will reset. Many of these loans were made in the FNC states. Many home owners will not be able to meet the substantially higher mortgage payments after the reset, putting further downward pressure on the housing market, which has just begun to revive, and increasing default rates further. So far there are no plans to rescue these borrowers.

The speed of the response of the global economy will have a significant impact on the Asian economies, both in their recovery and in their ability to address the various issues that are arising, particularly poverty and unemployment. In Chapter 10 we turn to the experience and challenges of individual countries against the backdrop of global recession.

Previous recessions in Asia

The IMF has examined previous recessions in some Asian economies to see if some insights that can be gained in terms of how long and how deep the current recession will be and also the vigor of the recovery when it does occur. The IMF looked at recessions in a mixture of industrial and developing countries in Asia. The industrial countries were Japan, Australia, New Zealand and the developing countries were China, India, Hong Kong, South Korea, Taiwan, Indonesia, Malaysia, the Philippines and Thailand. Poorer countries in South Asia and Southeast Asia were not included in the sample. Three major findings which emerged from the IMF analysis of these countries for the period from 1980 until 2007 (see IMF, 2009c, Chapter II) can be summarized as follows.

- Recessions accompanied by financial stress in domestic banking are longer and deeper than those without the accompanying financial stress. This is because the fall in credit that arises in a period of financial stress puts additional pressure on the corporate sector by depriving firms of working capital. It also prohibits households from smoothing consumption by making borrowing more difficult. Both of these developments reinforce the downward recessionary tendency that began in the real estate sector.
- Recoveries have been weaker than in other developing regions because they have been driven by exports alone. Other emerging economies had greater participation in recovery from other components of the economy, particularly investment. In Asian recoveries investment has been notably weak. Growth in the recovery phase has been a half percentage point lower in the recovery phase than in other emerging economies.
- Deep recessions in Asia have resulted in a permanent decline in potential output growth, resulting in a long tern permanent decline in potential output. Furthermore deeper recessions do not result in sharper and more vibrant recoveries.
- Exports have been the main engine of recovery while investment and consumption played limited roles.

There are several key lessons that can be drawn from the IMF analysis:

- Proactive monetary and fiscal policies have helped to both reduce the depth of the recession and speed up the recovery. While this conclusion is based on counterfactual models that assume there were no changes in monetary and fiscal policy and assumptions about the dynamic impact of monetary and fiscal policy on GDP, the conclusions are still powerful.
- Because policy impacts operate with lags, the gap between the actual and counterfactual paths do not become substantial until one year after the start of the recession, but after two years the GDP counterfactual is 3 percentage lower than the actual GDP (IMF, 2009c).
- In the current environment there appears to be room for further fiscal and monetary stimulus in developing Asian economies.
- The Asian model of excessive reliance on export-led growth is unlikely to be as successful in this recession because the industrial countries are also recovering and are unlikely to increase their import demand for Asian manufactured products at the same rate they have in the past.
- Structural reforms that put greater emphasis on lifting consumption by providing social safety nets, thereby reducing the need for households to accumulated large savings balances as well as the preoccupation with increasing industrial capacity to fuel further export growth.

Further examination of the status of Asian developing countries with regard to their status as the global recession unfolds suggests four groups of countries:

(a) Countries highly dependent on exports and whose export mix is composed of advanced manufacturing goods. These include South Korea, Malaysia, Singapore and Taiwan. All four are projected to have large shortfalls in years GDP growth according to Table 5.1. They are all higher income countries and have sufficient resources to provide strong stimulus to their economies. Their corporate sectors are not in a high risk category and poverty levels are low. We should add Hong Kong to this group even though its industrial capacity is small and it is more service oriented. It is, however, highly dependent on international trade in goods and services and is projected to have a high average yearly growth shortfall of over 6%.

(b) Countries in a middle income category that have high export to GDP ratios that are also susceptible to slower growth as export prospects are reduced. These include the Philippines, Thailand and Vietnam. Growth shortfall is also high in these economies, though not as high as countries in category (a). However poverty levels are also somewhat higher, particularly in the Philippines and Vietnam. Corporate risks to small-scale industries are also high. These countries have to tailor their stimulus packages to address the needs of small-scale industries and also the poor.

(c) Three large countries of India, China and Indonesia that have more modest expected average growth shortfalls averaging less than 3% without risk of negative growth in GDP and enough flexibility to address regional poverty concerns. The global recession is impacting different groups in the society. In China this would include workers in export-oriented industries who have migrated back to rural villages. In India workers involved in the Information Technology and Communications have been adversely affected. In Indonesia the impact has been more disperse and efforts to assist poor in the eastern regions should be intensified.

(d) Low-income countries with large poverty components that are not generally highly integrated into the global economy and are experiencing financial stress including large fiscal deficits and high levels of government debt. These include Bangladesh, Cambodia, Lao PDR, Nepal, Pakistan and Sri Lanka. With the exception of Cambodia and Sri Lanka, export share of GDP for these countries averages just over 15% and the expected shortfall in growth as a result of the global recession is modest, ranging from 0.4% for Bangladesh, 1.0% for Lao PDR, 1.1% for Sri Lanka, 1.2% for Nepal and 2.6% for Pakistan (see Table 6.4). The impact on Cambodia is expected to be larger, primarily because of the significant share of exports in GDP, a share that has increased dramatically in the last decade. The impact on Sri Lanka could also be larger depending on the cost of rehabilitation after the end of the conflict in the northern and western regions. Selectively, some export-oriented industries in other countries will also be affected including carpets in Nepal and apparel in Bangladesh and Sri Lanka. The risk in these countries is that poverty reduction programs will be setbacks as budgets are paired as a consequence of the crisis and related constraints.

Lost GDP growth and poverty

The yearly average GDP growth lost as a result of the global recession displayed in Table 6.4 and Table 6.5 can be roughly translated into increases in poverty. Work by World Bank (2000) and Ravallion and Chen (1997) conclude that on average 1% of growth will bring about a 2% to 3% reduction in the number of people living below the poverty line. Conversely a decline in growth of 1% results in a 2% to 3% increase in those below the poverty. Using these figures the global recession is resulting in a significant increase in poverty throughout the region. Though the impact is smaller in the poorer countries they are less well equipped to deal with it and will require assistance from international donors.

The growth shortfall from the global recession of 2008 and 2009 can be compared to the shortfalls from the Asian financial crisis of more than a decade ago which are shown in parenthesis in Table 7.8. The first numbers in column 2 of this table, the average yearly growth shortfall in the 2008/2009 recession are the same as column 4 of Table 6.4. Comparing the two recessions, it is interesting to note that the shortfalls for Indonesia, Thailand and Malaysia are more than 10% per annum in the Asian financial crisis, substantially higher than any of the shortfalls in the current crisis. Aside from the Philippines, the shortfalls in most other countries were less than 4% per year. The policy environment was quite different in the earlier Asian financial crisis. Rather than provide monetary and fiscal stimulus to provide liquidity and restore confidence in currencies, budgets were tightened to prevent further currency depreciation. This fiscal posture tended to exacerbate the decline in income.

Implications of a prolonged global recession

Much of the rhetoric concerning the global recession has been carried out against a backdrop of a return to a stable growth path either late in 2009 or early in 2010. The optimistic scenario suggested by Robert Gordon (Gordon,

Table 7.8   Average difference between yearly GDP growth in 2003–2007 and GDP in 2008, 2009 and 2010 (in %)

		Group
China	3.0 (4.0)	3
South Korea	2.9 (3.6)	1
Taiwan	5.9 (0.8)	1
Hong Kong	5.9 (4.4)	1
Indonesia	0.6 (**15.2**)	3
Malaysia	4.1 (**10.9**)	1
The Philippines	2.9 (6.1)	2
Thailand	4.9 (**10.8**)	2
Singapore	7.4 (3.6)	1
India	2.7 (0.2)	3
Vietnam	2.2 (3.0)	2
Sri Lanka	1.1 (0.1)	4
Cambodia	7.7 –	4
Nepal	–1.2 (0.0)	4
Bangladesh	0.4 (–0.7)	4
Lao PDR	1.0 –	4
Pakistan	2.6 (2.1)	4

Figures in parenthesis are growth shortfall from the 1997–98 Asian financial crisis using the same methodology. Double digit shortfalls highlighted.
Source: Authors' estimates

2009) puts the bottom of the recession in the United States in Q2 2009. First quarter GDP results in OECD countries and partial results for Asian economies suggest that this might be premature. While it is true that the large economies of the region which have large domestic demand (China, India and Indonesia) continued to grow although at a somewhat slower rate than in the past, the smaller economies with greater export dependence continued to struggle to recover from sharply negative exports and poor stock market and investment performance. Among these economies only South Korea has been able to recover quickly enough to record positive growth. The drag of financial restructuring on the US and European economies continues to pull down their economies and this is reflected in slower export growth, negative expectations and meager evidence that fiscal stimulus measures and looser monetary policy are having a tangible upside impact as the second quarter comes to a close. Time will tell whether the recovery will be more evident when fourth results come in. In early December it does now appear that the recovery is gaining momentum in Asia and, to a lesser extent in OECD countries.

The negative impact of potentially higher interest rates arising from the massive fiscal stimulus measures in many OECD countries has raised some concern that the recovery will be attenuated both in OECD countries and in Asia. The possibility that the global recession will be less V-shaped and more U-shaped, makes greater focus on the needs of the poor even more pressing. Stimulus measures already adopted and summarized in Table 6.2 have been targeted to address a variety of different challenges including boosting aggregate demand, particularly consumption. This has been done either by spending on a variety of "shovel ready" projects, tax breaks and investment incentives. There are only a few countries that have even mentioned assistance to those in poverty and these programs are tangential to the major thrust of the stimulus packages, which is to help the industrial and export sectors recover and move to a higher growth platform. The poverty reduction programs reviewed in the country analysis in Chapter 9 do little to dispel this notion. There is a preoccupation with restoring aggregate demand, keeping budget deficits in check while providing appropriate fiscal stimulus, the impact of budget deficits on possible currency depreciation as well as other macroeconomic and trade issues. Other issues including poverty are hardly mentioned. To avert a sharp increase in poverty sacrificing the gains of the past decade governments must also address the needs of the poor. This means reinvigorating the initiatives mentioned in Chapter 6 and mobilizing resources to address the plight of the poor. In cases where the economies of the region are slower to recover and move to a sustained growth trajectory there is a need for a continuing poverty reduction strategy. Such an effort will allow these economies to address poverty concerns within the context of more persistently slow economic growth. The most important component of this agenda is to keep a safety net in place to provide assistance for the chronically poor. Such a program is outlined in Chapter 9.

While poverty incidence is not perfectly correlated with the unemployment rate, particularly in developing countries where unemployment statistics are compiled for a limited component of the labor force, it is useful to remember that in industrial countries the time from peak to trough in the unemployment rate is much longer than the trough to peak. This is obvious from looking at the time profile of US unemployment in the postwar era, particularly since the mid-1980s when the rate hit a high of 10.8% at the end of 1982. It took six years and three months for the unemployment rate to fall to its next cyclical low of 5% in March 1989. The next trough to peak in unemployment took only three years and three months for unemployment to rise to the 7.8% in mid-1992 while the next secular acceleration in economic activity was seven years and nine months, taking the unemployment to a 3.8% in April of 2000, a level that had not been reached since early 1966, a period of over 34 years. In previous recessions the unemployment rate has receded somewhat more quickly from its peak. In the 1983 recession the unemployment fell from 10.8% to just over 7% in a year and a half and from 9% to 7% in two years following peak unemployment rate of 9% in May 1975. Of course "quickly" means something different if you are among the unemployed. There is no getting around the fact that this recession is exacting a toll on the labor market not only in the US but elsewhere in industrial and developing countries.

Is the past prologue? It is difficult to predict the evolution of unemployment and GDP in the US or the global economy. In Europe where people are used to higher unemployment rates because of more generous and comprehensive unemployment schemes, the rate has risen to about the same as the current rate in the US. Will it recede slowly as the global economy recovers? And how will this impact emerging economies in Asia? It is important to take steps to protect the poor in Asia and elsewhere, should such a recovery scenario come to pass. There is some good news the United States, where there was a marked decline in jobs lost in November 2009 of only 11,000, compared with over 135,000 in the three previous months. The unemployment rate also fell slightly to 10.0% from 10.2% and jobless claims fell to 432,000 in the week of December 26, the lowest level since July 2008. The highest level was 674,000 in the week of March 27, 2009.

Even if recovery is more rapid the crisis is continuing to extract its toll in rising poverty incidence, increased incidence of malnutrition, more begging and child prostitution, reduced school enrolment rates, rising infant and under age-five mortality rates and maternal mortality and morbidity. Asia can learn from its experience in the Asian financial crisis in 1997–98. Infant mortality increased, school attendance fell and malnutrition increased. There were few social protection programs and human development indicators were adversely affected as a result. A little more than a decade later the situation has changed little, particularly in the poorer countries. Millennium Development goals are threatened. According to UNICEF (2009) the current recession will bring significant setbacks in the process of improving human development outcomes and raising living standards. UNICEF (2009) estimates maternal anemia and low birth weight could increase by 10–20% and 5–10% respectively and infant mortality in severely affected countries could increase by 3–11%. Increases in budgets for social protection are absolutely crucial if the region is to avoid the mistakes it made a decade ago by failing to provide adequate funding for social protection.

Deleveraging

As the global economy began to recover in the 2H 2009 and Q1 2010 economists and policymakers have begun to discuss withdrawal of stimulus measures as well as the general issue of deleveraging. McKinsey Global Institute (2010) has analyzed a number of historical episodes of deleveraging. The most common feature of these episodes is a period of belt tightening where credit growth lags behind growth in GDP. The current global crisis, which is characterized by large increases in government debt, could delay the process of deleveraging. In the past several economies have built up export surpluses which have cushioned the process of deleveraging. This is unlikely in the current global recession. What is more likely is a gradual reduction in debt in the most highly leveraged sectors of developed and major developing countries. This could leave many developed countries with a high debt to GDP ratio. In Asia the build up in debt has not been as rapid and levels of debt to GDP are not as high as they are in developed countries. The features of the debt build up and particular sectors most likely to experience deleveraging as perceived by McKinsey Global Institute (2010) are displayed in Table 7.9. Of the three Asian countries covered South Korea is the only economy where the possibility of deleveraging of debt is high, in the case of the household sector. In all three Asian economies the debt to GDP ratios in the government and non-financial business sectors is low whereas in finance deleveaging has medium high probability. In general industrial countries have a higher chance of deleveraging than the Asian economies where debt to income ratios are generally much lower than in industrial countries. However the ratio of debt to GDP is growing faster in Asia than in industrial countries.

Turning to stimulus measures there is a risk in China that the rapid expansion in bank credit stimulated in part by lower interest rates and government incentives is creating something of a credit bubble. However recent steps by the central bank are seeking to address this problem. Risks

Table 7.9   Debt to GDP ratios and likelihood of deleveraging Q2 2009

Country	Debt as % of GDP 2008	Government	Nonfinancial business	Households	Financial institutions	Growth rate of debt 2000–2008 in local currency
South Korea	331	28 (L)	115 (L)	80 (H)	108 (M)	10.8
India	129	66 (M)	42 (L)	10 (L)	11 (M)	16.5
China	159	32 (L)	96 (L)	12 (L)	18 (M)	15.1
US	290	60 (L)	78 (M)	96 (H)	56 (M)	8.1
UK	469	52 (L)	114 (M)	101 (H)	202 (M)	10.2
Japan	459	188 (M)	96 (M)	67 (L)	108 (M)	0.3

In the US and UK the likelihood of deleveraging in commercial real estate, a component of nonfinancial business, is high.
Source: McKinsey Global Institute, 2010. Likelihood of deleveraging is noted as L (low), M (medium) and H (high).

of a comparable bubble in housing in China are also rising, although much of the rise in real estate prices is confined to large urban areas and is being fueled by draw downs in saving rather than through excessive mortgage lending. There is also a risk of overinvestment, which skyrocketed last year to an estimated 47% of GDP. Some of this investment has been for infrastructure while manufacturing investment share has fallen. Much of this investment has also been framed as part of the temporary stimulus package of measures and it also contributes to strengthening of the infrastructure base which will be helpful over the longer run. Nevertheless there is concern that excessive spending will result in a growth in excess capacity and reduced profitability. With the exception of South Korea, where household debt as increased dramatically in recent years, there is less risk that the stimulus is creating distortions and difficulties. With the exception of Thailand and China the stimulus measures have been relatively small relative to GDP (see Table 6.1 and Table 6.5) and in Thailand a good part of the stimulus was for the construction of a new airport. Continued monetary stimulus in the form of low interest rates and excessive bank lending is of concerned and bears careful monitoring.

Summary

By the end of 2009 Asia had rebounded very quickly from the impact of the global economic recession that began in the latter part of 2008. After a sharp downturn in Q4 2008 and Q1 2009 the region regained its growth momentum and as well as some of the ground lost in the previous three quarters (see Table 7.2). Analysis of leading indicators in Table 7.1 and Table 7.6 suggest the downturn lasted seven or eight quarters, from Q2 2007 to Q1 2009, making it one of the longer downturns on record. Economic conditions in the Asian economies at the beginning of the crisis were favorable and the region was well positioned to respond quickly and effectively to the crisis. Recovering from the financial crisis of 1997–98 required the region to clean up bank balance sheets and to adopt greater fiscal discipline. International reserves were all accumulated as a precaution against a future crisis. As a result the region's banking systems had few tainted assets and a generally low level of non-performing assets. For the region as a whole the levels of international reserves, current account and fiscal balances were strong and enabled economies to undertake fiscal and monetary stimulus measures without disruption to the domestic economy or the exchange rate. These measures were adopted and implemented quickly and effectively. In November 2009, the IMF (IMF, 2009d) estimated that the stimulus measures in the Asian-Pacific region added 1.75% to GDP growth in the first half of 2009 and was the linchpin of the recovery strategy that enabled the region to recover more rapidly than anyone anticipated a few months earlier.

While the details of the impact of these measures are still unfolding, the size of the stimulus measures, as detailed in Table 6.4 and Table 6.5, was equal to or larger than the estimate of the GDP shortfall. In other countries the fiscal stimulus was more moderate. As the region begins to recover exports, both intra-trade within the region and to industrial economics, are expected to recover and give added impetus to the recovery that is already beginning (see Table 7.2). The inflow of foreign capital to fuel rapid growth in the form of foreign direct investment and portfolio investment has already started (see Table 6.6). Remittance inflows have remained strong throughout the crisis and can be expected to continue to provide funds to fuel consumption of those in the lower portions of the income distribution as the recovery and expansion take shape (Table 6.7).

8
Asian and Global Initiatives for Rebalancing the Global Economy

It has become fashionable to talk about rebalancing the global economy to put greater stress on saving in the deficit industrial countries and on consumption in the surplus Asian economies. This approach is particularly important if one believes that the cause of the global recession originated in a persistent imbalance in global saving and investment. And even if one believes that the source was the result of increased financial risk taking and a flawed regulatory environment that encouraged excessive consumption and increased financial leverage, it is important to consider the implications of a continuation of the imbalance in global saving and investment moving forward. Certainly a return to the status quo of high saving and export-led growth by Asian economies combined with large US current account deficits and low saving rates is not tenable.

Much of the discussion regarding harmonization of rules and regulations governing financial products, controlling risk, increasing transparency within a global framework are beyond the scope of this chapter and are considered further in Chapter 11 and Chapter 12. Here we focus on two aspects of rebalancing the global economy. First, we explore the possibilities of coordinating fiscal stimulus measures in order to facilitate the unwinding of asset positions and the adjustment of international borrowing and lending. Such a process of coordinated stimulus measures would improve the outlook for all components of the global economy. The motivation for this approach is a set of simulations conducted by the United Nations (2009) based on policy simulations with the United Nations Global Policy Model. As we might suspect the results of these simulations suggest that the rebalancing should involve greater saving on the part of the major deficit countries including the United States and lower levels of saving in countries with large surpluses including China and other countries in East Asia. The United Nations asserts that

> a more coordinated global macroeconomic stimulus, as suggested, would yield significant global growth gains, compared with a scenario of

uncoordinated stimuli, as implied by the existing fiscal stimulus packages being individually undertaken by national Governments. In the coordinated scenario the stimulus efforts by countries which now have large external surpluses would be larger than in currently the case, while additional resource transfer would be made to developing countries for development finance (about $500 billion extra over 2009–2012 compared with the uncoordinated scenario). The additional resource transfers needed would include about $50 billion for the least developed countries (United Nations, 2009, p. 16).

The advantages of such a scenario are many. It would support the stimulus efforts of the least developed countries and assist in attacking poverty while strengthening social protection systems and programs. It would also result in coordinated efforts to provide developing countries with greater access to industrial country markets as a part of a enhanced Doha round of trade negotiations. If such a coordinated set of policy initiatives could be enacted by the major trading economies, the UN Global Policy Model results suggest that the global economy would recover to a robust growth rate of between 4% and 5% over the next five years. Developing countries would lead the way with growth of 7%. This compares with developed countries' growth of about half that rate, between 3% and 4%. The benefits of a doubling of developing country growth over the next few years are enormous. We know that faster growth results in a decline in poverty. Even with an elasticity of 0.5, a doubling of growth would result in a 50% acceleration in the rate of poverty reduction at a global level.

Such a coordinated policy scenario would also benefit industrial countries as well. GDP growth would accelerate to the range of 4%, up from between 2% and 3% in the uncoordinated scenario. Furthermore

the simulation results for the coordinated policy scenario predict a benign unwinding of global imbalances, keeping external asset and liability positions of major economies in check, which would, in turn, support greater exchange-rate stability (United Nations, 2009, p. 16).

The simulation results are strong evidence of a win-win situation evolving if policy coordination takes the path suggested. The transfer of resources to developing countries resulting from such policy coordination has a powerful positive effect on global growth which includes lifting of living standards in developing and developed countries alike. It will not be easy to convince enough governments of the efficacy of such proposals. And there are likely to be free riders that would undermine the overall thrust of these policy initiatives. A start has already been made by the G20 which has made a commitment to expand the resource base of the IMF by doubling its capital through increased subscription by its members. Additional reforms of the international financial system including review of the Bretton Woods institution and policies are also needed.

Second, we explore how developing countries with large surpluses reduce their saving rates while increasing domestic consumption. This is an important step which follows the policy coordination measures suggested above to develop a coordinated stimulus. Without continued reforms that lift saving in industrial countries while lowering savings rates in developing countries there is a risk of a return to a world of imbalances and a future global crisis.

At the outset it is important to realize that the contribution of exports to the recent rapid growth in Asia has been largely misunderstood. Clearly net exports are the relevant variable to consider when looking at the contribution of international trade to economic growth. Focusing on developing Asia, between 2000 and 2008 net exports contributed about 1.5 to 2 percentage points to GDP growth in Hong Kong, Singapore and Taiwan and slightly less for China. As a proportion of overall growth these figures are not large (see Table 8.1) and in the case of China relatively small – about 10% of overall average growth in China. Net exports were a much more important source of growth in Germany than they were in most Asian economies with the possible exception of Taiwan.

For all other Asian economies – Bangladesh, Cambodia, India, Malaysia, Pakistan, Sri Lanka, Vietnam – net exports either were a net drag on GDP or made a negligible contribution to growth in GDP (2% or less). These contributions to economic growth from net exports throw further light on the impact of the global recession on Asia moving forward. They reinforce the conclusions we came to earlier that only a few countries, mostly in Group 2 and to some extent Group 3 were hit hard by the global recession. The rest of the Asian economies will have to focus on domestic issues to raise incomes, increase economic efficiency and aid the poor. Furthermore

Table 8.1   Net exports as a source of growth: 2000–2008

Country	Net exports share of GDP growth 2000–2008 in %
China	10
Hong Kong	34
Indonesia	7
South Korea	29
The Philippines	20
Singapore	27
Taiwan	61
Thailand	10
Germany	64
Japan	33

Source: Prasad, 2009

analysis by the IMF (deBeck, 2010) suggests that exports tend to exert a countercyclical influence on GDP, reinforcing the notion that exports provided some offset to the boom conditions that existed during the boom years from 2000 to 2008.

Rather than focus on exports, the rebalancing of Asian economies should concentrate on saving and investment imbalances. Work by the Asian Development Bank (2009) and E.S. Prasad (2009) suggest a course of policy actions that will contribute to lifting consumption while at the same time increasing economic efficiency and addressing poverty issues. The components of such a strategy are outlined below.

Social safety nets

Research on the Asian economies suggests that lack of a government-sponsored social support package containing elements of social security, unemployment compensation, health insurance, pension benefits and other appropriate support programs is a major reason why Asian families have a substantial precautionary saving motive. As noted in the China country report in Chapter 9, such a comprehensive social safety net would weaken this saving motive and reduce the need to maintain a private nest egg. More generally,

> 'Improvements in the social safety net would pool risks associated with idiosyncratic income shocks and health expenditures, reducing the need for households to save in order to self-insure against these risks' (E.S. Prasad, 2009).

Such changes would help to reduce large current account surpluses over time and make a significant contribution to the reduction in global imbalances and stimulate consumption while reducing poverty. Evidence from Taiwan, where a package was introduced provides strong evidence that such a approach does have the desired impact on private saving, particularly household saving. Data from Taiwan also provide a nice natural experiment to test the impact of the provision of comprehensive national health insurance on saving rates. Chou, Lin and Hammitt (2003 and 2006) found that the introduction of health insurance in 1995 reduced average household saving rates significantly by as much as 14% while Athukorala and Tsai (2003) conclude that the increased availability of social security provisions and enhanced credit availability tend to reduce household saving in Taiwan (see also Prasad, 2009). The provision of social safety nets is also a pillar of policies to reduce poverty and raise living standards and the introduction of such programs if properly targeted to reach the poor as well as the well-to-do would serve to both reduce precautionary saving and help reduce the incidence of poverty.

The balance between consumption and saving

In analyzing the macroeconomic performance of developed economies it has long been common practice to recognize that the share of consumption (and of investment) to GDP tends to remain stable over time (see for example Klein and Kosobud, 1961 and a voluminous literature that follows exploring the "great ratios" of macroeconomics). This is not necessarily the case in Asian developing economies. While the share of private consumption in GDP has remained stable for many economies it has shown significant variation in others (see Charts 8.1–8.4). Of particular note is the rapid decline in consumption to GDP in China and the rather gradual decline in India and Vietnam as well as in Bangladesh and Cambodia. Consumption as a share of GDP in China fell from over 60% of GDP in the 1990s to less than 40% of GDP by 2008. Investment and government consumption took up the slack and accounted for the bulk of GDP and GDP growth. This pattern extended to other countries in the Asian region although were not as pronounced. According to figures assembled by Prasad (2009) higher saving and investment rates have been responsible for the bulk of growth in the three giant economies as well as in South Korea and Thailand for the period from 2000 to 2008 (see Table 8.2). Not all of the increase in saving was directed to investment. The excess savings in the region accumulated as current account surpluses and increased reserves, exacerbating global imbalances that already existed in the previous decades. According to Prasad (2009) China accounts for about half of the GDP of the Asian region outside Japan, yet accounts for nearly 90% of the region's current account surplus. Referring to Table 3.3, China has more than 56% of the region's foreign exchange reserves and these reserves continue to increase as does its current account surplus. China adds more than $30 billion a month to its already large holding of foreign exchange reserves. Therefore raising consumption in China is critical if

Chart 8.1   Consumption to GDP for Hong Kong, South Korea and Malaysia

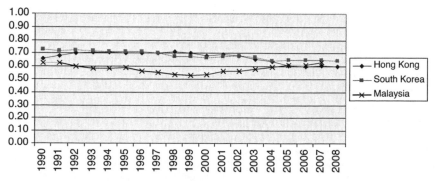

Source: World Development Indicators database

Chart 8.2   Consumption to GDP ratios for the Philippines, Thailand and Vietnam

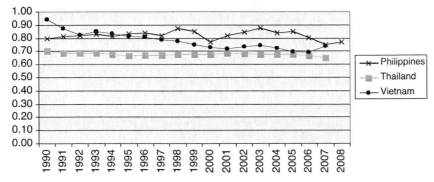

Source: World Development Indicators database

Chart 8.3   Consumption to GDP ratios for China, India and Indonesia

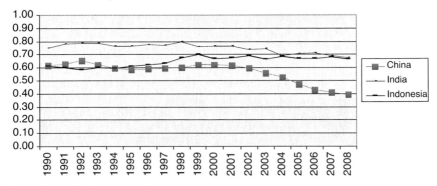

Source: World Development Indicators database

Chart 8.4   Consumption to GDP ratios for Bangladesh, Sri Lanka, Pakistan, Nepal and Cambodia

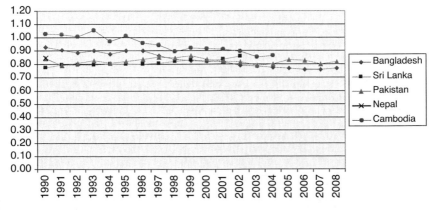

Source: World Development Indicators database

Table 8.2   **Shares of growth annually 2000–2008**

Country	GDP growth	Private consumption	Private investment plus government consumption	New exports	Employment growth
China	10.2	2.8	6.3	1.1	0.9
India	7.2	3.5	4.1	–0.3	1.9
Indonesia	5.2	2.5	2.0	0.4	1.6
South Korea	4.9	1.9	1.6	1.4	1.7
Thailand	4.8	2.4	1.9	0.5	1.6

Number many not add up due to rounding off
Source: Prasad, 2009

rebalancing of consumption and saving in Asia is to be achieved. The decline in consumption and the increase in saving and investment in China are largely the result of the rise in corporate saving and investment and a systematic neglect of consumers. Stimulus spending that focuses on more investment will continue rather than reduce the consumption imbalance.

J. Devan et al (2009) analyzed several possible tools for raising consumption (see Table 8.3). They suggest that improving healthcare and pensions would raise private domestic consumption by only about a percentage point above the current level of 38.7% of GDP in China. Further analysis is required to explore the validity of this conclusion and to consider how an improved pension and healthcare system could serve to raise consumption in other countries in the Asian region. Devan et al (2009) argue that while mobilizing resources to strengthen the safety net would ease anxiety

Table 8.3   **Private domestic consumption in China as % of GDP**

Methods to raise consumption	Moderate policy changes (% change from baseline of 38.7%)	Extreme policy changes (% change from baseline of 38.7%)
Direct stimulation	1.3	1.3
Mortgages	0.5	1.5
Consumer credit	0.6	1.2
Education financing	0.4	0.7
Healthcare	0.4	0.6
Pensions	–0.2	0.5
Investment allocation	2.8	4.8
Nonwage income	0.7	1.2

Note: In a moderate case scenario consumption increases from 38.7% of GDP to 45.2% while in the extreme case the increase is to 50.2%, still at the low range of OECD and Asian economies.
Source: Devan et al, 2009

Table 8.4   Private domestic consumption as a percent of GDP

United States	71
United Kingdom	67
Brazil	65
Russia	62
India	57
Japan	55
Germany	54
China	38

Source: Global Insight: McKinsey Global Institute analysis cited in Devan et al, 2009

about the future and improve consumer confidence, the cost of these programs would be partially borne by the government, raising its share of total consumption.

Recent figures for domestic consumption as a percentage of GDP in industrial and some Asian economies are displayed in Table 8.4. These ratios have changed little in the last couple of decades for industrial economies and for many Asian economies as noted above (see Charts 8.1–8.4). While some OECD economies and BRIC countries have ratios in the 60s, others have ratios in the 50s. However, only China has a ratio under 40%.

The focus on China should not distract attention from the other countries in Asia. Some of the poorer countries in the region including Indonesia and the Philippines and South Asian economies save and investment much smaller proportions of their income and consume more (see Charts 8.1–8.4). Since poorer countries have a much smaller capital stock than rich countries – somewhere between 2% and 6% of the capital stock in the United States according to estimates by Hedrick-Wong (2010) – it stands to reason that the marginal productivity of new capital would be much higher than it is in industrial countries and this would warrant a higher level of investment spending. The same holds true for South Asia, where consumption is around 80% of GDP.

Financial market development

There are other ways to lift savings aside from direct intervention. Banks are still the primary financial intermediary in developing economies in Asia. A more efficient financial system would enable financial resources to be made available for investment at lower costs and would lower the spread between borrowing and lending rates. Households in Asia now have a limited array of financial assets and borrowing instrument at their disposal. Purchases of durable goods and investment in housing are constrained by a lack of financial instruments that allow families to purchase these goods on credit or invest in housing without large down payments and short repayment periods. Systematic development of consumer credit and mortgage markets would provide greater flexibility and reduce liquidity constraints that force households to save substantial amounts out of disposable income to make large purchases. An efficient financial system that provides more opportunities for risk sharing and a larger set of instruments for both saving and investment would allow more opportunities for intertemporal smoothing of consumption. Firms would also be able to rely less on retained earnings for financing their investments if a broader set of financial instruments were available. For example, the recent rapid increase in profits by state-owned enterprises in China was largely responsible for the build-up in savings. Until recently state-owned enterprises were prohibited from distributing profit proceeds to share holders in the form of retained earnings. This contributed to the global imbalance between saving and investment. The build up of business savings as well as household savings also accounts for a major imbalance between consumption and saving in China and to a lesser extent in other countries in East Asia. Consumption and employment have been growing much more slowly than income in China; 2.8% and 0.9% respectively compared with 10.2% growth in GDP (see Table 8.2). As noted above consumption is now only 38% of income, a much smaller ratio than in other Asian and OECD countries.

In China the interaction between demographics and the lack of a well-developed mortgage market also plays an important role. As a result of the one-child policy and preferences for boys there are more young men than women. To compete for the ladies' hand, men in urban areas have to save enough to buy a place to live away from their parents. It is said that one of first questions women ask perspective suitors is the square footage of their apartment. With this pressure it is little wonder that consumer savings rates remain high.

This trend toward higher corporate savings in Asia is reinforced by Prasad (2009) who compiled estimates of saving rates for five Asian economies (China, India, South Korea, the Philippines and Taiwan) which show that the average corporate saving rate in these countries has increased from about 12% of GDP in 2000 to around 19% in 2008. A more liberalized financial system would allow firms the option of borrowing rather than having to finance all investment from retained earnings. These measures would also increase options to distribute retained earnings to shareholders. Improved access of rural communities to banks and other financial intermediaries would also allow rural residents to get better returns on their financial savings and would reduce the incentives for households to self-insure against health and other risks, particularly if financial social safety net development were interrelated. Furthermore, small businesses could borrow to expand their businesses without having to save up out of their own earnings.

Fiscal policy

Tax and subsidy policies can be effective instruments to redistribute incentive from saving to consumption. Taxes and subsidies which favor the manufacturing industry can be reviewed, taxes on business profits can be raised and the rich can be taxed at higher income tax rates. Since the rich save a higher proportion of income than the poor, these policies would redirect savings toward consumption. Furthermore, progressive taxation would also help to redress the deterioration in income distribution that has occurred in the past two decades in several Asian economies. Finally, restrictions on rural to urban migration could be relaxed to permit further flow of cheap labor to cities where labor intensive industries would benefit. This would raise consumption and income of the poor and middle classes.

Exchange rate policies

Policies that stimulate exports by tying exchanges rates to the US dollar, which has been generally weak, serve to implicitly continue a business-as-usual model where export-led growth is the way out of recession. This will not do. Following a more flexible exchange rate regime would allow economies to respond to changing international productivity differentials and could generate positive wealth effects through favorable changes in terms of trade. This could encourage private consumption while reducing reliance on foreign demand. A more flexible exchange rate would also allow for a more independent monetary policy which could have favorable impacts on productivity and income growth. By revaluation of the currency foreign goods would become cheaper and would help to replace reliance on foreign demand for exports. A more flexible exchange rate would also increase the efficiency of monetary policy and enhance macroeconomic stability (see Prasad and Rajan, 2006). In China there are political factors that make exchange rate adjustment difficult despite the fall in the value of the currency in recent months. The real trade-weighted exchange rate is now the same as it was in 2002, despite some subsequent revaluation against the US dollar. Communist party leaders and its banking and corporate sectors, particularly state-owned enterprises, all have a vested interest in maintaining low interest rates that sustain high investment and growth in industrial production. This system has resulted in rapid growth as well as sustaining the political power of the party elite. At the same time the regime shows little interest in consumers' welfare, despite the fact that living standards have increased and poverty rate have fallen. Considerably faster growth in consumption can be achieved if the exchange rate were to be revalued, more resources were devoted to consumer industries and the rate of investment growth in heavy state-owned industries reduced. Aside from these ramifications of exchange rate adjustment, there is genuine concern that a revaluation of the yuan could result in a similar fate that befell the Japanese economy after the revaluation of the yen following the Plaza Accord of 1985. By 1988, the yen had risen by more than 200% against the dollar – a shock from which the Japanese economy is still recovering 20-odd years later. The Chinese authorities want to avoid a similar scenario for China. However one could argue that Japan waited too long to revalue and as a result the value of the yen rose too rapidly. China risks a similar fate unless it takes action now to reduce the imbalances created by an undervalued currency. At the end of Q1 2010 speculators had begun to buy up the yuan, creating inflationary tendencies and putting additional pressure to revalue the currency. Furthermore, monetary policy needs to be watched carefully since the threat of a financial bubble remains in the background.

On a more ominous note, there is a genuine risk that if the Chinese authorities continue to resist pressure to revalue the exchange rate, their trading partners will react by raising tariffs and following other protectionist measures. This is not a good sign. A continuation of the standoff would jeopardize the gains the global economy has made in achieving freer trade over the past decades. It is not true that free trade is always good and protectionism is always bad. Paul Krugman in a recent article in *The New York Times* (Krugman, 2009c) quotes Paul Samuelson "With employment less than full ... all the debunked mercantilist arguments turn out to be valid". And Krugman continues to quote Samuelson who argued that misaligned exchange rates create "genuine problems for free-trade apologetics".

No one wants a return to the protectionist trade regimes that characterized the interwar period, where growth was slow and political tensions mounted, eventually culminating in the horrors of World War II. In a recent symposium on the world economy in 2010 sponsored by the Carnegie Endowment for the International Peace (Carnegie Endowment for International Peace, 2010) a group of well-known economists gathered to discuss the outlook for the New Year. Protectionism as a response to the imbalances resulting from an undervalued Chinese currency was highlighted as one of the major challenges facing the global economy. The question is how to convince the Chinese that if they continue to control their exchange rate the entire world could easily suffer a dramatic setback, making the current global economic crisis look like a cake walk.

Remove the bias against non-traded goods

Regulatory regimes that have promoted exports in the past should be dismantled in order to create a more level playing field for firms that are producing for the domestic market. This includes removal of tax breaks and subsidies for lending to exporters as well as other implicit subsidies to exporters. This is not to say that export-led growth should be discouraged as such. Rather policies should be even handed in dealing with firms, whether they are producing for the local or export markets. As part of this strategy there is a need to generally revive investment in many Asian economies which has been low since the 1997/98 Asian financial crisis (see Blanchard and Giavanni, 2006 and Park, 2009), which could be directed to raising capacity to facilitate the transformation from exports to domestic consumption, particularly China. If accompanied by an increase in capital inflows from industrial countries this would contribute to further rebalancing of the global economy and would, in the long run, contribute to a reduction in the debt overhang in industrial countries (see Martin Wolf, 2010).

Golden rules for saving

In a Solow type neoclassical growth model a simple golden rule (do unto others as you would have them do unto you by assuming the future generations enjoy the same level of growth in consumption as the current generation) for accumulation proposed by Edmund Phelps (1971) maximized the steady state level of the growth of consumption. In the steady state per capita consumption is both constant and maximized. The Phelps (1971) golden rule suggests that, in a closed economy where factors are paid the value of their marginal product, *the gross saving rate should be equal to the share of capital in national income*. These two variables are displayed in Table 8.5 for Asian economies and some industrial countries as well. The golden rule seems to apply pretty well to several economies in Asia

Table 8.5   Gross national saving and capital share of GDP 2008 – selected Asian and OECD countries

Country	Gross national saving rate as a % of GDP 2008	Capital share in GDP 2008 as a % of GDP	Investment to GDP ratio (2004–2008)
China	53.9	50.0	44
India	39.6	38.7	32
South Korea	30.3	39.0	30
The Philippines	19.2	35.0	na
Singapore	45.7	47.5	24
Taiwan	27.7	37.5	21
Thailand	32.3	31.5	27
Germany	26.0	26.0	18
Japan	27.0	26.0	23
United States	13.7	30.0	18

Sources: Prasad, 2009; Abu-Qarn and Abu-Bader, 2007; Singapore Department of Statistics, 1998; Felipe and Sipin, 2004; OECD database, 2009; Annex Table 24; Pholphirul, 2005; UNESCAP, 2009; Table 2 and Table 3

including Singapore, China, Thailand and India. In the US, Taiwan, South Korea and the Philippines the capital share is larger than the saving rate. The disparity is the highest by far in the US. That South Korea, the Philippines and Taiwan also fall in the low saving category is not a conclusion that is intuitively obvious from casual observation, given the recent build-up in foreign reserves in these countries. In the Philippines, this can be partially explained by the recent increase in remittance income. Some observers say the share of capital and the saving rate in China are both distorted by extensive government subsidies to capital which have raised its share of income so that it is out of line with economic efficiency.

A similar argument could be made for the saving rate, as we have discussed earlier. From the point of view of consumer welfare, high rates of saving should result from high rates of return to savers. In China and other Asian economies this is not the case. Real interest rates on household saving have been low or even negative. Furthermore, continued high economic growth is not being fully reflected in higher incomes and rapid growth in consumption. On the contrary, household income is growing more slowly than GDP and the share of household income in GDP has been falling over time. And saving rates have been increasing as well. This is also reflected in a slower growth in consumption (8% on average for the past few decades) versus income (10%). It is not that households are starving – 8% growth is the envy of the rest of the world – yet profitable state-owned enterprises are profiting even more.

How does the Chinese experience square with that of other countries in the region and with the experience of industrial countries? The overall impression is that there are only a few countries out of line with the golden rule and some of this can be explained by recent movements either in factor shares or in saving rates. The evidence suggests that among OECD countries, United States sticks out as the biggest deficit saver. Saving rates in Germany and Japan are in line with the simple golden rule as they are in Singapore and Thailand. Some of the other countries in Asia (South Korea, the Philippines, Taiwan) also fall in the low saving category, not a conclusion that is intuitively obvious from casual observation of the recent build up of foreign exchange reserves. In the Philippines, this can be partially explained by recent increases in the capital share of income from the range of 20% to 25% in the early 1980s to over 30% by the 1990s while in Taiwan and South Korea, the saving rate has been trending downward for some time. In South Korea the saving rate was over 37% in 1991 and even as recently as 1998. In Taiwan, the saving rate has not fallen as far but is still down from over 30% in the early 1990s to 27.9%.

This golden rule exercise gives a notional idea of possible imbalances between actual and optimal savings rates. The assumptions are restrictive and the golden rule does not specify the steady state levels of consumption and saving. It says only that the optimal rate of saving is the rate that generates the highest level of steady state consumption. In it simplest form, it holds only for a closed economy because it requires that saving equals investment. It also was developed for a Solow-type growth model in a closed economy where factors of production are paid the value of their marginal product.

Clearly Asian economies have developed a growth pattern where the saving rate is higher than it is in OECD countries and this is consistent with a higher share of capital in national income. This does not mean necessarily that Asian countries save too much or that industrial countries, with the possible exception of the United States, save too little. This exercise also demonstrates that it is not so much the rate of saving that is causing the imbalances but the shortfall in domestic investment which has led to the build-up in reserves and greater overseas investment in the US and Europe. This pattern is reflected by the difference between Asian saving and investment rates as reflected in Table 8.5. In the richer countries including China, Hong Kong, Indonesia, Malaysia, the Philippines, Singapore, Thailand and Vietnam the excess of GDS over GDI is more than 5% of GDP. This has sustained a build-up in foreign exchange reserves and facilitated FDI flows to industrial countries. In the poorer countries the pattern is reversed.

Note also that the countries with the largest holdings of foreign exchange reserves in Asia are generally the same as those that have large excesses of saving over investment (Table 8.6). Briefly, updating Table 3.3 to 2009, China, Taiwan, India, South Korea, Hong Kong and Singapore together have about $3.3 trillion in reserves. By slowly lowering current account surpluses and reserve positions, developing Asia could contribute to the rebalancing of the global economy.

More local investment opportunities related to the growth of domestic consumption should appear as part of the rebalancing exercise for the surplus countries. This would naturally lead to more domestic investment spending and a reduced outflow of resources.

To put matters in global perspective Oliver Blanchard, the IMF Chief Economist (Blanchard, 2009) argues that US net exports must increase if rebalancing is to take place and the US economy is to recovery smartly. He calculates that if the surplus emerging Asian economies were to lower their current account surplus by 4% of GDP this would improve the US current account by around 2% of GDP (emerging Asia's GDP is about half of the US GDP). The adjustment would have to be a bit more since not all emerging Asian trade is with the US. Blanchard also notes that the crisis is likely to decrease potential output and that the recovery in the US and the global economy will require an increase in US net exports and a shift from public to private saving worldwide. While the decease in potential output has been noted before, the results of an IMF study (see IMF, 2009e) reinforce the conclusion that output does not return to its old trend path. However

Table 8.6   **Gross domestic saving and gross domestic investment rates 2007**

	Gross domestic saving rate (GDS) as a % of GDP	Gross domestic investment rate (GDI) as a % of GDP	GDS – GDI in %
China	50.2	41.8	**8.4**
Hong Kong	33.8	22.2	**11.6**
South Korea	30.1	29.2	0.9
Bangladesh	19.5	26.0	–6.5
India	32.3	35.1	–2.8
Nepal	9.4	25.3	–15.9
Pakistan	16.1	23.0	–6.9
Sri Lanka	17.6	29.0	–12.4
Cambodia	15.2*	22.9	–7.7
Indonesia	30.5	23.7	**6.8**
Lao PDR	20.0	22.0	–2.0
Malaysia	44.8	20.6	**24.2**
The Philippines	20.0	14.6	**5.4**
Singapore	48.7	22.8	**25.9**
Thailand	33.0	26.9	**6.1**
Vietnam	31.1	37.0	–5.9

Countries with GDS more than 5 percentage points higher than GDI highlighted in bold.
* 2006
Source: UNESCAP Economic and Social Survey of Asia and the Pacific, 2009, Table 2 and Table 3

this work also notes that while crises permanently decrease the level of output they do not affect the long-term growth in output.

The process of adjustment has already begun as a result of the impact that the global recession has had on the balance between consumption and saving in both industrial and emerging economies. The US and UK current account deficits have fallen since 2007 – 5.3% of GDP to 2.3% of GDP in 2009 for the US and 2.9% to 2.6% for the UK. At the same time the Japanese surplus has fallen from 4.9% to 1.4% in 2009. The Chinese current account surplus rose in 2008 to $310 billion from $380 in 2007 before declining to $300 billion in 2009. Consumption has fallen and saving rates have risen in the United States in 2009. As the recovery accelerates there are good reasons to believe that the balance between saving and consumption will tend toward previous levels which will put further pressure on the rate of saving and investment in Asia (see Ashoka Mody and Franziska Ohnsorge, 2010).

9
Impact of Crisis on Poverty in Asia and Millennium Development Goals (MDGs)

Historical experience gives us some insights into impact that the global recession will have on Asia. Experience during the Asian financial crisis of 1997 and 1998 provides some useful clues. The sharp downturn in the second half of 1997 and 1998 resulted in a downturn in growth and an increase in unemployment and the incidence of poverty. Fallon and Lucas (2002) estimate that the headcount ratio in Indonesia and Thailand rose by 11% and 9.8% in 1997 and a further 19.9% and 12.9% respectively in 1998. More generally, the World Bank (2000) and Ravallion and Chen (1997) conclude that on average 1% of growth will bring about a 2–3% reduction in the number of people living below the poverty line. In Asia, further work by Hasan et al (2009) suggests that the impact on poverty will be more likely to impact factory workers in export industries as well as overseas workers. In the earlier crisis it was the very poor construction workers in the cities as well as some farming communities that were affected. Rising unemployment increases the vulnerability of these groups to poverty and has knock on effects on the extremely poor as well. Hasan et al (2009) estimate that the current global recession will result in an increase in dollar a day poverty of over 60 million people in Asia, which could rise to nearly 100 million in 2010. These estimates presuppose that growth in the Asian region will slow from 6.3% in 2008 to 3.4% in 2009 before rising to 6% in 2010. Simulations made in ADB (2009 Table 1.4.2) suggest the 60 million additional poor in 2009 and close to 100 million in 2010 is in line with growth projections for the region. These forecasts were made in the spring of 2009 and more recent estimates suggest these growth forecasts for 2009 and 2010 may have been overly pessimistic (see Table 5.1). As a result the net impact on poverty may be smaller than earlier estimates. Nevertheless the full impact is hard to determine. Hasan et al (2009) estimate the impact on GDP growth by assuming three different scenarios. First, growth in 2008, 2009 and 2010 will be 1% lower than growth in 2007; second, growth will be 2% lower in 2008, 2009 and 2010; and finally, that growth will be 3% lower in 2008, 2009 and 2010.

As outlined above in the discussion of Table 6.4, Table 6.5 and Table 7.8 we examined the realism of these alternatives by comparing actual 2008 and IMF projections for 2009 and 2010 with 2007 GDP growth. It is evident that even the most negative of the three alternatives suggested by Hasan et al is much more optimistic than the latest thinking on developments in 2009 and 2010 which are contained in Table 6.5 and Table 7.8. Only Indonesia has an average difference less than the most pessimistic of the Hasan et al (2009) growth scenarios. The NIEs are the most adversely affected as we would have suspected by their poor projected performance reviewed earlier. Yet even better performers such as Thailand, China, India and Vietnam all have high average growth shortfalls greater than 3%. Hasan et al (2009) and World Bank (2009c) also analyze the vulnerability of countries in Asia to the global financial crisis with respect to their ability to: (a) finance larger fiscal deficits necessary to fund the needed poverty reduction efforts, and (b) the institutional capacity to implement the additional poverty measures required to deal with the poverty impact of the crisis. The World Bank concludes that "countries in most critical need of external financial and technical assistance are those with high initial poverty and growth deceleration as well as low fiscal and institutional capacity" (World Bank, 2009c, p. 2).

The fiscal capacity measure takes into account the fiscal deficit, current account balance, international reserves, debt/GDP ratio and capital inflows. The institutional capacity measures the ability to manage and implement policies, provide services and provide transparency in administration and

Table 9.1   Fiscal capacity, institutional capacity and vulnerability of the poor in Asia

Country	Fiscal capacity	Institutional capacity	Vulnerability of poor to slower growth
Cambodia	Medium or high	Medium or high	High
Lao PDR	Medium or high	Medium or high	High
Bangladesh	Low	Medium or high	Low
India	Low	Medium or high	Medium
Indonesia	Low	Medium or high	Medium
Nepal	Medium or high	Medium or high	Low
Pakistan	Medium or high	Medium or high	High
The Philippines	Medium or high	Medium or high	High
Sri Lanka	Medium or high	Medium or high	Low
Vietnam	Medium or high	Medium or high	High
China	Medium or high	High	Medium
Malaysia	Medium or high	High	Low
Thailand	Medium or high	High	Low

Source: Hasan et al, 2009

spending of external funds as well as the institutional capacity to ramp up poverty spending.

Asian economies of interest are ranked in Table 9.1 according to fiscal capacity and institutional capacity as well as their vulnerability to increasing poverty incidence given a projected decline in growth.

Five countries are highly vulnerable to a decline in economic growth (Cambodia, Lao PDR, Pakistan, the Philippines and Vietnam). Indonesia has a medium level of vulnerability combined with a low fiscal capacity. Aside from Indonesia, none of these countries have a particularly low level of either fiscal or institutional capacity. Looking at it somewhat differently the World Bank (2009c) identifies Bangladesh, Cambodia, India, Indonesia, Lao PDR, Pakistan, the Philippines and Vietnam as countries with high poverty rates and decelerating growth as a result of the global crisis.

It would be useful to go one step further to investigate the ability of these countries to generate assistance internally without resorting to donors like the ADB and the World Bank. We explore these issues further in Chapter 10 where we look at individual country's issues and constraints. At this point we can also investigate hunger and poverty in these countries as ranked by the United Nations Development Program (UNDP) and the International Food Policy Research Institute (IFPRI). The UNDP reports the Human Development Index (HDI) each year and the rankings of some of the Asian countries at risk are displayed in Table 9.2 along with the Global Hunger Index (GHI) compiled by IFPRI and several other indices of poverty, hunger and social spending by these Asian countries at risk.

Six countries are identified as having general poverty and hunger issues which are likely to be exacerbated by the global financial crisis. We have added Nepal to the World Bank list and deleted Indonesia, the Philippines

Table 9.2   Poverty and hunger in Asian countries at risk

Country	SPIMP*	SPEXP**	% under nourished	% children under 5 underweight	HDI ranking of 179	Global Hunger Index (GHI)
Bangladesh	24	5.3	30	47.5	147	25.2 (alarming)
India	26	4.0	20	48.5	132	23.7 (alarming
Nepal	7	2.3	17	48.3	145	20.5 (alarming)
Pakistan	3	1.6	23	37.5	139	21.7 (alarming)
Cambodia	4	1.4	33	45.2	136	23.2 (alarming)
Lao PDR	7	1.3	21	40.0	133	20.6 (alarming)

Source: IFPRI, 2008; UNDP, 2008; ADB, 2008; ADB/ESCAP/UNDP, 2008
*SPIMP is the per capita social protection expenditures as a percentage of the national poverty line.
**SPEXP is social protection expenditure as a percentage of GDP.
A GHI over 20 is designated as alarming. Globally only seven countries in Africa have lower scores than the countries listed in Table 9.2, placing them in an extremely alarming category.

and Vietnam. The latter three countries have much stronger ratings both in terms of human development, poverty and hunger challenges. While they will still be at risk as a result of the global economic crisis they appear to be well-positioned to deal with it through stimulus measures. Furthermore, they are not expected to suffer a severe growth downturn as reflected by small shortfall values in Table 6.4 and Table 7.8 (0.6 for Indonesia, 2.9 for the Philippines and 2.2 for Vietnam). On the other hand, South Asia and the Mekong countries continue to suffer from severe human resource and hunger deficits. All six countries are in the alarming category of hunger risk and are rated very low on the HDI list. They have significant proportions of underweight children and undernourished children and adults. While Bangladesh and India do spread their social protection net to a wider group than the other countries the total allocation per family is still low. There is also significant leakage to the non-poor and to middlemen who siphon off some resources for themselves. The poor in these countries also receive a small share of government resources. The challenge for these countries is ongoing and will persist even after the global recession has come to an end. The situation in these six countries is discussed more extensively in the country reports in the next chapter.

Impact from slowdown in remittances

Aside from the impact on income generated domestically there will also be adverse impacts on poverty from a slowdown in remittances (see Table 6.7 for figures on remittance income in Asia). In Bangladesh, for example, remittances accounted for 8.8% of GDP in 2005 (see Ahmed, 2006) and are a vital part of the fabric of the social network support which the poor depend on. Remittances by Nepalese migrants in India and elsewhere to family households rose by four times to 12% of GDP by end of 2004 compared with a decade earlier (World Bank, 2006). Results of a recent study by M. Lokshin et al (2007) indicate that one-fifth of the poverty reduction in Nepal occurring between 1995 and 2004 was because of increased remittances. Adding to traditional remittance sources from India and Hong Kong recent Nepalese migration to the Middle East has also swelled the flow of remittances to close to 20% of GDP (see Table 6.7). In the Philippines remittances are lowest from the poorest provinces and only 15% of those who migrated had less than a high school education (see Capistrano and Sta. Maria, 2007). Therefore it is unlikely that the poorest quintile of the population will be able to afford to send a migrant overseas. There is the option of pooling assets among members of extended families to facilitate these costs and this is a viable strategy even in tough times. This strategy is particular pertinent in countries where the average level of education is relatively high, enhancing their chances of getting an overseas job. International migration is particularly attractive for India and the Philippines, where English is widely spoken. Total remittances from overseas migrants to the

Philippines now contributes 11.6% of GDP (see Table 6.7) and remittances are the most important foreign exchange earner, outpacing export income. While remittance income goes mostly to the upper quintiles of the income distribution the lower quintile also benefits. In the Philippines income in lowest quintile increased over 20% as a result of international remittances and 16% from domestic remittances (see Pernia, 2007) and Vietnam reports a similar result (see p. 98). In India, Lipton (1988) argues that high emigration rates are found in villages where there is a high degree of inequality. The rate of internal migration in Asia is probably much higher than international migration. Evidence from Bihar province suggests that nearly half of all households reported at least one migrating member and migrating rates were higher among the lower castes and classes (see http://www.bihartimes.com/poverty/anup.html). There had been a sharp decline in the growth of remittances since the beginning of the crisis in early 2008. The World Bank (2009) suggests that remittance to East Asia are expected to fall by 4–7.5%. In the Philippines, forecasters are scaling back on remittances growth estimates for 2009 to 6–9% from 10–14% in 2008 on the assumption that workers in IT, finance, housing services (maids), construction and entertainment will lose their jobs. Nevertheless, remittances income will still be higher than it was in 2007. Workers in healthcare in the US are unlikely to be affected. In Bangladesh, remittances are falling and workers are being repatriated from the Middle East and Malaysia. In South Asia, the World Bank indicates that remittances will also soften (see Bauer, 2009). Even though the bulk of remittances go to families in the upper three quartiles of the income distribution a reduction in remittances has extensive trickle down effects to the rest of the population. A decline in remittances will have an adverse impact on the spending patterns of poorer households as education completion rates fall, malnutrition increases and girls' education are all adversely affected. There will also be a drop in the rate of internal migration from rural to urban areas and even reverse migration as recent migrants are retrenched and have to return to their home towns in the countryside. Estimates of 20 million Chinese and 10 million Indians returnees are rumored.

Impact on Millennium Development Goals (MDGs)

The Millennium Development Goals were developed by the United Nations and codified in a resolution signed by 189 countries in September 2000 and from further agreement by member states at the 2005 World Summit and a resolution adopted by the UN General Assembly. The Goals and Targets are spelled out in Table 9.3.

MDG1 poverty and hunger

The focus on economic poverty reduction, including reducing hunger, which is Goal 1 of the MDG, has been made emphatically by many development

Table 9.3 Goals and targets from the Millennium Declaration

Goal 1	Eradicate extreme poverty and hunger
Target 1.A	Halve, between 1990 and 2015, the proportion of people whose income is less than $1.25 a day
Target 1.B	Achieve full and productive employment and decent work for all, including women and young people
Target 1.C	Halve, between 1990 and 2015, the proportion of people who suffer from hunger
Goal 2	Achieve universal primary education
Target 2	Ensure that by 2015, children everywhere, boys and girls alike, will be able to complete a full course of primary schooling
Goal 3	Promote gender equality and empower women
Target 3	Eliminate gender disparity in primary and secondary education, preferably by 2005, and at all levels of education no later than 2015
Goal 4	Reduce child mortality
Target 4	Reduce by two-thirds, between 1990 and 2015, the under-five mortality rate
Goal 5	Improve maternal health
Target 5.A	Reduce by three-quarters, between 1990 and 2015, the maternal mortality ratio
Target 5.B	Achieve by 2015 universal access to reproductive health
Goal 6	Combat HIV/AIDS, malaria, and other diseases
Target 6.A	Have halted by 2015 and begun to reverse the spread of HIV/AIDS
Target 6.B	Achieve by 2010 universal access to treatment for HIV/AIDS for all those who need it
Target 6.C	Have halted by 2015 and begun to reverse the incidence of malaria and other major diseases
Goal 7	Ensure environmental sustainability
Target 7.A	Integrate the principles of sustainable development into country policies and programs and reverse the loss of environmental resources
Target 7.B	Reduce biodiversity loss, achieving by 2010 a significant reduction in the rate of loss
Target 7.C	Halve by 2015 the proportion of people without sustainable access to safe drinking water and basic sanitation
Target 7.D	Have achieved a significant improvement by 2020 in the lives of at least 100 million slum dwellers
Goal 8	Develop a global partnership for development
Target 8.A	Develop further an open, rule-based, predictable, nondiscriminatory trading and financial system (including a commitment to good governance, development, and poverty reduction, nationally and internationally)
Target 8.B	Address the special needs of the least-developed countries (including tariff- and quota-free access for exports of the least-developed countries; enhanced debt relief for heavily indebted poor countries and cancellation of official bilateral debt; and more generous official development assistance for countries committed to reducing poverty)

Table 9.3   **Goals and targets from the Millennium Declaration** – *continued*

Target 8.C	Address the special needs of landlocked countries and small island developing states (through the Programme of Action for the Sustainable Development of Small Island Developing States and the outcome of the 22nd special session of the General Assembly)
Target 8.D	Deal comprehensively with the debt problems of developing countries through national and international measures to make debt sustainable in the long term
Target 8.E	In cooperation with pharmaceutical companies, provide access to affordable, essential drugs in developing countries
Target 8.F	In cooperation with the private sector, make available the benefits of new technologies, especially Information and communications

Source: United Nations, 2008

economists. What is perhaps less understood and appreciated is the relationship of poverty and hunger with the other components in the MDG agenda. The ADB/ESCAP/UNDP 2008 report and also the World Bank (2009b) both emphasize the importance of the global crisis' impact on other aspects of the MDG. The MDG agenda lists halving the proportion of the population that goes hungry as a goal. In 2007 only about half of the Asian economies were on track to achieve this objective. The proportion of children under five years of age that are underweight combined with the percentage of the population that is undernourished reflects the extent of hunger and food deprivation. These ratios are displayed in Table 9.4 and Table 9.5. Only about half of the countries in Asia are on track to achieve this goal of halving hunger by 2015. The ADB/ESCAP/UNDP report (2008) suggests that those countries will have to increase their investment in

Table 9.4   **Proportion of population undernourished (in %)**

Cambodia	33
Bangladesh	30
Pakistan	23
Sri Lanka	22
Thailand	21
Lao PDR	21
India	20
The Philippines	19
Nepal	17
Vietnam	17
China	12

Source: ADB/ESCAP/UNDP, 2008

Table 9.5   **Children under five years of age who are underweight (in %)**

India	48.5
Nepal	48.3
Bangladesh	47.5
Cambodia	45.2
Lao PDR	40.0
Pakistan	37.8
Sri Lanka	29.4
Indonesia	28.2
The Philippines	27.6
Vietnam	26.6
Thailand	17.6

Source: ADB/ESCAP/UNDP, 2008
Note: China not reporting.

hunger reduction programs by at least 20% in order to accelerate progress in this critical area and by so doing achieve the MDG objective.

The strain that the global crisis is putting on budgets makes meeting that objective much less probable. Furthermore, there is a very real risk that budgets will be cut further, making it even more difficult to recover lost ground and make further progress in alleviating hunger. It is therefore critical that social programs be protected. It is important to note in this regard that income growth and undernourishment are not that highly correlated. More important is the emphasis that governments make and their commitment to improving nutrition. History tells us that Sri Lanka has made significant improvements in social development even though its income per capita is still low. The same can be said for Kerala, a state in India with much better human development markers than the rest of India. This demonstrates that it is possible to improve education and health outcomes without necessarily also raising the rate of economic growth. Both Kerala and Sri Lanka allocate larger shares of their government budgets to social sector programs than other countries and regions.

In the same vein, Dowling and Yap (2009) summarize the results of a comprehensive analysis recently completed by the Asian Development Bank on social protection in the Asian region (ADB/ESCAP/UNDP 2008). Three components of social protection are summarized in Table 9.6: (a) social protection expenditure (SPEXP) as a percentage of GDP; (b) the percentage of the poor receiving some social protection (SPDIST); and (c) per capita social protection expenditures as a percentage of the national poverty line. Social protection expenditures as a percentage of the national poverty line (SPIMP) are the most revealing. Aid reaching the poor is a fraction of the poverty line requirements of around a dollar a day. If each individual received a dollar a day SPIMP would be 100.

Table 9.6   Social spending and HDI in selected Asian economies

Country	SPEXP	SPDIST	SPIMP	HDI ranking
China	4.6	69	44	82
Indonesia	1.9	71	8	107
The Philippines	2.2	30	6	90
Vietnam	4.1	71	17	105
Lao PDR	1.3	40	7	130
Cambodia	1.4	43	4	131
Bangladesh	5.3	53	24	140
India	4.0	100	26	128
Nepal	2.3	35	7	142
Pakistan	1.6	8	3	136
Sri Lanka	5.7	85	26	99

Source: Asian Development Bank, 2008b, Chapter 4 and UNDP, 2008
Note: HDI is the UN Human Development Index – ranked from high to low, SPEXP is social protection expenditure as a percentage of GDP, SPDIST is the percentage of the poor receiving some social protection and SPIMP is the per capita social protection expenditures as a percentage of the national poverty line.

Six of the 11 countries (Indonesia, Philippines, Lao PDR, Cambodia, Nepal and Pakistan) had SPIMP values less than 10%, an abysmal performance of assisting the poor through social programs. Social programs in Bangladesh, India and Sri Lanka were somewhat more effective. In these countries social capital expenditures were about one-fourth of the per capita poverty line. China stands out among the Asian countries with an SPIMP of 44, nearly twice as high as Bangladesh, India and Sri Lanka. Aside from the higher ranking of China, note that the HDI rankings do not properly reflect the variation in SPIMP within the Asian countries.

Higher food prices have also put the goals of reducing poverty and hunger at risk. The poor are particularly at risk when food prices increase since they spend two-thirds of their income on food versus around 40% for the non-poor. As prices increase the poor tend to substitute foods of lower nutritional value that lack the nutrients of higher priced alternatives. As a result nutrition as well as caloric intake are compromised. In the first part of 2008 food prices increased dramatically as reflected by research (see Bauer et al, 2008, p. 14) that shows that the poverty incidence increased by anywhere from 3% to 8% as a result of the 2008 food price increases for grain and resulting in an commensurate increase in the incidence of poverty. In the Philippines, on study suggested that a 10% increase in food prices would result in 2.6 million more people falling below the poverty line (see ADB, 2008c). While food price hikes have subsided recently there is a longer-term risk of rising food prices in the future, particularly if the economic crisis diverts resources from addressing the needs of agriculture, including infrastructure and research and development.

Resource mobilization is a general problem for the countries in South Asia, particularly in India. This constrains the ability of the central government and provincial authorities to mobilize resource for poverty reduction. The EIU points out that the tax base in India is extremely narrow. Only 4% of the working-age population is estimated to pay income tax and as a proportion of GDP India's annual revenue is among the lowest in the world. In fiscal year 2007/08 revenue was equivalent to just over 12% of GDP putting India 145th out of 149 countries according to EIU calculations. Although spending was about 3% higher this was achieved through public borrowing. This puts the figures in Table 9.6 in a somewhat different perspective. While SPIMP for India is still low it does not seem neglectful of the poor but rather reflect the general weakness in resource mobilization. The budget is complicated by the sometimes contradictory and irresponsible actions of state governments which tend to run up even higher fiscal deficits than the national government – between 6% and 9% in recent years compared with around 3% at the national level. Past debt servicing further reduces the ability to address poverty issues – between 30% and 50% – although at the lower end of the interval in recent years. All of these difficulties constrain the ability of the government to mount a significant fiscal stimulus directed toward the poor. These issues are discussed further in the India country report.

As a result of the slowdown in global growth, the United Nations 2009 estimates that between 56 and 80 million people will either remain poor or fall into poverty. About half of this number will be in India alone. In China, 20 million workers were displaced in the last months of 2008. This will bring a significant setback to plans for meeting the Millennium Development goal for reducing poverty by half between 2000 and 2015. Poverty incidence will rise by between 1% and 2% in Asia in 2009 as a result of the slowdown in the global economy.

MDG2 Primary education

The relationship between income and the other MDGs is less direct than is the relationship of income with poverty. Social and environmental poverty is only weakly related to income growth. Bauer (2009) and ADB/ESCAP/UNDP 2008 report that the correlation between income and growth and the share of the population with income below $1 per day is high at –.858 but that growth and other MDGs is weaker (see Table 9.7).

Correlations with other MDGs such as primary school completion rate, enrolment in primary education were negligible. This suggests that higher government expenditure does not necessarily translate directly into better social indicators. Resources have to be allocated sensibly and honestly and directed effectively to the target group. Often this is not the case as others siphon funds meant for the poor.

Table 9.7   Link between growth and MDGs in Asia

Variable	Correlation between variable and economic growth
Population below $1 per day	–0.858
Poverty gap ration	–0.781
Percentage of population undernourished	–0.483
Infant mortality 0–1 year (per 100,000 births)	–0.482
Under age five mortality (per 100,000 births)	–0.430
Maternal mortality rate (per 100,000 births	–0.304

Source: ADB/ESCAP/UNDP, 2008; Bauer, 2009

Nevertheless, as incomes increase less rapidly and unemployment rises, families and governments have fewer resources to devote to education. If we roughly equate MDG2 with literacy, then most Asian economies have achieved close to 100% youth literacy. In 2001, only South Asia and a few countries in Southeast Asia were far from achieving 100% literacy for youth between the ages of 15 and 24. Cambodia and Lao PDR were at 80% while Pakistan (58%) and Bangladesh (49%), Nepal (62%) and India (73%) have further to go. The rest of the countries in developing Asia were at 95% literacy or higher. This risk is that fiscal constraints could threaten civil service budgets with adverse impacts on educational quality. At the same time poorer families might be unable to send their young children to school because the costs of uniforms, transport and meals are too high. As a result, the economic crisis is likely to further delay the achievement of universal primary education. There will also be detrimental impacts on secondary and tertiary education as well, particularly as response to the crisis will require labor force adjustments and retraining for both men and women. Technical and vocational education will be a critical component of this adjustment. There is also a risk that enrolment rates will fall as poor families pull their children out of school to work and that families that could formerly afford private school are forced to send their children back to public school.

MDG3 Gender equality and empowerment

Significant progress in gender equality has been made throughout the Asian region both in terms of equal pay for equal work and also in human resource development. Female literacy is still lower on average than that of men. However in many countries the differences are now much smaller than in the past (see Table 9.8). South Asia still lags behind. In the current global downturn we have seen that exports from Asia have been adversely affected, and this has had an adverse impact on women's employment. In the formal sector in urban areas women are generally employed in export-oriented

Table 9.8   **Literacy rates for adults and females**

Country	Adult literacy (2001)	Female literacy (2003)
Bangladesh	41	31
India	58	48
Nepal	43	35
Pakistan	44	35
Sri Lanka	92	89
Cambodia	69	64
Indonesia	87	83
Lao PDR	66	61
Malaysia	88	85
The Philippines	95	93
Thailand	96	91
Vietnam	93	87
China	86	86

Source: Dowling, 2008, Table 4.13

labor intensive industries such as textiles and apparel, footwear and leather products, simple electronics, handicrafts and tourist and household services. As the export industries have been adversely affected by the downturn across the region, employment of women and their livelihood has been adversely affected.

We do not yet have the full measure of the gender impact for the current global recession. However, analysis by the ILO conducted recently gives some guidance. Women dominate the occupational structure of these industries in Thailand, the Philippines and Vietnam, anywhere from 2 to 5 women per man in the workforce (See ILO, 2009a; Bauer, 2009). See also Table 9.9. In the Asian crisis, the vast majority of those laid off were female – 95% in the garment sector and 88% in toys (Mahmood and Aryah, 2001). A larger proportion of labor-intensive industries are located in South Asia relative to East and Southeast Asia. Therefore we would suspect a larger impact on women's employment. However, this is likely to be more than offset by the fact that South Asia is much less dependent on exports and is also projected to suffer less both in terms of loss in exports and in income growth (see Table 6.4). There will be a more than proportionate impact on livelihood in agriculture as laid off workers in urban locations return to rural villages. More than 60% of all female employment is in agriculture. Women are also over represented in vulnerable occupations, about 8% or so in South Asia than men according to the ILO (ILO, 2009b). Given the projection of a rather deep global recession in 2009 and 2010, ILO foresees a rise in the percentage of workers in vulnerable occupations which would wipe out more than ten years of progress in reducing vulnerable employ-

Table 9.9   Gender composition of selected industries – employment ratio of women to men 2004/2005

Industry	Thailand 2005	Philippines 2005	Vietnam 2004
Textiles	3.22	1.25	2.85
Garments	3.75	3.41	
Electronics	2.14	1.64	2.30
Footwear and leather	1.67	0.25	1.80
Tourism (hotels, food)	1.77	3.67	2.99
Auto plants and parts	0.27	0.47	0.22
Construction	0.17	0.28	0.10

Source: ILO, 2009

ment rates worldwide. Many of these jobs are in low-skilled occupations such as domestic work, and sub-contracted home work in the handicraft and garment industries. As women lose their jobs, it is also more likely that the education of their female children will be compromised, since families under stress are more likely to educate boys rather than girls, particularly in South Asia, where gender equality in education has made less progress than in the rest of developing Asia.

Furthermore, public infrastructure programs which have great potential in addressing unemployment created by the crisis need to pay closer attention to the special needs of women. In this regard social service projects including healthcare, childcare and education could be crafted to employ more women while at the same time raising the human development level of their communities. These lessons were learned during the Asian financial crisis when female participation in Indonesia's public works programs was low compared with South Korea's program which included activities specially designed for women (ILO, 2009, p. 10). Microcredit was also a valuable resource for women during the Asian financial crisis. Care should also be taken to recognize that as men become unemployed they can force unemployed women to the sidelines because of the perception that men are a more important component of the workforce than women. In addition, a reduction in social spending on families close to or already in poverty has a number of undesirable social consequences including reduced food consumption and healthcare, reduced school enrollment rates as children are put to work and a heavier burden on women who are forced to work harder to help support their families as well as taking care of their children. Decision-making in the allocation of resources to crisis programs is usually put in the hands of men. Women's role in this process has to be increased.

Gender inequality is also related to the loss of remittance income. There is evidence that female migrants remit larger amounts of money to families at home than do men and a survey of urban to rural migrant Philippine workers showed that when a male worker lost his job, 65% of households reported a loss in income whereas when a woman lost her job, 94% of households reported a loss in income (see Bauer, 2009). Furthermore, since women do double duty as caregivers as well as workers, if they are forced to work longer they and other members of the household are put under greater stress. This often results in increased tension, violence and substance abuse.

MDG4–MDG6 Health

As noted above, six of the 11 countries (Indonesia, the Philippines, Lao PDR, Cambodia, Nepal and Pakistan) had SPIMP values less than 10%, an abysmal performance of assisting the poor through social programs. Social programs in Bangladesh, India and Sri Lanka were somewhat more effective. In these countries social capital expenditures were about one fourth of the per capita poverty line. This lack of effort is nowhere more evident than in the health sector. Bauer et al (2008) point out that total expenditures on health in South Asia were $26 per capita per year, lower than in any other region in the world, including Sub-Sahara Africa. Many countries spent less that the WHO recommended minimum of $35 per capita. Government spending on health (netting out private expenditures) were only $3 per capita in Pakistan, $7 per capita in India and $10 in Vietnam. Because the public sector health budgets are so meager households have to spend if they want better care. For the poor this leads to further impoverishment. Any major illness results in bankruptcy and further impoverishment and debt. The Asian Development Bank estimates that nearly 40 million people in India were kept below the poverty line through spending on health and 78 million people fell into poverty in other countries in Asia (see Bauer et al, 2008; Bauer, 2009). While it is hard to imagine the public sector reducing its level of public health spending further, the impact of the global recession on the sector will be immediately felt as incomes are reduced, unemployment increases, tax revenues dip and the ability to fund public sector health programs is further compromised. Health spending by the private sector, particularly for the poor, is also likely to suffer.

The World Bank projects that infant mortality will increase, particularly among girls and the poor will be additionally stressed by having less money to buy nutritious food, contributing to susceptibility to disease and the cost of drugs in countries where the exchange rate as depreciated and the local pharmaceutical industry is unable to deliver drugs without a large import component. While estimates for Asia are not available, the World Bank (2009d) and also Bauer (2009) estimates that girls are more likely to suffer from a decline in GDP. The result of the financial shock will be between 200,000 and 400,000 additional infant deaths per year worldwide between 2009 and 2015. Although economic growth in Asia has been outstanding the same cannot be said for infant and maternal mortality. The disparities in life expectancy and infant mortality are particularly troublesome in poor

Table 9.10   Life expectancy and infant mortality

Country	Life expectancy at birth in years, 2001	Infant mortality per 1,000 live births, 2004
Bangladesh	62	56
India	63	62
Pakistan	63	80
Sri Lanka	73	12
Cambodia	54	97
Indonesia	66	30
Lao PDR	54	65
The Philippines	70	26
Thailand	69	18
Vietnam	69	17
China	70	26

Source: UNESCAP, 2004 and Save the Children, 2006

Table 9.11   Demographic indicators by state

State	Female life expectancy (1992–94)	Infant mortality per 1,000 births (1992–94)
Poorer states		
Assam	54.4	78
Bihar	56.4	69
Madhya Pradesh	53.2	102
Orissa	55.1	109
Rajasthan	56.7	85
Uttar Pradesh	54.5	93
Richer states		
Andhra Pradesh	61.5	66
Gujarat	60.5	63
Haryana	63.2	69
Karnataka	63.6	68
Kerala	73.4	15
Punjab	67.2	55
Tamil Nadu	62.5	58
West Bengal	62.3	61

Source: Population Census and Registrar General of India

countries and regions. Cambodia has life expectancy at birth which is 19 years less than Sri Lanka and infant mortality rates that are nearly ten times as high (Table 9.10). A similar comparison holds for comparison between the states of Kerala and Assam in India (Table 9.11). Yet these disparities in human development are not reflected nearly as much in per capita income. Cambodia's per capita income is slightly less than half of Sri Lanka and Kerala's income per capita is about 1.6 times that of Assam. The difference is primarily in commitment and efficiency in the allocation of health expenditures.

The secondary effects of the crisis on health are manifold. These include lower nutrition, higher rates of starvation and stunting and fewer resources to pay for essential medicines resulting in higher rates of morbidity and mortality. As the cases of Kerala and Sri Lanka demonstrate, the cost of increasing expenditure on preventative medicine is not high, particularly if efforts are focused on reducing infant mortality and improving the health of newly born and their mothers. Clean air and water, better sanitation, and preventative measures to reduce the incidence of malaria, tuberculosis and other communicable diseases are more general challenges and will take more resources. Partnerships with NGOs such as the Gates Foundation should also be encouraged and current efforts expanded.

The relative neglect of healthcare is further reinforced by the results of a UNESCAP study which calculates the coverage of social protection programs in 30 countries in Asia and the Pacific (see J. Wood, 2009). Wood finds that over 20 countries had less than 20% of the population covered by healthcare assistance. Only a few countries had more than half of the population covered. Health received the lowest level of coverage compared to other social programs like assistance to the elderly, labor market assistance, social assistance, assistance to the disabled and child protection.

MDG7 Urban and municipal services

MDG7 turns to the spatial distribution of poverty and measures to help the poorest members of society, both in the cities and in rural areas. It also deals with environmental challenges and policy issues including climate change and health and sanitation in urban slums and in dry land areas. While many of these issues are of longer-term duration and interest, the current and ongoing economic crisis is also creating a number of challenges. These include dislocations as many newly arrived urban residents are losing their jobs and are being forced to return to the former homes in rural areas as a matter of economic necessity. This trend has gathered momentum in China and to a lesser extent in South Asia. For those that remain in the cities the loss of jobs and income is making life more difficult. The crisis is increasing the incidence of both rural and urban poverty, although the exact extent of the impact of the crisis is yet to be determined. Clean water and improved sanitation in urban areas is particularly at risk, given the continued rapid increase in population in cities and the pressure on government resources that is being increased by slow growth in personal, corporate and excise tax revenue as well as lower trade taxes as import and export growth collapses. The growth of large cities is a characteristic of urbanization in the last few decades. Asia, including Japan, has 11 of the 20 largest cities in the world (see Table 9.12). And these Asian cities, particularly those in developing economies, are continuing to grow at a rapid pace. This population growth is accompanied by an increase in urban poverty as the balance of poverty issues slowly shifts from a rural to an urban setting. By its nature the global crisis will have a much greater initial impact in urban as opposed to rural areas. Industrial production and exports are hard hit by the recession. For the most part these goods are manufactured in urban areas and layoffs and unemployment are highest among workers in the manufacturing and processing sectors. Urban poverty presents a different agenda from rural poverty. In Asian cities many of the poverty issues have to do with urban services including housing, water, sanitation, health and education as well as social services. The special needs of vulnerable groups including the young, elderly and the ill and disabled are also important and somewhat easier to deal with logistically as opposed to rural settlements that can be geographically isolated. Slums are a particular problem for most Asian cities and while the crisis may not have a direct economic impact on them, the indirect effect of lower economic growth of the city itself and growing unemployment of its residents is felt through its impact on informal market for goods and labor which sustain those living in these neighborhoods. The impact on poverty and well being of those working in the informal sector is indirect and difficult to measure. Some urban workers in the formal sector who are laid off or fired as a result of the impact of the global recession will, of necessity, move into the informal labor market. This will put further pressure on those already working in the informal sector, both in terms of finding and holding a job, keeping their place of residence and being able to afford healthcare, sending children to school and maintaining the other necessities of life. Others will manage to remain out of the informal sector, perhaps looking for a job or relying on help from family and friends. In any event they will be spending less on a variety of goods and services, some of which are being supplied by informal sector businesses.

To mitigate the social impact of the crisis on the existing urban poor and those who have recently joined the roles of the unemployed, governments can ramp up existing social programs such as conditional cash transfers, public works employment programs, workfare programs and food aid for those unable to work. Bangladesh and Indonesia already have these modalities in place (see, for example, Dowling and Yap, 2009) and have a commendable track record (see Box 9.1 and Box 9.2). What is required now is better focus on the needs of the vulnerable groups that are being impacted

Box 9.1   Conditional cash transfers

Most aid programs designed to address chronic poverty come with certain conditions. Cash (or sometimes food) is offered to chronically poor families in exchange for the family commitment to send their children to elementary school. Such programs, commonly called conditional cash transfers (CCT) have become quite popular in Latin America. These programs have recently been extended to Asia. For example, in Bangladesh a food for education program began in 1993 and continued for ten years until 2002, when it was replaced by a similar program using cash transfers. Indonesia had a school scholarship and grant program implemented in 1998/99 as a social safety net in response to the Asian financial crisis which lasted two years and has recently begun a pilot CCT program. CCT programs give cash transfers to targeted poor households. They offer cash transfers to households as a carrot to induce households to send their children to school and adopt more progressive healthcare treatment regimes. Families also attend nutrition and hygiene classes. The objective is to focus on the children's health, nutrition and education.. The programs target families and villages which have been identified as locations where chronic poverty is most prevalent. The grants are conditional upon the participation of the households in education and or health programs for their children. These programs are designed to build up human capital of the younger generation of these families as a way to break the unending cycle of chronic poverty and prevent the transmission of poverty to the next generation.

CCT programs have a number of advantages besides the human capital components. They work both to build up the supply of human capita and satisfy a demand side need for funds to meet household expenses as well as expenses of children going to school. They instil a feeling of mutual responsibility and doership among the recipients. Households feel that they are investing in their own future and that of their children. The programs can also build support within the local community by building pride in the students and in the school system. Such programs are designed to balance current poverty reduction objectives against future reductions in poverty for the next generation. CCT programs are beginning to be recognized within the international community and have drawn support from donors. However Bangladesh and Indonesia are the only countries in Asia that are currently developing such a program.

Source: Dowling and Yap, 2009

Box 9.2   **Work fare**

Public works programs, sometimes called work fare, can have two objectives. The first is to provide income for the poor in exchange for work contributions to a government project. The second is that workers can benefit from the project itself through skill enhancement and experience. In the past the first component was given greater emphasis. The work programs themselves were generally designed to benefit the wider community. Roads, irrigation systems, sewers and other civil works infrastructure were the focus of these social projects. Recently such projects have included components of the village infra-structure such as schools and primary healthcare facilities that can directly benefit the poor and the local communities where they live. Direct assistance to the chronically poor comes from wages received by those who work on the project.

If the poor have to give up other jobs to participate in the project it will subtract from the overall benefit. Therefore projects should be designed to be implemented during the slack season when agricultural workers, who make up the bulk of the chronically poor involved, are not employed elsewhere as day laborers. Secondly, the wage rate should be enough to attract poor laborers yet not too high to attract the non-poor. In India, for example, looking at the poorest households defined as those where the family head is an unskilled casual worker supplying unskilled labor in the market, primarily in agriculture, we note that the average wage for these workers was around 40 to 50 rupees per day in India about ten years ago or about $1.00 or a little more. In Maharastra a government scheme was implemented in the 1980s that employed laborers at these kinds of wage rates to work on small-scale projects constructing and maintaining roads, irrigation facilities and undertaking reforestation.

The project was successful and recently India has implemented a Maharastran type scheme for the entire country which has been phased in over a three-year period beginning in 2006. It is called the National Rural Employment Guarantee Act (NREGA) and guarantees one person in every poor household in the country employment 100 days out of every year. In 2007 it provided 30 million families with an average of 43 days of work. The program is eventually designed to provide 100 days of work per year for up to 60 million families per year. The wage per day is about $1.50, low enough to attract only the poorest but high enough to make a difference in their living standards. (See the Oxfam website www.fp2p.org for further details.)

Source: Dowling and Yap, 2009

Table 9.12   **Population of urban areas with 10 million or more inhabitants (2005)**

	Population 2005 in million inhabitants	Population 2015 in million inhabitants	Average annual increase in % 1975–2005
Tokyo	35.2	35.5	**0.93**
Mexico City	19.4	21.6	1.99
New York	18.7	19.9	0.55
Sao Paulo	18.3	20.5	2.15
Mumbai	18.2	21.9	**3.15**
Delhi	15.0	18.6	**4.08**
Shanghai	14.5	17.2	**2.28**
Kolkata	14.3	17.0	1.98
Jakarta	13.2	16.8	3.37
Buenos Aires	12.6	13.4	1.20
Dhaka	12.4	16.8	**5.81**
Los Angeles	12.3	13.1	1.07
Karachi	11.6	15.2	**3.56**
Rio de Janeiro	11.5	12.8	1.39
Osaka	11.3	11.3	**0.45**
Cairo	11.1	13.1	1.82
Lagos	10.9	16.1	5.84
Beijing	10.7	12.9	**1.91**
Manila	10.7	12.9	2.53
Moscow	10.7	11.0	1.12

Asian cities in bold.
Source: United Nations 2008 and http://www.peopleandplanet.net/graphs/Megacities.png

by the crisis. This is made more difficult by the many other competing uses for government funds and the budget constraints that have become more binding as a result of the crisis. It is important to remember that poverty reduction and reaching the MDGs should be a cornerstone of public policy for all emerging economies in Asia.

Rebalancing aggregate demand to address the perceived problem of over-saving among emerging Asian economies is an additional challenge that can be addressed by programs to improve social safety nets. This can be accomplished if a more comprehensive system of social safety nets can be developed and implemented that have the support of the people.

Balancing social and economic development

While it is important to set MDGs for the various components of social development it is equally important to develop an overall framework that addresses economic and social development in a coherent and coordinated fashion. Many of the efforts to stabilize economies in the face of a global

Table 9.13   Comparison of HDI and SPI ranks for Asian economies

Country	HDI 2008	SPI 2006
South Korea	25	2
China	94	11
Indonesia	109	18
Malaysia	63	14
The Philippines	102	22
Vietnam	114	13
Cambodia*	136	25
Lao PDR*	133	23
India*	132	10
Bangladesh*	147	17
Nepal*	145	24
Pakistan*	139	26
Sri Lanka	104	9

Note: HDI rank of 179 countries, SPI Rank of 31 countries in Asia.
* indicates country identified as at risk for compromised human development.
Source: UNDP, 2008 and Asian Development Bank, Social Protection Index (SPI)

recession necessarily focus on raising living standards and increasing the rate of growth in aggregate income. This is an important task. At the same time it is also critical that the poor and those vulnerable to falling into the poverty trap are protected. The analysis of Chapter 5 demonstrated that the crisis has impacted the region's four groups differently, depending on level of development, geographic location, degree of integration into the global economy, the mix of industries and services, the skill set of the labor for and the competence of government. The response to the crisis is further discussed in the regional and country analysis in Chapter 10. Nevertheless, it is important to also recognize that social protection is a concept that binds together a number of different aspects of social and economic development. In this regard the Asian Development Bank has developed a Social Protection Index (see http://www.adb.org/Poverty/knowledge-products.asp?q=social+protection+index&submit=Submit+Query&c=ALL) that ranks countries according to the scope, coverage, targeting effectiveness and efficiency of their respective social safety nets. This Index provides a useful tool for the detailed analysis that follows in Chapter 10 and also as a useful complement to the Human Development Index which has been developed by UNDP and is widely employed as an indicator of social development (see Table 9.13).

Although there are differences in rankings there are some similarities between the HDI and SPI approaches. For example, India ranks very high in SPI but quite low in HDI.

10
Individual Country Responses and Prospects

As the details of individual country responses to the global crisis will vary, this chapter is designed to provide more details regarding individual country prospects. As a preamble, we have assembled a couple of tables giving details of the amount of social protection that is provided in the Asian economies. Expenditure in Table 10.1 is comparable to SPEXP in Table 9.6. The Impact variable in Table 10.1 is comparable to SPIMP in Table 9.6. There are some differences between figures in these two tables. This is because the two studies used different sampling techniques and methodologies We will refer to these two tables in the country reports that follow. Briefly we note here that there are wide variations in the social protection coverage in Asian countries. Nepal and Pakistan rank at the bottom, both countries with low levels of Coverage/SPDIST and Impact SPIMP. Bangladesh, China, Sri Lanka and Vietnam rank high both in Impact and Coverage. Higher levels of Expenditure/SPEXP do not necessarily translate into high impact on the poor as some social programs are either directed to the non-poor or diverted to other groups.

Table 10.1   Social protection indicators by country in percent for selected Asian economies

Country	Expenditure	Coverage	Target	Impact
Bangladesh	3.8	10.2	34	15
Indonesia	1.9	34.6	73	11
Nepal	2.2	10.5	26	7
Pakistan	2.0	6.5	5	2
Vietnam	3.5	3.5	52	12

Note: Expenditure on all social projection programs as a percentage of GDP; Coverage as percentage of reference population of total poor; poverty target is percentage of poor receiving some social protection benefits; impact is the proportion of the poor who benefit from social protection measured as a percentage of the national poverty line.
Source: Baulch et al, 2006

Box 10.1   Cost of eliminating chronic poverty in Asia

The Chronic Poverty Research Center 2008 estimates that there are around 800 million poor people in Asia and that the number of chronically poor is between 175 million and 250 million (Chronic Poverty Research Center 2008, Annex E). Using the low estimate of chronically poor and assuming that it would take a dollar a day to lift everyone of the chronically poor out of poverty, then the bill for eliminating chronic poverty in Asia for one year would be 175 million times 365 days in a year or around US$64 billion. This assumes that every dollar appropriated by the government would get to the chronically poor. This is overly optimistic. Administrative costs can eat up some of the resources of poverty programs. However, research in Latin America suggests that these costs are not that high, averaging only around 10% of total program costs (see Caldes et al, 2004; Coady et al, 2005).

On the other hand, the chronically poor are not all completely indigent, so that it would take less than a dollar per day per person to lift all of the chronically poor out of poverty. Allowing for these distortions it still seems useful to work with the dollar a day benchmark as a way to assess both the cost of dealing effectively with eliminating chronic poverty and the capacity of governments to deliver the needed assistance.

The subsequent ongoing cost of keeping the chronically poor above the poverty threshold would be lower still, since some of the chronically poor would find jobs as a result of the dollar a day subsidy. So let us take US$64 billion as a first round guess as to the cost of eliminating chronic poverty in Asia, leaving aside the logistical problems of identifying where they are, the costs of delivering the assistance, keeping greedy government officials from subverting the money to their own pockets and the possible negative impact on work efforts of the poor.

We can compare this US$64 billion to wipe out chronic poverty in Asia with a variety of budgetary items for industrial and developing countries. For example, the United States spent almost three times this much (about US$170 billion) on the wars in Afghanistan and Iraq in 2007. US official development assistance to poorer countries was US$23.5 billion in 2006 of which US$18 billion went to Iraq. The next largest donor was the United Kingdom ($12.46b) followed by Japan ($11.19b), France ($10.60b) and Germany ($10.43b). Other European countries along with Australia and New Zealand gave smaller amounts.

Current estimates of the budgetary costs of all forms of social protection in a few countries are reported in Table 9.6. These estimates range from under 2% in Cambodia, Laos PDR, Indonesia and Pakistan to

5.7% in Sri Lanka. For our set of chronic poverty countries and using 3% as a notional average for the region as a whole, this amounts to about US$150 billion at current exchange rates.[1] From these notional calculations and assuming that the full allocation of social spending is spent on the chronically poor, it does appear that there are sufficient resources available in the Asian region to wipe out chronic poverty if these resources were used efficiently.

If we look at the budget for chronic poverty reduction from a more disaggregated point of view a somewhat different picture emerges. Comparing the 3% of GDP figures with the dollar a day costs on a country by country basis there are three countries that would not have sufficient resources – India, Bangladesh and Nepal. A few countries would have somewhat more than needed and a few would have a large surplus. The calculations are displayed in Table 10.2. China and Indonesia have the biggest surplus resource gap. Three percent of GDP is about 10 times as big as the cost of a dollar a day subsidy for all the chronically poor in China and around 15 times the dollar a day resource cost in Indonesia. In the Philippines, Pakistan and Vietnam the surpluses are somewhat smaller.

For the other three countries (shown in bold face) – India, Bangladesh and Nepal – there is a deficit. The cost of a dollar a day poverty reduc-tion program for the chronically poor is 11% of GDP in Nepal, 5.5% in India and 3.3% in Bangladesh. Assuming that a dollar per day per person would eliminate chronic poverty for a family, even in the best case scenario where the chronically poor were well targeted and over-head expenses were low, these three countries would still not be able to eliminate chronic poverty without outside assistance. This assumes that they could not muster more than 3% of GDP to address chronic poverty.

In a prior study one of the authors investigated the incidence of chronic poverty in Asia. In this study some estimates of the cost of eliminating poverty were made. This analysis is summarized in Box 10.1. Using a figure of 3% of GDP as the resource commitment it suggests that if Asian govern-ments are committed to eliminating chronic poverty, most have the avail-able resources achieve this objective. However three South Asian econ-omies (Bangladesh, India and Nepal) would need external assistance to achieve this objective and several others (the Philippines, Pakistan and Vietnam) have only a small margin of error if they were to achieve this objective. Note that only China, Bangladesh, India and Sri Lanka are currently allocating 3% of GDP for overall social protection expenditures (see Table 9.6).

Table 10.2   Cost comparisons of a dollar a day subsidy for the poor with a social spending allocation of 3% of GDP for a panel of Asian economies (in billion US dollars)

Country	Cost of a US one dollar a day program for the chronically poor given to all chronically poor in the country (billion US)	Cost of a US one dollar a day program for the chronically poor given to all chronically poor in the country (as percent of GDP)
China	11.92	0.003
Indonesia	0.92	0.002
The Philippines	1.42	0.010
Vietnam	1.49	0.020
Bangladesh	**4.01**	**0.055**
India	**35.92**	**0.033**
Nepal	**1.18**	**0.110**
Pakistan	2.50	0.017

Note: Highlighted countries have a ratio in column 3 of over 0.03. Assuming that US$1 equivalent is given to all the chronically poor, the number of chronically poor calculated as the lower bound estimate of the proportion of poor who are chronically poor by CPRC 2008/2009, GDP estimate at current exchange rate from CIA factbook.
Source: CIA Factbook, 2008 and CPRC, 2008

The point of this exercise is not to give accurate estimates of the cost of poverty reduction but rather to point out that the financial capacity of countries to finance a comprehensive poverty reduction effort varies dramatically. World Bank estimates that 64 million more people will be living in extreme poverty (on less than $1.25 a day) by the end of 2010. India, Nepal and Bangladesh would need additional resources to eradicate chronic poverty while China and Indonesia are quite capable of handling the financial burden should they wish to embark on such a program to tackle chronic poverty. Also note that this ignores the resources required to deal with other families in poverty that do not fit into the chronically poor category. Whatever the nature of government efforts to address chronic poverty these financial realities have to be kept in mind (Dowling and Yap, 2009, pp. 480–483).

Group 1 – Richer countries in East Asia

Hong Kong

Hong Kong's economic fortunes are closely related to that of China. The current global downturn has had a dramatic impact on exports from the southern coastal provinces of China and this has had a negative effect on Hong Kong. Hong Kong exports growth fell to 2.5% in 2008 after increasing by over 7% in the previous four years. According to the latest data from the government, exports contracted by 12.6% in 2009. Re-exports from China, which make up the bulk of Hong Kong exports, fell dramatically. The IMF estimates that GDP growth will be –4.5% in 2009 (see Table 3.1). In Q1 2009, GDP fell 7.8% and exports fell by 22.7% (year-on-year) and 16.8% (quarter-on-quarter). Service income fell less, by 8.2%, as a result of still strong tourism revenue from the mainland. Investment was down 12.6% and unemployment rose to 5.2%. The prospect of reduced FDI inflows into China will have a secondary impact on Hong Kong, further reducing investment. Aside from the IMF estimate of –4.5% growth in GDP mentioned above, other forecasters are predicting negative growth of 5.5 to 6.5%. Unemployment rose in 2008 and was expected to increase further to over 6% in 2009. By Q4 2009, there was some pick up in economic growth due to the recovery in China. In actual fact, real GDP contracted by 2.7% and was less than initially expected. Economic growth in Hong Kong is projected to increase between 4–5% in 2010 and mainly led by a revival in consumption and investment expenditure especially from the mainland. Exports are likely to remain weak still.

Given constraints on monetary and fiscal policy and the anticipated lack of stimulus to the Hong Kong economy from the fiscal stimulus by the Chinese authorities it was not difficult to understand the contraction of the economy in 2009. Hong Kong does not have an independent fiscal policy since it is part of China. Hong Kong was not expected to benefit from the fiscal stimulus put in place by the Chinese government which was designed to stimulate infrastructure, consumption and some investment. Exports, private investment and household discretionary spending remained weak in China and these are the categories of expenditure that are important for Hong Kong. Slower net capital inflows to China also had an adverse impact on Hong Kong which has a large financial sector. However Hong Kong continued to have a positive balance on current account, albeit a shrinking one (from 10.8% of GDP in 2008 to 9% of GDP in 2009 according to the Asian Development Bank, 2009). Inflationary trends have abated and Hong Kong is faced with the possible prospect of deflation which could entice consumers to hold off purchases anticipating further price declines.

Hong Kong does not have an independent monetary policy since its currency is tied to the US dollar. What it can do is lower the Hong Kong interbank lending rate (HIBOR) to provide additional liquidity for banks that have to borrow in the interbank market. Lower interest rates will also ease debt repayment for households. The property market slumped in 2008 as transactions fell by around 20% compared with 2007. Further declines were expected in 2009 although low mortgage rates and price declines would have attracted some buyers. A decline in share prices of nearly 50% in 2008 also had an adverse real wealth effect on the economy.

Given the constraints of a fixed exchange rate and limited fiscal discretion the Hong Kong Monetary Authority has taken a range of measures to support the economy. In Q4 2008 the money supply has been increased through open-market operations and it has lowered the discount rate to 50 bps over the US federal funds target rates. Both of these measures were designed to supply liquidity to the system. The government also agreed to guarantee all customer deposits without an upper limit to authorized banks in Hong Kong. It also signed an agreement with China for a swap facility. Owing to the loose monetary policy adopted earlier, there has been a surge in speculative activities in the Hong Kong stock market and property market. In a bid to fend off the formation of asset bubbles, the government has begun to increase mortgage requirements in 2010 so as to calm the property market. Stamp duties have also been raised on luxury property sales to prevent excessive speculation. The government is also looking into the use of land sales to further stabilize the heating property market.

Fiscal policy measures were provided to support small- and medium-sized firms at the end of 2008 and the budget for 2009 has a deficit equivalent to 2.4% of GDP. Spending measures include generation of 62,000 jobs and internships, infrastructure spending and increased social spending. The recently unveiled 2010/11 fiscal budget continues to stress spending on public work projects. The fiscal budget has slightly improved with the revival of economic growth and rising tax revenues in 2010. However there is likely to be increased pressure for government expenditure especially on social spending for the vulnerable groups like the elderly and the lowly skilled. Aging in Hong Kong is on the rise and the number of elderly who depend on their children to support them in the midst of rising cost of living is growing. The current means-tested US$128 per month is often regarded by many Hong Kongers as "fruit money" and insufficient to support monthly expenses. In the future Hong Kong would need to further cement ties with the Pearl River delta area of China, where Hong Kong accounts for over 70% of cumulative foreign direct investment (ADB, 2009). Hong Kong also supplies logistics, shipping and finance to firms in the delta. To gain the full benefit of closer integration with companies in the Pearl River delta it has to improve infrastructure linkages and reduce custom clearance bottlenecks. It also needs to upgrade its workforce tertiary skills in order to supply skilled professionals that are comfortable working in both economies.

South Korea

Highly dependent on exports (exports are 43% of GDP and net exports still account for 90% of economic growth) economic performance of the South Korean economy deteriorated in 2008 and 2009. GDP growth fell to 2.5% in 2008 after growth at double that rate in the previous five years and registered a mere 0.1% in 2009. Both exports and investment contracted in 2009. South Korea's financial sector was also highly exposed to the global financial crisis with its commercial banks being highly reliant on short-term external debt financing. Stock prices fell by about 40% and the won depreciated from 900 won/$ to nearly 1,600 won/$ over the course of 2008 with most of the depreciation occurring in the fourth quarter. Hedge funds and other foreign resident's withdrawals were largely responsible for the rapid decline. US$55 billion in foreign exchange reserves in the form of swaps or loans were provided to banks involved in trade financing by the Bank of Korea to shore up support for the financial sector. Other efforts included the setting up of a 40 trillion won fund to aid local banks recapitalize their balance sheets and another 40 trillion won to purchase toxic assets. In October 2009 the trade balance was up 35% for the latest 12 months and a current account surplus of around 4% of GDP was realized in 2009. By spring 2010, the recovery had manifested in further strength in international trade and payments and economist Lee Jyung-tae writing in *The Korea Herald* at the end of 2009 predicted exports to rebound at 13% in 2010 as the global economy recovers further (http://www.koreaaherald.co.kr/NEWKHSITE/DATA/html_dir/2010/01/01/201001010011.asp).

To address rapidly deteriorating export performance during the peak of the crisis, South Korea enacted a stimulus package of around $10 billion at the end of 2008 and provided further stimulus of $100 billion package in early 2009. In sum these measures amounted to about 5.6% of GDP (see Table 6.2). Around a quarter of the package consisted of revenue measures, primarily permanent cuts in the personal and corporate tax rates. The remainder of the stimulus measures (75%) comprised higher expenditure measures, consisting primarily of income support for low-income households, active-labor market policies, support for SMEs, and investment spending. Reflecting this, the overall fiscal balance is expected to switch to a deficit of around 2.75% of GDP in 2009. Initially this did little to slow the downturn. Early forecasts of modest growth in 2009 of 0.7% by KDI and 0.3% by the central bank, bad enough for an economy used to growth in excess of 5% replaced by a negative growth rate of 4% projected by the IMF in the spring of 2009 (see Table 3.1). The level of household debt was high and could have slowed the economy further if not for the two fiscal stimulus packages that were adopted in late 2008 and early 2009. Currency depreciation of around 30% in 2008 also aided in boosting exports. Recent trade figures show exports contracted by over 17% in 2008 and capital investment was projected to fall by 7.7% in 2009. Export prices for their key South Korean products were falling as competition to maintain global market share intensified. A decline in export volume of over 15% was predicted for 2009, particularly to China, South Korea's largest export market (see Table 3.4). In November 2008, shipments were down nearly 30% including a wide array of products such as personal computers, home appliances, semiconductors, automobiles and petrochemicals. South Korea's exports, which are mainly durable exports to industrial countries, are highly sensitive to the drop in global economic activity.

The central bank cut the policy interest from 5.25% to 2.5% at the beginning of October 2008 and kept it at a record low of 2% for 2009. In mid-2009 most economists doubted that the economy could keep from falling into recession. Employment growth has slowed and unemployment was expected to reach nearly 5% in 2009, up from 3.2% in 2008. In addition to the hardship created for the families of the unemployed this also put a damper on consumption. The housing sector was also weak in Q4 2008 and in the first half of 2009. The inventory of unsold apartments increased putting downward pressure on prices. The government has announced various measures to prop up the property market including buying 10,000 to 15,000 units and land from construction companies as well as extending loans to construction companies. These measures along with the stimulus and other measures helped to turn around the economy in the latter part of 2009. Quarter-on-quarter growth in Q2 and Q3 was 2.9% and 2.6% respectively and overall economic growth for 2009 was slightly positive along with a modest decline in export volume of only 0.1%. Authorities are also predicting stronger growth in 2010 of over 5%. Stimulus to pull the economy back amounted to about 5.6% of GDP, just about the same amount as the predicted shortfall in growth between 2008 and 2010 and perhaps even substantially more if recent forecasts are accurate (Table 7.8). Total government spending is projected to have increased in 2009 by 27% from 2008, resulting in a budget deficit of around 4.5% of GDP. (The OECD estimates that the general government fiscal deficit will be smaller at 1.8% of GDP.) An additional boost in investment can be expected from stimulus measures that reduced corporate tax rates. The low cost of credit has also resulted in a turnaround in the housing market which has resulted in a jump in housing prices and pressure on the government to curb housing loan to value ratios.

Despite continued strong growth in 2H 2009, in early January 2010 some economists were predicting that it would be some time before government stimulus measures would begin to be phased out. In March the government announced that 60% of its annual budget would be committed to job programs, construction and income re-distribution. The budget deficit is likely to continue until 2014. With the recovery of the global financial market since April 2009, the government has used less than half of the 40 trillion won recapitalization fund. Similarly, the toxic asset fund was also largely unused since local banks did not invest heavily in the US subprime loans. Interest rates continue to be held at a record low to prevent disrupting the ongoing economic recovery. However monetary policy is likely to be tightened in Q2 2010 due to fears of excess liquidity and emergence of asset bubbles. Longer-term measures could be considered to offset the impact of global growth cycles on the economy by introducing stronger counter-cyclical measures such as an expanded unemployment system and other automatic stabilizers. This would also serve to cushion the impact of recession on the poor. Structural reforms are also needed in the non-manufacturing sector to improve productivity and contribute to stronger growth in the medium term.

Malaysia

Malaysia is highly exposed to foreign trade. Its exports are larger than its GDP (117% in 2007) whereas the rest of the Southeast Asian economies have a smaller export share; from about 30% for Indonesia to over 70% for Thailand (see Table 6.4). It also has a relatively small domestic market and this will make it difficult to make up for the loss of foreign business. Forecasts of growth for 2009 made by the IMF and ADB in Q3 2009 were for negative growth in the range of 3.5% (see Table 5.1) while more recent estimates by EIU in February 2010 were more optimistic, lowering the negative growth rate to 2.4% for the year. Exports recovered somewhat in Q4 2009 after registering negative growth in the first three quarters of 2009. The recovery was led by a rebound in demand for electrical products and components and petroleum products. China is a major export destination. Real GDP is expected to grow within a range of 2–3% in 2010 led by a rebound in private consumption and investment.

In Q1 2009, MIER slashed its growth forecast for the year and called for a second economic stimulus package to boost aggregate demand in the face of a deteriorating export environment (MIER, 2009). This package of around 8% of GDP was announced in early March 2009. It provides subsidies for capital investment, both private and public by the government's investment holding company. It also provides tax incentives for consumers and private investors as well as funds for expansion of the Kuala Lumpur airport. It followed a $1.9 billion package announced in November 2008 (equivalent to 1% of GDP) designed to focus on high-impact projects including roads, schools and low-cost housing. Together these two packages, designed to be tranched over several years, amounted to around 9.0% of GDP. Table 6.2 shows the stimulus to be only 5.5% of GDP for a shorter period of time. The stimulus will be accompanied by generally looser monetary policy and lower interest rates and would imply an increase in the budget deficit to over 7% of GDP. Public debt was projected to increase although financing costs are expected to be minimized given the low interest rate environment. Most of the debt is domestic and the sovereign debt rating is high. Whether these policies will be effective or not will depend not only on the response of private sector demand in Malaysia but also on the recovery in exports to industrial countries. Electrical machinery and products comprise nearly 40% of Malaysian exports and shipments of office machines and other machines and parts fell rather dramatically in Q4 2008. To offset weakness in traditional markets in industrial countries Malaysia is focusing on new and emerging markets as well as providing financial support for small- and medium-sized enterprises. MIER is also concerned about the secondary effects on a slowdown in China which will have an adverse impact on Malaysian suppliers of intermediate products to this large market. Future growth will require concentrated efforts to increase total factor productivity (TFP) and promote knowledge and technology intensive industries.

Poverty rates are generally low, although Sabah has a high rate of 16% and rural areas have generally higher poverty incidence than the cities. World Bank (2009e) reports that poverty incidence in Malaysia remained unchanged from 2007 to 2008 at 3.6% of all households. Social services access and income support for the poorer sections of the country as well as investment incentives and increased market access for more isolated rural areas will be needed to address poverty and promote greater regional income equality as the economy experiences slower than historical growth rates in the next two years. Estimates suggest that rural poverty deteriorated from 7.1% in 2008 to 7.4% in 2009 (World Bank, 2009e).

Currently, fiscal considerations appear to be forcing the government's hand in tightening fiscal policy before the recovery seems secure as global economic conditions stabilize. Although the fiscal deficit of 7.4% in 2009 is considered relatively small when compared to the budget position of some OECD countries, this is Malaysia's biggest deterioration in its fiscal position since 1987. The 2010 budget is only 90% of the revised allocation for 2009. Large cuts are expected to be made to operating expenditure to balance fiscal budget in 2010. EIU anticipates the budget deficit to narrow to 5.8% in 2010. There is greater urgency to foster growth in private and foreign investment if Malaysia is to recover quickly from the economic downturn.

Singapore

Singapore is the most volatile of the open economies in Asia. Extraordinarily high dependence of trade (exports of goods and service are around 250% of GDP, higher than any other Asian economy) is the primary reason for the volatility. Hence the economy is quite sensitive to the global trading climate. In the 2001 global recession, economic growth was −2.4% compared with over 10% the previous year. The turnaround in 2009 from 2008 is not going to be as dramatic since the economy was already feeling the signs of the recession in early 2008. Growth in 2008 was 1.5% and economic performance weakened throughout the year. This was following a strong 7.7% growth performance in 2007. As expected, weak exports were the major driver of the economy although all sectors were hit hard. The economy contracted by 14.6% on a quarter-on-quarter basis in Q1 2009. Manufacturing contracted by 26.6%, pulled down by weakness in electronics, biomedical manufacturing, and precision engineering and chemicals. However there was a significant recovery later in the year and by January 2010, Singapore's exports were posting double-digit growth. Non-oil domestic exports soared by over 20% year-on-year in January and the economy experienced the most rapid growth in exports since June 2006. The upturn was led by external demand from US, EU, Hong Kong and Taiwan. There was stronger demand for electronic exports (integrated circuits, disk drives and other PC components) and non-electronic goods (pharmaceuticals, petrochemicals and primary chemicals). However analysts predict that it will take some time for exports to return to pre-crisis levels since Singapore's major trading partners are still in the midst of gradual economic recovery. Real GDP declined by only 2.1% in 2009 and a rebound to between 4% and 5% growth in 2010 is expected according to the latest forecasts from EIU.

Construction and services grew slightly in Q4 2008 but did not hold up well in 2009. A weaker real-estate market and the negative wealth effects that accompany it are an additional downside development. By early 2010, the construction sector has improved with the recovery in the property sector. It was also supported by the government investment program and the development of large-scale project like integrated resorts. Amidst concerns about excessive speculation in the property market during the second half of 2009, the government has stepped in with measures to cool the real-estate sector to prevent overheating.

The Monetary Authority of Singapore (MAS) shifted its exchange-rate policy stance from gradual appreciation of the trade-weighted Singapore dollar to control import price push pressures to 0% appreciation in October 2008. By then, oil prices had weakened and the economic horizon looked bleak due to the slowdown in economic growth with its major trading partners. To ensure that financial institutions were not overly exposed to the subprime crisis and that they could access US dollar liquidity, MAS entered into a swap arrangement with the US Federal Reserve in October 2008. As of August 2009, MAS has yet to make use of this facility.

On the fiscal side, the government has announced a stimulus of $20.5 billion at the end of January 2009 (about 9% of GDP, higher than the earlier United Nations estimate reported in Table 6.3 of 5.9% of GDP) which was designed to save jobs, provide tax breaks and build infrastructure, stimulate bank lending and enhance international competitiveness through tax relief and grants to businesses. $1.7 billion was also allocated to infrastructure and upgrading of health and educational facilities. The corporate income tax rate was cut from 18% to 17% and the government provided personal income tax rebates of 20% with a ceiling of S$2000. The major components of the stimulus are two programs. The first gives companies access to working capital with much of the default risk borne by the government. The second is a job-credit scheme that prevents mass layoffs by offering cash grants to employers to cover part of their wage bill. The subsidy amounts to a 9% cut in the employer's contribution rate to the Central Provident Fund (CPF), the Singaporean social security system. This is a change from policies followed in previous recessions where the employer's contribution rate was cut. The burden is now shifted to the

Government (see ADB 2009, p. 256 for further details). By September 2009, more than 100,000 employers had received up to S$890m (US$640m) from the Job-Credit scheme. The stimulus may also help to shore up capital formation which probably declined by 10% or more in 2009. The workfare program that gives cash grants to poor working families is allocating an increase in payments of 50% to help these families cope with the recession. The government will use reserves of S$4.9 billion to fund the stimulus program and will not undertake any borrowing initiatives. Due to legislative changes passed in January 2009, the government can finance its spending up to 50% of the expected long-term real returns on reserves invested by the MAS and sovereign wealth funds. The various stimulus measures should help to keep the recession from being severe but not enough to keep it out of negative growth territory in 2009.

The Job Credit scheme is expected to be gradually phased out by the end of 2010. The size of the subsidy paid to each employee on the CPF will be cut from 12% of the first S$2500 of the employee's salary to 6% in March and halved to 3% in June. Provision of government-backed financing loans under the Special Risk Sharing Initiative (SRI) would only phase out in January 2011, but terms of condition has been revised in line with Singapore's recovery from recession. The cap for such loans to small and medium enterprises has been cut from S$5m to S$2m while the government's share of the default risk will be lowered to 50% from 80%. In the long term, Singapore continues to emphasize skills, innovation and productivity as a strategy for sustained economic growth. Productivity is targeted to increase to 2–3% over the next decade and levies were also raised on foreign workers to prevent Singapore's over-reliance on foreign labour.

Taiwan

Taiwan is a small, open, highly export-dependent economy not unlike its neighbors in East Asia. Taiwan's economy had grown at about the same rate as its companion East Asian NIEs (see Table 5.1) but weakened considerably more in Q4 2008 (–8.4% versus –3.4% and –3.7% for South Korea and Singapore). By the end of 2009, there was a sharp jump in industrial orders and exports picked up by 53% in Q4. Exports are expected to recover to close to pre-crisis levels in 2010. According to EIU February estimates, economic growth in 2009 is estimated to have contracted by 3.5% with recovery to around 4% expected in 2010.

In retrospect, export performance in 2008 was particularly weak, falling by 20% year-on-year in the fourth quarter and a more rapid –36.3% in the first two months of 2009. Industrial production fell by 43.1% in January 2009. Becoming an outsourcing location for Chinese manufacturers did not help as shipments to China also fell dramatically in Q4 2008 and shipments to China fell by a whopping 43.1% in January and February 2009. The slowdown was broad based with all major export categories

– machinery and electrical equipment, chemicals, precision instruments all being adversely affected. Exports and imports each account for 70% of GDP and there is little compensating demand from consumption and investment which are both weak. Construction investment also fell at the end of 2008 (–14% in 4Q 2008 versus –20% in 3Q 2008). However the outlook for a turnaround in the sector was colored by negativities surrounding the rest of the economy and was not expected to revive quickly despite low interest rates. A weak stock market has also had a negative wealth effect on consumption and the economy in general. The global financial crisis has also hit the trade credit market as exporters have had trouble securing letters of credit to finance imports. Weakness in the euro also began to hurt Taiwanese exports. The fallout from weak exports also took its toll on the domestic economy as consumption and investment also declined. Despite the expected upturn in 2010, exporters have to face several obstacles. Competition in the international arena is increasing with the FTA signed between China and other ASEAN countries (Brunei, Indonesia, Malaysia, the Philippines, Singapore and Thailand).

Furthermore fiscal and monetary stimuli implemented in 2008 and 2009 have so far failed to stem the tide toward slower growth. The discount rate has been cut and further cuts are expected but there is not much room for further easing since the discount rate is now close to 1%. The story is complicated by inflows of speculative capital since late 2009 which have caused an upward pressure on the Taiwan dollar. The Taiwan government responded by implementing capital controls in January 2010 to prevent an asset bubble. The fiscal stimulus enacted in 2009, composed of a multiyear infrastructure package and issuance of consumption coupons, averaged about 3.9% of GDP (see Table 6.2). The package is expected to bolster the construction sector which declined by 14% in Q4 2008. Additional fiscal stimulus is needed and is well within the capacity of the government. International reserves are huge, the current account is in surplus and expected to remain so despite the crisis, public debt is around 35% of GDP and until last year the government deficit was less than 1% of GDP. Investment spending has also fallen although not as far as in the 2001 recession. However there is not much evidence that the fiscal stimulus is directed to supporting private sector capital formation. Rather it is being directed to consumption and infrastructure. Unemployment which has been higher than levels in the other NIEs, has been increasing and it might have reached 7% at the end of 2009. Putting all of this information together it appears that without further fiscal stimulus the Taiwan economy sank further into recession in 2009 with GDP growth somewhere between –3.0% and –5.0%. A government program to enhance the social security system while providing short-term benefits to the unemployment and some tax relief for middle-income wage earners could work to rebalance consumption and saving. A robust retirement program would reduce the incentive to save and provide a much needed stimulus to consumption. The combination of stimulus measures and some revival in exports in Q4 suggest that the economy will recover to a satisfactory growth rate of around 4% in 2010.

As of January 2010, many of the fiscal stimulus measures have yet to be implemented and the emergency fiscal stimulus package will be gradually phased out by 2012. Taiwan continues to emphasize government support for key industries particularly for the electronic sector. However monetary policy is expected to be tightened beginning in mid- 2010 and corresponding guarantees on loans and emergency liquidity measures will be withdrawn. Given the heavy dependence on the China export market, Taiwan will be carefully monitoring stimulus measures in the mainland before undertaking an exit strategy.

Group 2 Economies – Middle-income group (the Philippines, Thailand and Vietnam)

The Philippines

In 2008 the Philippine economy performed very well through the first three quarters of the year, following on from successively strong years in 2005 through 2007 when the economy grew from 5% to 7.2%, one of the highest in the Asian region. In the third quarter GDP growth was 4.6% year-on-year led by rapid growth in government spending. However results for Q4 2008 and early 2009 performance suggest that the global downturn that has descended upon the rest of the Asian region began to pull down the Philippines as well. In Q1 2009 GDP grew by a negligible 0.4% and fell by 2.3% in April and May. Exports fell by 18.2% in Q1, particularly electronics which fell by 34% in Q1. However there are some signs of recovery as the rate of decline leveled off later in the year. Exports are concentrated in electronics, which accounts for 60% of shipments and exporters anticipated a decline in overseas orders of 5–8% by the end of 2009 (Semiconductor and Electronics Industry of the Philippines quoted by CLSA 2009 report on the Philippines). This translates into an estimated decline in export volume of 11% in 2009. This is a smaller decline than experienced in Hong Kong, Singapore and Thailand but more than in the rest of Asia (See Table 3.5 column 5). Capital formation was also weak. Economic growth slowed to 0.9% after a mild recovery in Q4 2009. World Bank, EIU and ADB predicts that real GDP growth will improve to between 3.1% and 3.3% in 2010 but the Philippine economy is still underperforming owing to pre-crisis structural bottlenecks.

Government stimulus came in two ways – through lower interest rates which still are sticky because of continued inflation of over 5% and a larger fiscal deficit which will fund a series of tax breaks for consumers and business as well as increased physical and social infrastructure spending. The scope of the fiscal stimulus, 5.8% of GDP (see Table 6.2) is slightly higher as a fraction of GDP although the same order of magnitude as stimulus measures taken by the other Asian economies in East and Southeast Asia with the exception of China. Half of the stimulus will go to boost welfare payments to the poor as well as in labor-intensive infrastructure projects including roads, reforestation and classroom construction for public schools. Thirty percent of the spending package will be spent on large infrastructure projects as well as tax breaks for corporations and individuals. Diokno (2009) also argues that the fiscal stimulus package is not large enough to make a big difference in creating enough jobs during the economic downturn. This is because many of the provisions included in the package have already been factored into behavior of firms and individuals. Furthermore, the stimulus will be constrained by the public sector deficit which is projected to have increased to as much as 3.4% in 2009 from 1.6% of GDP in 2008. Remittances have risen over the past decade and have provided a strong boost to consumption. It is estimated that more than 10% of the workforce is employed overseas at any time and that one in four people in the Philippines benefits directly from remittances. As the global recession impacts the Middle East through softer oil prices and other countries which host Filipino guest workers through lower income growth, it is expected that remittance income flattened out in 2009 but did not decline. It is possible that remittances will remain strong going forward and this could help maintain growth at a reasonable level. Fiscal responsibility has risen in the past decade. This is reflected in a slow decline in government debt as a percentage of GDP from 75% to 56% over the past few years. However interest payments are still 25% of total government expenditure. Tax effort need to be improved by widening the tax base and improving enforcement. Tax revenue is a low 14% of GDP. Initial plans to balance the budget by 2010 have been postponed. With elections due in mid-2010, there is little intent for the government to re-impose fiscal discipline. The fiscal stimulus will only be rolled back over in 2011 and 2012. EIU estimates a fiscal deficit of 3.2% of GDP in 2010.

Poverty has been rising in recent years. ADB (2009) indicates that poverty rose from 30% in 2003 to nearly 33% in 2006, the latest date available. In addition, the typhoons Ondoy and Pepeng which hit the Philippines in late September and early October 2009 are expected to throw many more households into poverty. Stimulus spending in the Philippines has been credited with being pro-poor in nature. The spending on agricultural and social services has been targeted at the lowest income groups. Since June 2008, the government has increased funding for conditional cash transfers under the Pantawid Kuryente programme with each beneficiary household receiving a cash grant of US$11. The allocation to poor households who send their children to school and undergoing medical checks also doubled under the Pantawid Pamilyang Pilipino programme. Over 600,000 households have benefited from the scheme. Livelihood and emergency employment schemes have been implemented to create jobs in agriculture, education and healthcare. Reconstruction efforts by the government as well as increased remittances from overseas workers to affected relatives back home helped to prop up consumption in Q4 2009. Hence the Philippines was able to enjoy stronger growth at 1.8% for Q4 2009.

Despite the strong fiscal stimulus undertaken, World Bank (2009f) estimated that the 1.4 million Filipinos will be pushed into poverty by 2010. Resources for addressing the Millennium Development Goals of improving health and education indicators need to be augmented by additional budget allocations and/or support from external donors. Perennial problems of weak governance, poor implementation capacity continue to constrain efforts to improve economic efficiency and attract foreign investment.

Thailand

At nearly 75%, Thailand has the greatest export dependence among Southeast Asian economies outside of Malaysia and Singapore (see Table 6.4). After contracting by an estimated 3.2% in 2009, its worst performance for ten years, the outlook for Thailand is muted with a return to modest growth in 2010. As the global crisis has impacted the financial sectors of industrial countries, commercial banks have become reluctant to make new loans and to extend trade credit. The closure of the international airport in late 2008 along with continued political uncertainty has also damaged confidence of international investors and foreign importers of Thai products. According to the Thai News service the International Monetary Fund projected a decline in the value of Thai exports to the US of 0.7% in 2009. Exports to the EU and Japan were also expected to decline by 0.5% and 0.3% respectively. The outlook for agricultural exports was guarded. Thai rice exports were expected to drop by 15% in volume and 20% in value in 2009 compared with 2008. Processed food exports were projected to show no growth in 2009 as global consumer demand softened. Produce value was expected to drop as consumers bought lower-priced goods. Textile and apparel exports might have grown at around 5% in 2009, the lowest growth in a decade with a possibility of zero growth. This compares with 10% growth in a normal year and some small manufacturers may have to close down. Industry sources expected negligible export growth in the electronics sector. Hard disc drives and integrated circuits exports will also drop as investment has been shifting to other countries including Taiwan. The automobile and auto-parts sector was adversely affected by the global slowdown in new car sales. Exports were expected to drop by at least 5% and perhaps by as much as 20% in 2009 (see Table 3.5) compared with an increase of 12% in 2008. In Q4 2008 exports declined by 8.7%. Export demand for gems, furniture and toys also softened in 2009, although toy exports may have picked up somewhat as product safety and recalls dampens demand for Chinese toy exports. However in Q4 2009 there was a rapid rebound in real

GDP, fueled by a recovery in export and tourist arrivals. Exports grew by close to 10% year-on-year in Q4 2009 and tourist arrivals rose by 28% over the same period. However sectors related to trade and tourism like transportation, storage, communications, hotels and restaurants are still suffering from weak external demand. Growth in 2010 will be fragile, improving to the range of 3.0% to 4.0%. Consumer and investors' confidence are likely to remain muted owing to continued political unrest in Thailand.

Tourism has also declined beginning in late 2008. Arrivals fell in the last few months of 2008 by 13% and this trend continued in 2009. Thailand has been hit harder than some other Asian economies due to the relatively larger role of the tourism sector. Tourist arrivals started to pick up beginning in mid-2009 but are unlikely to reach pre-crisis level till 2011 or later (World Bank, 2009g). Private investment flows will also be adversely affected by the global slowdown. Board of Investment approvals fell dramatically in the second half of 2008. The Thai banking system remains sound and exposure to foreign assets is limited. Non-performing loans were only 3.3% of total loans in Q3 2008 and the guarantee of all bank deposits has been extended through 2011. Growth in other markets including Eastern Europe and the Middle East may offer some offset to weaker demand in industrial countries and lower oil prices will reduce the import bill. To offset lower exports and reduced financial inflows, Thailand needs to speed up the pace of public investment to reduce overhead costs and increase productive efficiency. It also must improve the investment climate to attract foreign capital and upgrade its human capital resources. Private investment is also expected to weaken along with consumption as stock and real-estate markets continue to be weak and political turbulence could resume.

To address the weaknesses in the Thai economy that have resulted from the ongoing global recession the government enacted a fiscal stimulus package of $39 billion in 2009, a whopping 14.3% of GDP, even more than the Chinese stimulus (see Table 6.2). The package, which will be paid for by domestic and international borrowing includes supplements to low-income earners, students and the unemployed. There are also provisions for better healthcare, aid to rural communities and senior citizens. The package also includes infrastructure projects and support for the tourism industry including expansion of airport facilities. The government also extended concessions introduced last year covering free electricity and water supply and public transport for poor households. Tax measures will be taken to reduce the tax burden on the real-estate sector, venture capital companies, small and medium industries and the tourism sector. Liquidity support for the financial sector is also envisioned. The package is projected to increase GDP by at least 1% and ensure positive growth for 2009. However, most observers say that growth was a negative 3% for the year (see Table 5.1). The government also plans to spend 2 trillion baht on infrastructure projects over the next three to four years to increase economic efficiency and create jobs highlighted by extending mass transit lines in Bangkok. Higher spending is expected to have resulted in a widening of the budget deficit to about 5% of GDP in 2009. To offer further support to the economy, monetary policy was further eased as the policy interest rate was lowered to 1.5%. While the recession will put a damper on the amount of deficit spending that can be sustained these measures should work to raise income growth. The private sector investment climate is clouded by infrastructure constraints and a burdensome regulatory environment. There is, however, room for further fiscal expansion as the public sector debt limit is still manageable (a 50% self imposed debt limit has still to be breached). Foreign exchange reserves are substantial and external debt in relation to GDP has fallen more or less steadily since the Asian financial crisis to 24% of GDP. Programs to aid the poor are particularly welcome. Social safety nets should be expanded to provide greater security for poor and lower middle classes (lower 30% of the income distribution). This would allow these families to eventually amass some precautionary savings to meet emergencies, invest in small-scale business and purchase agricultural and business equipment to help raise productivity.

By end 2009, Thailand has kept to its stimulus plan and has disbursed funds accordingly. Nearly 9 million people benefited from the cash handouts. However the second stimulus spending on social and infrastructural development projects has yet to fully take off. Despite the large size of the second stimulus package, total expenditure is a mere 21.4 billion baht out of the 2 trillion baht. Only 14% funds under the total three-year budget has been approved (EIU, 2009a) and further delays are expected. The main concerns that face Thailand include political uncertainty, graft allegations as well as financing issues. Public sector debt has risen from 38% of GDP in 2008 to close to 60% of GDP with an increase in off-budget spending anticipated over the next three years. Fiscal stimulus measures are set to continue but the Bank of Thailand is likely to raise interest rates in 2010 if inflationary pressures occur. This forecast assumes that political disruptions will be resolved by the end of 2010.

Vietnam

From one perspective, Vietnam is in a similar situation to other countries in the region. Export revenue, foreign direct investment and remittance income has been falling and were estimated to have fall further throughout 2009. However from the perspective of possible government policy actions to provide stimulus to offset the fall in demand Vietnam is under more constraint than its neighbors. It has lower levels of international reserves and ballooning current account and fiscal deficits, both of which constrain further fiscal expansion. In addition firms which have borrowed abroad to finance local investment find themselves in a bind as the dong continues to depreciate. Taking these factors into account, the government's goal of maintaining growth of 6.5% in 2009 was not realized. World Bank (2010a) and EIU estimated GDP growth rate at between 5.0% and 5.5% in 2009 (see Table 5.1). Real GDP growth rate is estimated to recover to around 6% for 2010 but will still be below pre-crisis economic levels.

Owing to the global economic crisis, GDP growth in Vietnam slowed toward the end of 2008 but less than its neighbors. Consumption growth was resilient in 2008 as a result of higher commodity prices which translated into higher earnings for farmers and also urban salaries. This did not continue in 2009. Industrial production began to fall in December 2008 and exports are estimated to have fallen by around 6% although there are also some observers who show more dramatic declines (latest EIU estimates from Table 3.5). Foreign direct investment also weakened as a result of reduced appetite for risk given the global recession. Tourism income also declined putting further pressure on Vietnam's external balance. Arrivals from mainland China, Singapore, Thailand and Malaysia increased by 14.7%, 14.3%, 14% and 13.5% respectively in 2008 compared with 2007. However arrivals from higher income countries (US, Canada, Japan, South Korea and Taiwan) which account for 40% of foreign arrivals decreased and fell further in 2009. Remittance income, another important source of foreign exchange has also weakened, not only because of a decline in growth in the Middle East but also because of reluctance to remit in the face of a depreciating local currency. While inflation has moderated as economic growth has fallen, a gradual weakening of the dong is expected to continue. In an attempt to ease the downward pressure on the dong caused by a large trade deficit and high inflation, the State Bank of Vietnam devalued the dong on several occasions. The dong was devalued by 3.4% against the US dollar in February 2010. The devaluation was the government's fourth since June 2008.

Monetary policy has been supportive of economic growth. Interest rate cuts are expected to continue and state banks are also expected to make loans available to businesses. Vietnam cut the benchmark interest rate from 8.5% to 7% in February 2009. Discount and refinancing rates were also lowered respectively. The amount of fiscal stimulus is still unclear. One source mentioned a $6 billion stimulus equivalent to 6% of GDP (Citibank, 2009) and another to a 1% stimulus (CLSA, 2009). If PPP figures are used the 6% stimulus using the exchange rate method translates into a 2.5% stimulus which would be similar to the stimulus in Taiwan and somewhat greater than the other countries in the region (see Table 6.2). Latest figures from EIU (February 2010) puts the size of the fiscal stimulus package at $7.7 billion. However due to the lack of transparency in Vietnam's fiscal accounting EIU says that there are difficulties in estimating how much of the fiscal stimulus is actually new spending rather than duplication of existing spending. So far, the stimulus is aimed at improving infrastructure and there will also be a reduction in corporate income tax and deferred tax on dividends. SMEs were given 30% reduction in their corporate income tax for Q4 2008 and the entire of 2009. Another aspect of the package is a 4% interest rate subsidy on new bank loans denominated in local currency. This subsidy is designed to provide working capital to local businesses and there has been strong demand for them. The objective is to maintain production levels and employment. About 60% of the loans have been taken out by private companies with the balance going to state-owned enterprises. According to the central bank of Vietnam, total lending under the interest rate subsidy reached $23 billion in 2009. By end of 2009, Vietnam has already terminated the interest rate subsidy scheme for short-term lending. However loans for discounted medium- and long-term lending and the lowered corporate tax rate has been extended till end 2010. There is also a new credit guarantee scheme to support lending to small- and medium-sized businesses. However this scheme was less effective owing to red tape and stringent lending criteria and only 813 guarantees were authorized. As the stimulus will require additional borrowing there will be pressure on the external balance and the current account deficit which will be compounded by falling remittances, weaker exports and tourism revenues as well as the planned fiscal stimulus. If the saving-investment gap is financed by foreign direct investment then Vietnam will be able to sustain a fairly large current account deficit of close to 15% of GDP in 2009. If not, there is a threat of further currency devaluation, reduced fiscal support and even greater decline in aggregate activity. Fiscal strain has been exacerbated by a reduction in crude oil royalties as the global oil market has weakened. To raise additional funding for various stimulus projects the government is contemplating a dollar denominated domestic bond issue of as much as $1 billion and is continuing to seek additional assistance from international donors. The rise of domestic credit and pressures of food and fuel prices have triggered inflationary pressures. Consumer price index rose at 12% in 2009 (World Bank, 2010a) and the inflation rate is expected to exceed 10% for the next two years. ADB and IMF have urged for Vietnam to tighten monetary policy to slow credit growth and controlling inflation. With the swing of the pendulum from sustaining economic growth in 2009 towards maintaining price stability in 2010, Vietnam needs to tread a fine balance to prevent any major scale social impact from rising cost of living and yet not reverse the recovery in economic activity.

After a steep reduction in the poverty rate from 58% of the population in 1993 to around 22% in 2007, many households in Vietnam have since slipped back into poverty with the economic turbulences brought forth by the global financial crisis. A review of the social impacts of the financial crisis carried out by World Bank in February and April 2009 highlighted certain groups to be more vulnerable to poverty than others. They include high numbers of migrant workers, informal sector workers and household-based enterprises. Vietnam has created community-based small-scale infrastructure projects to provide temporary job opportunities. The government is also reviewing the 2005 criteria list for poor households to receive state assistance. The criteria list was meant to be used till 2010. But in view of the global economic crisis, natural calamities and inflation at home, the review aims to better target the poor and enable them to access state-assistance schemes. There is also a pressing need to develop Vietnam's social protection system which lags behind other countries. The unemployment insurance law has been in effect since 2009 but workers will only benefit in early 2010. The government has to do more for poorer regions with high concentrations of ethnic minorities. The poor ethnic minorities face a significantly larger poverty gap of 19.2% which is more difficult to bridge (Swinkels and Turk, 2006). Investment in education and training of workforce is of high priority so as to prepare Vietnam for the different type of economy that could emerge after the recession.

Group 3: Large economies – China, India and Indonesia

China

Official figures from the National Bureau of Statistics showed that China managed to achieve a V-shaped recovery, with a 10.7% year-on-year increase during Q4 2009. China was relatively less affected than other countries due to strong domestic spending. However export-oriented industries especially small and medium enterprises were quite badly hit during the onset of the global economic crisis. One-fifth of SMEs were reported to have gone bankrupt and another one-fifth heavily cash strapped and lack of access to credit. Toward the end of 2008 and in early 2009 there were reports of substantial layoffs in the export processing zones in Southern China and some recent migrants to the cities were returning to their homes in rural villages. The extent of the recessionary buildup is reflected by estimates of export shipments. After falling by 2.2% in late 2008, exports declined much more rapidly in January 2009. Shipments were down by 17.5% while imports fell even further by 43%. Further export contraction continued for the remainder of Q1 2009. A large fraction of imports are for inputs to exports. In the middle of the year, the IMF downgraded Chinese growth prospects to 6.5% for 2009 and Euroframe (2009) also predicted slower growth in 2009 and 2010 of 7.6% and 7.1% respectively. The Consensus Economics forecast (Consensus Economics, 2009) was somewhat higher at 8.1%. Latest figures from EIU are even more optimistic with 8.7% growth expected to be reported for 2009 and 9.6% in 2010. Remittance income was also expected to decline slightly. China is now the second largest recipient of overseas remittances after India with over $25 billion remitted in 2007. As growth slowed, unemployment rose and many migrant workers returned to their villages as factories closed. Income distribution deteriorated as the share of income of the poor declined further.

In response to softer expected GDP growth, China took steps to shore up its economy by announcing a US$583 billion infrastructure investment program to be implemented over 2009 and 2010 (about 13.3% of GDP according to the United Nations estimates, Table 6.2). The stimulus projects included low-income housing, electricity, water, rural infrastructure, environmental protection and technological innovation. Corporate tax rate was reduced and farm quotas removed. Monetary policy changes were also included as part of the package and a reduction in policy lending rate and lending rates to business resulted in growth of investment in government projects. However, small and medium industries without access to concessional lending had a rough time. China could well afford such a large stimulus package since government debt is less than 20% of GDP. A similar though smaller package was implemented following the 1997 Asian financial crisis. By comparison, this package is more than double the $700 billion financial sector bailout in the United States when measured as a percentage of income (the US bailout package is about 5% of GDP) and is being spent at a rapid pace. However, some commentators argue that the package includes investment projects already planned. Furthermore, the package will be tranched over several years. Exporter tax rebates which were suspended in 2008 have been restored and new laws on wages and work rules that added to costs have been relaxed. According to the Ministry of Human Resources and Social Security, China created 11 million new jobs in 2009, an additional 2 million ahead of the government's target. The composite lending indicators of the OECD suggest that the recession may have already reached a trough in the Q1 2009 with further recovery continuing throughout the year. Chinese economists are now predicting the economy will grow by 10% in 2010.

Results from 2H 2009 suggest the Chinese economy did begin to recover quickly. Fixed investment grew at the fastest pace since 2006. However, investment growth was far from uniform. Investment grew faster in central and western provinces than the formerly booming coastal provinces. Consumption spending was also strong. The OECD composite leading indicators series suggests that the recession began later in China than elsewhere (Q1 2008) and ended a year later. China is also using is vast foreign exchange reserves to make investments in minerals and oil companies in Russia and Australia. FDI inflows to China increased for the fifth month in a row, rising to $12.1 billion in December 2009. Foreign exchange reserves also increased, reaching nearly $2.4 trillion at the end of December 2009. At the same time the real-estate market, which had been rising rapidly in 2H 2009 began to cool off in December 2009. However, bank lending accelerated in December and early January 2010 prompting the central bank to order some banks to temporarily halt lending as fears of another asset bubble and inflation grew. Lending in the first two weeks of January far exceeded the targets for the year set by the central bank. The central bank also raised the reserve requirements for banks in early January. As economic activity accelerated toward the end of the year Q4 growth was 10.7% lifting growth for the year to 8.7%, nearly a full percentage higher than estimates made only a few months earlier (see Table 5.1).

Funding for China's large stimulus package is largely raised from bank lending than from central sources, provincial and local government funding (EIU, 2009a). Financing from the central government comprises less than 50% of total stimulus package. Total new bank lending for 2009 is believed to have doubled that lent out in 2008. Hence China's fiscal balance appears to be more manageable than many other countries that have similarly embarked on fiscal stimulus to spend their way out of recession.

In the medium term, efforts will have to be made to rebalance growth by stimulating consumption and reducing the preoccupation with saving, investment and exports. As it is

> the composition of the demand stimulus and production boost is completely wrong. The government has simply done more of whatever it was doing in the past: increased investment in the production of exportable goods and heavy industry (metals and chemicals), increased production of semi-finished manufactured goods and increased investment in infrastructure. The inevitable result of this investment boom will be increased excess capacity in exportables and unprecedented environmental destruction ... The green shoots we may be seeing in China will therefore not endure unless the country manages, very rapidly, a radical change in the composition of its production and consumption. This is possible but not likely (W. Buiter quoted in www.salon.com/tech/htww/2009/05/01/china surges ahead/print.html).

One way to do this would be to introduce a comprehensive social safety net which would ensure all workers of a pension, reducing the need to maintain a private nest egg. Such changes would help to reduce large current account surpluses over time and make a significant contribution to the reduction in global imbalances and stimulate consumption while reducing poverty. A second approach would be to allow the yuan to appreciate in value. This would stimulate consumption as opposed to exports and further contribute to the shift away from capital intensive exports. As a result net exports will contribute less to overall growth than in the past and the shortfall will be made up by consumption and investment in factories, equipment and services geared to the domestic market. A third policy, which might be difficult to implement but an effective measure nonetheless, would be to force SOEs to pay dividends. This would reduce the tendency for reinvestment of profits. Fourth, the government could reduce taxes and subsidies which favor the manufacturing industry. Fifth, policies could be adopted to increase taxes on business profits, which have risen as a share of GDP to 20% of GDP from 12% a decade ago. Sixth, the government could introduce a change in the income tax rate so that the rich are taxed at higher rates. The rich save a higher proportion of income than the poor and progressive taxation would also help to redress the deterioration in income distribution that has occurred in the past two decades. Finally, restrictions on rural to urban migration could be relaxed to permit further flow of cheap labor to cities where labor-intensive industries would benefit. All of these changes would help to stimulate consumption which is only 35% of GDP, a fraction of the share of consumption in GDP in most other Asian countries which is in the range of 50% to 60% of GDP (refer also to the rebalancing discussion in Chapter 8).

Work by Guo and N'Diaye (2009) suggests that it will be extremely difficult for China to continue increasing its share of world exports of manufactured goods. Chinese machinery exports now account for close to 50% of total exports, about the same rate as South Korea a decade ago. They indicate that a scenario of zero net export growth combined with higher consumption would result in a relative decline in the growth rate of exports without a significant decline in economic growth over the next decade. For example, growth rates of steel and shipbuilding would decrease to 15% per annum from much higher rates in 2007 (66% and 31% respectively). Machinery exports would continue to grow at 15%. These growth rates would enable China's exports to grow at about the same rate as world demand with some price reductions for steel and machinery. Under this scenario consumption would grow at the same rate as income and the contribution of net exports to growth would decline from its current high rate of around 30% to a much lower level. Growth in consumption and investment in services would help to make up the difference.

With the massive increase in credit growth, there are concerns over emergence of asset bubbles and overinvestment in infrastructure in 2010. Investment to GDP ratio in China was over 40% in 2008, and strikingly similar to the level in Thailand before the latter succumbed to the 1997 crisis. The Shanghai stock market in 2009 was up by 90% from a year ago. Housing prices in Beijing and Shanghai have increased by about 50%. Bank lending in 2010 will be triple that of 2009 and has appeared to have favored large SOEs with political connections more than SMEs. Beneficiaries of stimulus spending include the rail sector, the construction and energy sectors as well as manufacturing sectors like the automobile industry. Sales of automobiles have surged. However, this deliberate boost to productive capacity is likely to aggravate China's strained trade ties with its trading partners as other countries accuse China of dumping and fostering an anti-competitive edge. China is also under growing pressure for its currency to strengthen from its pegged rate of 6.83 reminbi to US$1. A resurgence of protectionist action is expected in 2010. To avoid a stock market and real estate bubble, China is trying to develop an appropriate strategy for reducing monetary and fiscal stimulus measures. China is already cautiously tightening its monetary policy in early 2010 in anticipation of inflationary pressures as the latest purchasing managers' index indicates higher price expectations. Reserve requirements for banks were raised twice in January and February. Again this could favor SOEs at the expense of SMEs. According to Xu (2010), SOEs in China control roughly about 30% of the total secondary and tertiary assets, or over 50% of total industrial assets. The average size of SOEs is about 13 times that of non-SOE peers. The silver lining is that the risk associated with non-performing loans will be borne by the state rather than SMEs.

China has done an admirable job in lowering poverty rates, which have fallen from over 80% in the early 1980s to under 20% by 2005 (see M. Ravallion, 2009). The effort has been balanced so that its substantial spending on social programs as a percentage of GDP (4.6%) reaches a large proportion of the poor (69%) and spending on the poor is a large proportion of their per capita income (44%). See Table 9.6. for details. Greater focus needs to be directed to the poorer regions in the south and southwest regions of the country (particularly Guizhou, Yunnan and Guangxi) where poverty rates are still often in excess of 50%. The rapid growth in income in the coastal regions has also resulted in growing income inequality (Gini coefficient of 29.1 in 1981 deteriorating to 41.5 in 2005). This has been exacerbated by the continuation of the *hukou* personal registration system imposed by the local authorities that restricts rural to urban migration.

The World Bank (2009e) investigated the impact of the global financial crisis in East Asia and forecasted that an additional 14 million people will remain in poverty in the region in 2010 as a result of this crisis. China is estimated to have nearly 9 million of the additional estimated poor. The actual poverty figure is dependent on the extent of economic recovery. China has stepped up efforts to increase the minimum living allowance (*dibao*) for the lowest social level groups and providing one-off income support for 74 million poor Chinese citizens. Enterprise development in poorer regions has been implemented. Funds to speed up earthquake reconstruction efforts in Sichuan Province have been increased significantly. In addition, pension benefits, rural pension schemes and rural health insurance have been expanded. A rural pension program for farmers aged over 62 years to receive a life time pension conditional on the payment of a one-off fee (approximately 1.5 times of annual income) was piloted in August. The program is dependent on subsidies from the central and local governments. Rural net income per capita actually rose due to the rise in transfer payments. Enrollment in medical insurance schemes has been astronomically on the rise from 19 million to 337 million in urban areas and 160 million to 830 million by end 2008 to June 2009 respectively (World

Bank, 2009h). Ministry of Health aims to cover more than 90% of the population by 2011. China has also actively implemented enterprise development in poorer regions to provide employment and the usage of purchasing vouchers to help the poor cope with rising cost of living. Special skills training program have also been implemented. However, there are constraints such as ensuring the transferability of pension accounts across regions in China's segmented system and the financial burden for the government especially in poorer regions. See Dowling and Yap, 2009, Chapter 7; M. Ravallion, 2009; and World Bank, 2009e and 2009h.

India

By early 2010, growth in India appeared to be fast approaching pre-crisis levels after taking a battering from the global economic crisis and experiencing the worst monsoon in nearly 25 years. Real GDP growth rate is projected around 7% for 2010. Initially many observers believed that India would be only marginally affected by the global crisis. However, the collapse of Lehman Brothers and the global liquidity crisis that ensued resulted in a sharp reduction in the availability of foreign financing for business ventures and a resulting shift to domestic financial markets. This put pressure on interest rates and spreads as well as creating further risk aversion and a reduction in credit expansion as domestic liquidity tightened. There was also a sharp increase in outflows of foreign capital and falling stock prices. Higher interest rates and currency depreciation have followed. However, policies were undertaken in late 2008 and early 2009 that served to stabilize interest rates, increase domestic liquidity and reduce the outflow of capital. The economy grew at 5.9% in 2009, slightly lower than the most recent projections by EIU (see Table 5.1). Banks are still tightly regulated in India, resisting the trend toward deregulation followed in many other developing countries. As a result, Indian banks were not heavily invested in the assets and derivatives backed by subprime mortgages issues in the US. According to Panagariya (2009), only about a billion dollars out of total banking assets of 500 billion fall into the toxic asset category. However, there have been withdrawals by US firms and a sharp decline in US imports of Indian products. Foreign exchange reserves fell by nearly $40 billion in October 2008 alone resulting in a tightening of liquidity in India. Equity markets lost more than 60% of their index value between January 2008 and March 2009 and there was a massive value outflow of foreign portfolio investment. However, this outflow reversed in 2009 as capital began to flow back. India is one of the few countries in the region where economic growth has remained relatively buoyant. Nevertheless, the economy remains fragile. Merchandise exports demand softened in Q4 2008 following a tripling between 2002 and the first part of 2008. Exports have fallen in every month since October 2008 although the pattern of decline slowed in the second half of 2009. Exports of gems and jewelry, textiles and plastics and farm products have not done well. Even though export dependence in India is lower than in other Asian economies the sector is employment intensive and the Federation of Indian Export Organization fears that ten million jobs could be lost as the recession's impact spreads. Remittance income has also been adversely affected. Some economists were predicting that remittance flows, which comprise about 3% of India's GDP, would also decline. In 2007, India was the largest recipient of remittances at $27 billion followed by China at $25.7 billion and the Philippines at $17 billion. However remittance flows strengthened through 2009 and were over $12 billion in Q3, substantially higher than they were before the crisis began in 2007 when they were about $8 billion a quarter. Although the World Bank is predicting a slight decline in global remittance flows in 2009, a recent World Bank report (World Bank, 2009c) argues that non-resident Indian remittances (NRI) will hold up well despite the slowdown in the global economy. This is despite some remittance shortfalls following the financial problems in Dubai.

Bank lending has been weak since the beginning of the crisis. In response the Indian government has loosened monetary policy by cutting interest rates and reserve requirements. Although constrained by a large fiscal deficit and debt to GDP ratio of more than 80%, India was initially able to mount a modest fiscal stimulus package of 3.2% of GDP (refer to Table 6.2). However, Kumar and Vashisht (2009) suggest that India has since adopted an expansionary budget FY 2008 (April 2008 to March 2009) which amounted to about 4% of GDP. When added to the three fiscal stimulus packages adopted in December, January and March of 2009, Kumar and Vashisht suggest that the total stimulus was about 6% of GDP. Measures to cut interest rates, reduce duties and increase subsidies for exporters have been taken and a scheme to subsidize export credit has been extended. Other measures have also been adopted to assist exporters by offering subsidies, particularly in employment-intensive industries including leather and textile products. Pre-election spending provided temporary fiscal spending that help bolster income of low- and middle-income families and the elections in May 2009, which the Congress party won handily, accelerated government spending independently of the fiscal stimulus. Will these measures be enough to help the Indian economy sustain growth in the range of 7% or higher in 2010 and beyond? Chances are good, if only because India has not globalized as rapidly as other countries in the region. Fifty percent of GDP is generated by the services sector which has not been affected significantly by the global recession. Furthermore, its financial sector has not been adversely affected by the build up of toxic or other non-performing assets. The economy also benefited from the fortuitous increase in stimulus spending that was implemented even before the deepening of the global economic crisis. Spending on fertilizer subsidies, handouts to civil servants, debt relief for farmers and the National Rural Employment Guarantee Scheme helped to support fragile domestic demand during the downturn. However it must continue to deregulate its domestic economy and pursue measures to increase economic efficiency, particularly with respect to industrial policy and by relaxing labor market restrictions. There are positive signs that the fiscal measures are having a positive impact on the industrial sector. In June 2009, the industrial output of India grew by 7.8% which has been caused by the stimulus package and low-interest rates by the lenders. Montek Singh Ahluwalia, Deputy Chairman, Planning Commission, said that he had always expected the positive growth. For the third straight month, beginning in September 2009, the Indian Industry has been showing positive growth which shows the country is on the road to economic recovery. This progress is also reflected in the improvement in the OECD leading indicator series for India in Q2 and Q3 2009.

At the same time, efforts to address poverty issues must be accelerated and its programs refined to reach the poor more effectively. India is one of the few countries in Asia that is expected to fall short of its millennium development objective of halving poverty between 2000 and 2015. Budget allocations for poverty reduction and health and education improvements need to be increased and better targeted if progress toward achieving the MDG is to be made. Dowling and Yap (2009) outline a number of ways in which poverty is being attacked in India. Including food subsidies, workfare, new schools for villages and conditional cash transfers to encourage students from poor families to attend school. One of the most successful has been the National Rural Employment Guarantee Act (NREGA) which guarantees 100 days of minimum wage employment on public works projects to every rural household that asks for it. The program began in 2006, when India implemented the (NREGA) for 200 backward districts. The residents in these districts make up 70% of India's poor. They are mainly located in arid and semi-arid regions. The scheme guarantees one person in every poor household in the country employment 100 days out of every year. In 2007, it provided 30 million households with an average of 43 days' work. Three million got the full 100 days between 2007 and 2008 (CPRC, 2008). The scheme aims to reduce severe rural livelihood distress by creating a short-term need for unskilled labor. It also aims to improve agricultural productivity of the arid and semi-arid lands with projects relating to water conservation, drought proofing (including reforestation/tree plantation), land development, flood control and protection works (including drainage in waterlogged areas) and rural connectivity in terms of all-weather roads. Farmers are guaranteed short-term casual employment and with the completion of the NREGA project, the farmers can plant a second crop and earn additional income, thus providing a sustainable livelihood in the long term. Beginning in April 2008, the NREGA has been extended to all 604 districts of the country.[2] However, its effectiveness appears to be varied. The poorer states of Andhra Pradesh (25.37 person days), Uttar

Pradesh (22.23 person days), Bihar (18.46 person days), Chhattisgarh (38.65 person days), Orissa (32.27 person days) and Madhya Pradesh (39.9 person days) still fall short of the desired target of 100 days. Furthermore, NREGA was not intended to provide fiscal stimulus and there have been delays in implementing the delivery of assistance under the program. Poverty programs poverty and hunger rates continue to fall slowly. India is in a group of 24 countries where IFPRI views the hunger situation as alarming. It ranks 66 out of 88 countries ranked by IFPRI in its Global Hunger Index. Only Bangladesh ranks lower among Asian countries. Some of the poverty programs have been very successful while others have met with difficulties. It is important to learn from these experiences and focus on allocating more resources to programs that have achieved greater success in reducing poverty. Provincial governments in Kerala and to a lesser extent in Madya Pradesh have made significant progress in introducing health and education programs that have been successful in targeting the poorest groups. Other provinces can learn from their experience, particularly as Asia and the globe emerge from this costly recession. The strong political showing of the Congress party in the May 2009 election should help renew the government's commitment to addressing the poverty issue as well as undertaking additional reforms to the subsidy and education systems. Doing so will require strong commitment, particularly in view of the constraints imposed by the global recession.

The general war on poverty will continue to be constrained by weak resource mobilization and continued resort to deficit finance. According to the OECD, a fiscal deficit of 10% of GDP in 2009/2010 is not unlikely (10.3% on a 2009 calendar year basis). This is slightly higher than the current year but higher than the government would like. The global recession will not help India in its efforts to contain the fiscal deficit, increase resource mobilization and widen the tax base. Of particular concern is the low level of fiscal effort in India. Tax revenue is a smaller proportion of GDP than in many other economies, the tax base is narrow and tax avoidance is widespread. The EIU estimates that tax revenue in India was just 12.4% of GDP placing the country near the bottom (145th) of the nearly 150 countries analyzed. As a result, the government does not have resources to aid the poor. Healthcare spending per capita is less than half that of China ($47 versus $116 according to EIU). By relying on deficit spending the government has built up a substantial deficit, so much so that interest payments eat up nearly 30% of the government budget. The risks of relying on foreign borrowing to fill the funding gap are also high, particularly in a recession when exchange rates are at risk of depreciation and there is general volatility in markets. In addition, an increase in the budget deficit that is predicted to rise to 4% or 5% of GDP brings added pressure on interest rates and the cost of financing the deficit. Therefore in the medium to long run, the challenge will be to increase the tax base and fiscal effort in order to raise revenue, increase spending for poverty reduction and reduce the fiscal deficit. The Fiscal Responsibility and Budget Management bill passed in 2003 is designed to establish a statutory limit on government borrowing, to increase fiscal transparency and close the gap between revenue and spending. However, these goals have been sidetracked by the global recession and the need to provide fiscal stimulus to prop up the economy. While necessary in the short run, there is a risk that the longer run agenda of providing more funds for poverty reduction will be compromised. The 2010/2011 budget in particular has emphasized fiscal consolidation and has for the first time included an explicit target for reducing the debt to GDP ratio. Funds are expected to come from higher tax revenues from a recovery in economic growth, sales of shares in state-owned companies, auctions of 3G telco licenses and the easing of the fuel subsidy regime.

To date India has had moderate success in reducing poverty. Despite allocating nearly as large a proportion of GDP to human resource development as China (4% versus 4.9%, see Table 9.6) it has been able to reduce poverty from 60% to 40% between 1980 and 2005 (see Ravallion, 2009) and social spending as a percentage of family income is substantially smaller (26% versus 44%, see Table 9.6). Ravallion, argues that the caste system and poor state schools have inhibited the ability of the government to mount successful programs to reach the poor (see also Dowling and Yap, 2009, Chapter 7). Furthermore, even if India were to focus all of its human development efforts on the chronically poor, it would not have sufficient resources to lift them out of poverty (see Table 10.2). Also, India is in the alarming category when it comes to the extent of poverty and hunger (see Table 9.2). For all these reasons foreign assistance would still be required.

An additional challenge is the resurgence in inflationary pressure that has surfaced as the recovery has gathered steam in 2010. Reducing the fiscal deficit will be a key to address these pressures. While there are plans in place to withdraw its fiscal stimulus measures, it is likely that these support measures will stay in place at least in the first half of 2010. Approval has been passed for subsidies on food and fertilizer prices at end 2009. India has also committed another additional Rs 5 billion to support exports of goods like engineering, electronic and chemical products. However monetary tightening is already underway with tighter rules on overseas borrowing by local firms. The ceiling on interest rates that local firms pay for external commercial borrowing has been re-introduced with effect from January 2010. India is projected to grow at 7.5% and 8% in the financial year 2010–11 and 2011–12 respectively according to World Bank estimates (estimates made by EIU displayed in Table 5.1 are slightly lower for 2010). External demand from the resumption of growth in high-income countries and FDI inflows are expected to increase. The latter is due to the simplifying of investment procedures and relaxing investment limits in certain sectors.

Indonesia

The global slowdown had a modest impact on the Indonesian economy. The slowdown in Q4 2008 was less dramatic than in some of its neighbors in Southeast Asia. Economic growth in 2009 was 4.5% and is expected to accelerate to over 5% in 2010. Although exports have been rising faster than GDP in recent years, they are still a much smaller proportion of GDP than in other Southeast Asian economies and manufactured exports are also a smaller fraction of total exports than in their neighbors in the region. In addition manufactured exports including textiles, electronics, footwear and wood products have weakened suggesting that Indonesia has been losing its competitive advantage. Increasing reliance has been put on traditional exports such as coal and palm oil. While these products are not expected to be hit has hard as manufacturing, the markets for minerals and agricultural products are volatile. Prices softened toward the end of 2008 and remained low as the global recession has sapped demand. Furthermore, underinvestment has limited the growth in oil production. In manufacturing, there have been significant layoffs that are expected to increase before the global outlook stabilizes. Twenty-five thousand workers have been laid off since November 2008 in the manufacturing sector (see *The Economist, 2009*). However the rest of the economy is still performing reasonably well. Indonesia achieved rice self-sufficiency in 2008 for the first time in more than two decades and the informal sector has yet to feel the impact of the crisis. There were some warning signs, such as predicted softness in new car sales, that the global crisis could create additional downside risks. Furthermore, unemployment increased rapidly and the stock market has weakened as foreign investors have been selling. Net capital outflows have increased and the rupiah depreciated by 20% from March 2008 to February 2009. Bank lending has also softened in light of increasing uncertainty and export proceeds are down. The National Development Planning Board estimated that export value would fall by 6% in 2009 and non-oil exports would fall by 20% (see also Table 3.5 where ADB projected exports to fall by 25% in 2009). Nevertheless, the financial sector remained healthy and the level of non-performing loans has been reduced as a result of reforms undertaken following the Asian crisis a decade ago.

To address the crisis the government has taken a series of policy measures. The initial concern was the balance of payments would be adversely affected. It was later amended to place greater emphasis on the potential decline in output and rising unemployment. To offset the negative impact of the crisis, the government has allocated the equivalent of $6.1 billion (about 1.4% of GDP) as a stimulus package in 2009, about $1 billion for infrastructure and around $850 million to create new jobs and to bring nearly a million unemployed back to work. The fiscal stimulus will be continued in 2010 and a proposed 2% of GDP or nearly $9 billion will be allocated for that purpose. The amount of the stimulus distributed over two years is the equivalent of 3.4% of GDP, which is the same magnitude of the fiscal stimulus provided in the US and China. It seems appropriate given the strain that it will put on the budget. However, Indonesia does not appear to be spending as much as planned. By October 2009, only two-thirds of the planned expenditure has been realized according to EIU estimates. Certain ministries were singled out by the finance minister for failing to meet fiscal spending targets. Construction sectors did not particularly benefit from the 2009 budget. This shortfall in infrastructural spending is likely to pose a problem for Indonesia's long-term sustained economic growth. The stimulus packages this year and in 2010 will put pressure on the budget and the deficit is projected to be 2.6% of GDP in 2009 compared with a deficit of 1% of GDP last year. (The OECD is predicting a smaller fiscal deficit of 1.8% of GDP.) To cover the deficit, Indonesia will need to raise capital from both domestic and foreign sources. It raised $3 billion by the sale of treasury notes in February 2009 although at a premium of 800 bps above US treasury yields.

Monetary policy has been relaxed to provide additional stimulus to the economy. By August 2009, the benchmark interest rate has been cut eight times since December 2008. However, commercial bank lending rates have not followed suit and they have been pressured to lower rates further, particularly in light of a moderation in inflation as a result of the weaker economy and lower oil prices. By August, interest rates have been cut by a total of 300 bps. However lending rates fell only around 100 bps over the same period. There was also concern then that liquidity has been adversely affected by fears of a deepening crisis. However with the resilience of the Indonesian economy in the face of the crisis and concerns of inflation in 2010, the policy stance has since reversed.

Given the evolving outlook for the global economy and export prospects for manufactured goods, the rather optimistic forecast of 6.2% growth for 2009 made at the end of 2008 has been reduced to the range of 4% by many economists including Bank Indonesia which reduced its forecast in March to 4.5%. Preliminary estimates for 2010 suggest the reduction is more in line with performance in 2009. Real GDP is forecasted to expand by 5.5% in 2010. Private consumption grew strongly in 2009 being stimulated by higher salaries for public sector employees and election campaign spending. With the recovery in the economy and a rise in inflationary pressures to 5.8%, Indonesia looks set to raise interest rates. Capital controls are also being considered to halt the appreciation of the rupiah. Financial speculators have been borrowing from countries with low interest rates such as US and Japan and purchasing assets in Indonesia, thereby stroking upward pressure on the rupiah.

The poor will need to be protected in the global slowdown. te Velde et al (2009) estimates that household poverty count likely increased as a result of slower growth. Poverty rates remain high in the outer islands, which are unlikely to be heavily influenced by the recession. However, there has been a decline in formal sector employment and many workers have been forced into the informal sector where wages are low and job security is limited. Those families who were close to the poverty line are now likely to be falling below it. Some of the stimulus will be directed to infrastructure projects including water supply, low-cost housing, roads and ports. Some of these could create employment in the rural sector. A small component of the package is devoted to encouraging village-level participation in rural infrastructure, health and education projects. A greater emphasis on such programs would be welcome particularly since regional governments have been lacking in their capacity to implement development projects at the local level. Lower oil prices at the end of 2008 and in the early months of 2009 also enabled the government to make direct cash transfers to nearly 20 million poor families. This program has been enough to solidify the present government's position as the leader going into the July 2009 election and in fact Susilo Bambang Yudhoyono (affectionately called SBY) won the election by a comfortable majority over his two opponents, Megawati Sukarnoputri and Jusuf Kalla. Indonesia has also launched the "Hopeful Family Programme" in January 2009, which is a form of conditional cash transfer to poor families. Recipient households need to ensure that expectant mothers undergo medical checkups during maternity and schooling children complete schooling till junior high school with minimum 85% attendance. Past efforts to reduce poverty have been successful as the poverty rate has fallen from over 50% in 1975 to around 20% or lower according to some estimates (see Dowling and Yap, 2009, Chapter 7). However, the amount of resources now being devoted to human resource development when measured as a percentage of GDP is less than half that spent in China and India (see Table 10.2). Indonesia's current fiscal stimulus has focused its priority on the promotion of macroeconomic sustainability rather than significant expansion in social protection expenditure (te Velde et al, 2009). Funds allocated to social spending from the 2009 budget has been primarily for healthcare provision, community development projects and a modest increase in allocation of subsidized rice for the poor. Nevertheless, Indonesia has existing social protection schemes (especially in rural areas) and seem to be well-targeted as over 70% of the poor ostensibly receive some aid, although it is less than 10% of per capita income. Furthermore, should Indonesia concentrate its efforts on eliminating chronic poverty it does have sufficient resources to accomplish this objective (see Table 10.2) Greater efforts need to be made to reach the poor in the Eastern provinces of Papua and Maluku and also in parts of Sumatra.

Group 4 – Poorer countries in South Asia and Mekong

Bangladesh

Bangladesh was relatively less exposed than other Asian countries to the global economic crisis since its export sector accounts for a relatively small share of GDP. Economic growth in 2010 is expected to remain stable at over 5%. The Bangladesh economy has mainly been buffeted by the global economic recession through a loss in export revenue and a potential slide in the pace of remittances. Exports and remittances together account for around 30% of GDP. Garments, which comprise about 75% of manufactured exports and which have been the mainstay of manufactured export growth over the past few years, have been facing weaker external demand since the end of 2008 when the global economic slowdown began. In the first few months of 2009 global demand has softened, despite Bangladesh's strengthened position as the low end of the market displacing China, whose competitive position has suffered from currency appreciation. However, Bangladesh is vulnerable to shifts in demand from the US and Europe since the bulk of its textile exports are directed to these two markets. In addition, foreign direct investment in the textile industry has been on a downward trend as policies have favored domestic producers after the multifibre agreement ended a few years ago. This has led to a slowdown in technological innovation and perhaps damaged export competitiveness to some extent. Export growth has been declining continuously since Q3 2008. Efforts are being made to diversify products and export destinations. However, agriculture has been doing well and this has helped to sustain the rural economy. Although the agricultural sector only contributes one-fifth of overall GDP at factor cost, it is the country's largest employer and hires up to 50% of the labor force. Output rose by around 4.6% in FY 2009 (ending July 1, 2009) up 1.4% from the previous year. Irrigated area has been expanded and output increased as tube wells have been widely adopted by farmers. One negative aspect of this development is the rising incidence of arsenic poisoning from the pumping of ground water. Cheap methods are available for testing and cleaning up the water are available but there are literally thousands of tube wells that must be tested and remedial actions taken. It is estimated that between 28 and 77 million people drink arsenic-laden water from shallow tube wells. At the levels observed in Bangladesh, arsenic poisoning has a longer-term impact on health resulting in skin lesions and an elevated risk of cancer (see Mathieu et al, 2008). The contribution of remittances to GDP has swelled from 4% in 2001 to 10% by 2008. This compares with export revenue of 20% of GDP. Remittances, primarily from low-skilled overseas workers employed in the Middle East and Malaysia, have remained relatively firm in 2009 though this is likely to moderate in 2010. The number of overseas job fell by nearly 40% in Q1 2009 compared with the same quarter in 2008 (see Reuters' economic outlook is more uncertain – IMF at http://in.reuters.com/articelPrint?articleId=INIndia-39727320090519 and UN, 2009b). If this trend continues, remittances may fall after some time lag. Another factor to consider is the fact that many Bangladeshis are in low-end jobs and the recession has not hit them as hard as higher-skilled blue-collar workers. At the beginning of the global slowdown, labor markets for unskilled overseas workers in the Middle East were not affected but that situation is likely change as the crisis spreads to all global regions. There is also a growing market for more highly skilled workers as a result of greater emphasis on training centers designed to supply workers for overseas assignments. These developments are expected to result in a slowdown in economic growth in Bangladesh from over 6% in 2008 to 5.6% in FY 2009 and 5.2% in 2010. Consumption and investment are likely to be the two main drivers of growth in 2010.

The fiscal balance will be adversely affected by slower growth as revenue sources weaken. Import cuts associated with slower growth in international trade will erode custom duties and other tax revenues will also be adversely affected. Bangladesh has loosened monetary policy twice in 2009 to support domestic demand. Generally Bangladesh's monetary policy works through the repo and reverse repo rate rather than the discount rate. The reverse repurchase was slashed from 6.5% to 2.5% in October 2009. The ratio of bank credit to GDP increased 12 percentage points (World Bank, 2010a). Monetary policy is likely to remain loose in 2010.

While lower oil prices in Q4 2008 and Q1 2009 eased inflation and also helped the budget by reducing subsidies, lower food prices have also had a beneficial impact on incomes and living standards for the poor. This is particularly relevant since there is a high level of food insecurity and widespread malnutrition. The economic downturn is having a negative impact on labor markets where data are available in urban areas. The UN estimates over a million peoples' livelihoods could be compromised as a result of job losses. More children are being sent to work and indebtedness is increasing. Social protection programs such as food for work should be expanded and accelerated. While the growth prospects for Bangladesh are more optimistic than for some of the highly export-dependent economies in Southeast Asia, the new global environment will put substantial pressure to improve economic prospects in agriculture by selective investments, some requiring capital imports. Research and extension and roads and water management are also important to boost productivity and incomes in rural areas. Power investments, particularly in natural gas, which supplies 80% of power generation, are also critical to avoid service interruption and adverse impacts on factory productivity.

About half of all families in Bangladesh are in poverty and further deterioration in overall welfare will result from loss in income as a result of the global recession. Two poverty programs have been successful in reading the poorest segments in society. The Cash for Education program has been successful in helping the poor and it has also reduced the incidence of child labor. However, spending on the program is still a fraction of the level required (less than 0.2% of GDP) to raise educational attainment levels to the desired standard and about 40% of the funds have leaked to non-poor students (CPRC, 2008; Dowling and Yap, 2010). Further improvement can be made by focusing the grants to the chronically poor and raising more money for the program. Another program provides an unconditional transfer of US$2 per month to recipients and targets a fixed number of the poorest and oldest beneficiaries in each ward and individual selection is then decided by the local communities. Although it is a small amount of money, and hardly enough to raise these women out of poverty, up to 1.4 million women have so far benefited from this unconditional cash transfer system (CPRC, 2008). Ramping up both of these programs would be needed to make a significant dent in the well being of these groups of needy women. This would be possible without much additional fixed cost because the women and the administrative apparatus are already in place. Additional social safety net programs can also be developed with the help of foreign donors and fiscal stimulus funds amounting to Tk 30 billion that have recently been allocated by the newly elected Awami League coalition government. This is equivalent to about 1.5% GDP and further stimulus may be provided later on. Forty-three percent of the stimulus is allocated to the agricultural sector with power and agricultural recapitalization also a significant share of the stimulus budget. Bangladesh may also apply to the IMF for funding support. The stimulus will put additional stress on the budget, although the budget deficit is projected to remain around 4.5% of GDP, half of which will be provided by foreign sources. The fiscal stimulus should be sufficient to close the potential output gap, which has been calculated at a low 0.4% of GDP for three years (see Table 6.4) or 1.2% of GDP for three years. Bangladesh has made some progress in reducing poverty. However estimates by the Asian Development Bank put poverty at over 50% of the population (see A. Bauer et al, 2008). Further estimates of the costs of eliminating chronic poverty and the ongoing efforts being made to generally reduce poverty as reflected by estimates contained in Table 9.6 suggest that despite a resource commitment of 5.3% of GDP to human resource development programs and a modicum of success in reaching the poor (estimated 53% from Table 9.6) considerable foreign assistance will be required to substantially reduce poverty levels in the medium term (see Table 10.2), and reduce hunger.

Cambodia

Cambodia suffered an estimated contraction in GDP of 1.5% in 2009 owing to the adverse impact of the global economic crisis on garment exports, tourism and foreign investment. Before the onset of the crisis, Cambodia was able to sustain double-digit economic growth due to a rapid growth in exports (close to 20% per annum between 2004 and 2007) and a dynamic industrial sector led by garment production. Garment exports grew at an annual rate of 28% between 1997 and 2007 growing from virtually nothing in 1994 to a $2.7 billion industry in 2007. Garment factories support a workforce and family members estimated at 1.5 million. Given a potential total workforce of around 7 million, garment provided the bulk of formal sector employment, mostly women. The sector accounted for close to 20% of GDP in 2007. However by the end of 2008 garment exports, mainly to the United States, had fallen off dramatically. In January 2009, garment exports fell by 25% compared with a year earlier. Garment exports were also hurt by higher domestic inflation which led to a 20% rise in garment workers' minimum wage. Overall exports were expected to have contracted by 2.5% in 2009 and economic growth to slip into negative territory. Unemployment was on the rise and many of the laid-off workers were forced to return to their family homes in farming communities. The ILO forecast job losses will be greatest in textiles and clothing and construction followed by tourism. It is estimated that over 50,000 jobs will be lost and some of the workers will be absorbed back into agriculture. Others may take jobs in the informal sector and stay in the urban ring. Some workers may have working hours cut and overtime reduced to cut the wage bill of employers. A slackening of tourist arrivals was experienced in 2008 as a result of the global recession and as fallout from the political turmoil in Thailand. Along with higher oil prices, this contributed to an increase in the trade and current account deficits. Tourist arrivals in 2009 weakened further as a result of the recession in Europe and the declining value of the won *vis-à-vis* the US dollar which depressed tourists arrivals from South Korea. Cambodia is a favored destination of South Korean tourists. The ILO estimated a slowdown in the growth of tourism receipts to 5.5% in 2009 compared to 15.7% in 2008. The only bright spot is agriculture. Agricultural production expanded in 2009 following good growth of 4.5% in 2008. It also continued to attract most investment with close to US$40 million approved through January 2010. Agricultural productivity is expected to increase as a result of improvements in irrigation, farm extension including planting of higher yielding varieties of rice and other grains as well as better disease and pest control. Lower growth in exports and tourism translated into weaker aggregate demand and lower tax revenues. Remittances from overseas Cambodian workers declined from 4.2% to 3.4% of GDP from 2007 to 2008 and probably fell further in 2009 as the majority of such workers are often employed in unskilled and informal occupations (te Velde et al, 2009). Out migration is likely to fall further as demand for workers in Malaysia and Thailand's plantations softens. Malaysia has also announced tighter controls on foreign labor. The rate of growth in foreign direct investment also decelerated in 2009 as a result of slower growth in its main investors, China and South Korea. However recent indicators show that both of these countries are recovering rapidly and there may be a pickup in FDI later in 2010. Concessional lending from international donors such as the Asian Development Bank and World Bank as well as bilateral assistance has increased in order to offset some of the fallout from the global recession. The United Nations has asked donors to speed up farm aid to Cambodia to help the country increase rice exports and assist in further productivity gains in the agricultural sector. This will provide a crucial offset to losses in revenue from tourism and garment exports and will also provide a boost to the sector as it absorbs some laid-off workers from the garment industry.

To address the crisis the government has indicated it will increase spending on transportation, public infrastructure and irrigation as well as adopt a larger budget than originally planned. The government has also announced plans to reduce costs for garment exporters and implement skills training schemes for laid-off garment workers. Additional options proposed by the government include further easing of monetary policy by reducing reserve requirements, beefing up social safety nets, suspension of profit tax on textile and clothing manufacturers, intensification of efforts to diversity export promotion and market diversification of textile and clothing exporters. Budget allocation is set to increase to US$2 billion of fiscal spending in 2010 (a 14% increase from last year's budget). However its effectiveness will be limited by the budget deficit. Oil revenue from the fields of the Gulf of Thailand is not expected to come in till 2013. On the other hand, monetary policy will be limited by the high degree of dollarisation in the economy. The non-performing loan ratio increased during the first six months of 2009. Banks are reluctant to loan and credit is tight. As a result, GDP growth is likely to remain muted in 2010 at around 3%.

Cambodia made good progress in reducing poverty during the period of rapid growth from the late 1990s until 2007, down from 47% in the 1990s to less than 40% by 2007. Nevertheless the levels of chronic poverty, infant mortality and hunger are still among the highest in Asia and it is critically important to maintain the level of progress already achieved (stunted growth affects 45% of children under five years old, over 50% of children between seven and 14 years of age in labor force and under five year old mortality is 141 per 1,000 live births). Government spending on human resource development is a meager 1.4% of GDP, one of the lowest in the region (see Table 10.2). While over 40% of the poor receive some support from the government, the amount of social protection is a small fraction of the amount needed for the poor to escape poverty. Furthermore, Cambodia is one of the countries where poverty and hunger have reached alarming proportions (see Table 9.2). Higher food and fuel prices as well as inflation put some of this progress at risk in 2008. Reducing inflation and providing additional social spending are crucial in this regard. About one in five households have a job in sectors directly impacted by the global crisis (garments, construction and tourism). The poor make up about 30%, 40% and 14% of the workers in the garment, construction and tourism sector respectively (World Bank, 2009e). Male workers in the construction sector and female workers in the garment sector are particularly at risk. Wasting among poor urban children has exceeded the 15% wasting threshold for a humanitarian emergency, from 10% in 2005 to 16% in 2008 (UNICEF, 2009). While garments and textile exports along with tourism have provided much of the impetus for rapid growth over the past decade, it is important to remember that 80% of the population still lives in rural areas where the bulk of the poor reside. Therefore raising agricultural productivity is the key to further progress in poverty reduction. The World Bank predicts that the rate of poverty in Cambodia will increase, as 200,000 more will fall below the poverty line in 2009, a nearly 5% increase in the number of poor. Hence programs are urgently needed to protect further increases in poverty as a result of the crisis. Cambodia has significantly increased the coverage of poor through a one-off extension of crisis response program; though this was more so due to external assistance from World Bank and ADB rather than on its own policy formulation. The former has committed $10 million to be directed towards social protection expenditure. Cambodia's existing social programs mainly include public works programs, food distributions for poor and school feeding programs, education scholarships and government subsidies. However existing coverage is limited and patchy. Targeting could be further improved. Social protection for those retrenched workers who return to their villages can be enhanced by a dedicated fund which would lighten the household burden and could provide income generating opportunities and employment in the village. A central job information system would also be helpful to reduce search costs for recently retrenched workers.

Lao PDR

Owing to its isolation from global trade and investment flows Lao PDR was one of the countries in Asia least affected by the global economic crisis (see Chart 5.4d). World Bank estimates that real GDP rose by 6.4% in 2009 due to rapid expansion in its mining sector and recovery in exports. Only China had a faster rate of economic growth in 2009. Still, Lao PDR remains one of the poorest countries in Asia. It is a highly agrarian society where more than 80% of families reside in rural villages. Rates of poverty and malnutrition are high, particularly in the northern region where over half the population is poor. Stunting and high infant mortality rates are common. The industrial sector, which has been the driving force behind rapid economic growth of over 7% between 2004 and 2008, is dominated by hydropower (which is mostly sold to Thailand) and copper and gold mining. Agricultural productivity has also increased and the sector has also contributed to higher rates of growth and is responsible for some reduction in poverty. The country also has a small apparel sector which has developed into a source of exports and foreign exchange. Inflation, which was in the range of 10% between 2003 and 2007, has come down as global oil and food prices eased toward the end of 2008 and continued to be moderate in 2009.

The global recession has resulted in a deterioration of export revenue and in economic growth. Garment exports are down by an estimated 15% to 20% in Q1 2009. Prices for gold and copper, Lao PDR's main mineral exports were weak in late 2008 and early 2009. Prices have strengthened considerably since the collapse of Lehman Brothers in September 2008. Gold prices are now 50% higher and copper prices have doubled. For the year as a whole gold and copper export earning are expected to increase as demand from China and other importers continues to strengthen. Income from tourism is expected to soften. The bulk of tourism arrivals are from neighboring countries that are members of ASEAN, all of which have also been hit by the global crisis. Lao PDR foreign direct investment is also expected to fall as global demand softens, particularly in the garment and mining sectors. Early estimates put GDP growth at 2.5% in 2009. However recent forecasts suggest growth will be more in the range of 5% to 6%. With the recovery in global growth and higher prices for international commodities, growth figures are projected to move further upwards in 2010. Foreign investment has been on the rise with Chinese and Vietnamese SOEs and Thai investors entering the mining and hydropower projects respectively.

The government has some room for fiscal and monetary stimulus and a package amounting to 3% of GDP was recently adopted. Given the relatively limited impact of the global recession on the economy, this amounts to 150% of the growth shortfall (see Table 6.5 and Table 7.8). During 2009, Lao PDR lowered its main policy interest rate by a total of 200 bps to 5%, a record low. Funds were directed into state-owned banks and loans extended to infrastructure developmental spending to stimulate domestic demand. Stronger than anticipated copper and gold prices will result in more stable tax revenue and the fiscal deficit is expected to remain stable at around 4% of GDP in 2009. Although revenue sources are limited and expansion of credit by the banking system could further weaken balance sheets and lead to a higher level of non-performing loans, the improved outlook for gold and copper along with further growth in hydropower exports to Thailand suggests some improvement in financial conditions. While earlier forecasts highlighted a definite possibility that rather than provide stimulus to the economy and greater safety nets for the poor, the government will be forced to cut back on poverty programs and reduce the already stretched safety net that gives some protection from further deterioration in poverty and general human development. This now seems a much less likely scenario as the implementation of fiscal stimulus suggests. Nevertheless, available developmental resources should be directed to lifting living standards, output and productivity in the agricultural sector.

Particular attention to the needs of the poorest in the 72 districts that have been identified by the government. Some of the stimulus funds should be used for these programs. At the same time it has to be recognized that Lao PDR is heavily dependent on external funding. Official development assistance makes up 85% of public investment and almost 40% of total public expenditure (IMF, 2008). Heavy reliance on such off-budget funds risk compromises in the effectiveness of programs that rely on continual funding. Revenues from taxes on hydropower and mining projects can be used to provide continual maintenance of pro-poor services including schools and health services for mothers and children. The emphasis of these programs should be concentrated in the 25 poorest districts as identified by the government requiring intervention based on the household, village and district level indicators of basic minimum needs. Several initiatives such as village development funds and provision of basic services to remote areas appeared to have yielded results. By focusing scarce resources in this way, Lao PDR can establish greater ownership of its poverty programs and develop a viable long-run strategy for implementing poverty reduction programs. These initiatives could earmark a portion of taxes on gold and copper exports as well as hydropower revenue for poverty reduction programs. Regional initiatives are also planned in the Northern region of the country. The government has plans to spur economic development and income levels in this lagging region, where there are a substantial number of poor districts. For instance, there are plans to develop the Luang Prabang City into a provincial capital which will also serve to attract tourists to the region. The government also aims to increase the share of the non-agricultural sector in the Northern region, to provide alternative employment opportunities for the rural poor. Greater emphasis is to be placed on industries like mining, community forestry and agricultural processing. The Luang Namtha Industrial Zone will serve to further promote the industrial sector. There are also opportunities for tourism in the north, particularly from China which has relaxed its tourist travel policy to Lao PDR (see Dowling and Yap, 2009, Chapter 7, for further details). Further efforts will also be required to reduce poverty and address the needs of the hungry. Lao PDR is one of the countries identified as having alarmingly high rates of poverty and hunger in Table 9.2. Government spending on human resource development is a meager 1.3% of GDP, one of the lowest in the region (see Table 10.2). While over 40% of the poor receive some support from the government, the amount of social protection is only 7% of the amount needed for the poor to escape poverty. Its efforts to address poverty are being supplemented by development assistance since its domestic allocations are insufficient to lift large numbers out of poverty.

Nepal

According to the National Planning Commission, economic growth in Nepal likely remained below 5% in 2009. This was due to the slow growth in the manufacturing and agricultural sectors. In addition, Nepal also faces the challenges of excess liquidity in its financial sector, weak business climate, power shortages and labor market concerns. Difficulties in resolving the civil conflict that had been ongoing for several years have already caused Nepal's economic performance to lag behind other countries in South Asia and its per capita GDP is the lowest in the region ($256 in 2008 in 2000 prices compared with $462 for Bangladesh, $678 for Pakistan and $724 for India). Resolution of this conflict and a recommitment to maintain macroeconomic stability and a smooth political transition will determine the pace of future economic growth and the ability to overcome the risks that accompany the global economic slowdown. Remittances and tourism income are at risk as the crisis impacts the global economy. Remittances are a cornerstone of the poverty reduction effort. Combined with migration and investment in rural infrastructure remittance flows have helped to cut the incidence of poverty in Nepal in recent years. According to M. Lokshin et al (2007), one-fifth of the poverty reduction in Nepal occurring between 1995 and 2004 was because of increased remittances. This powerful poverty impact occurred despite the fact that most of the remittance income accrued to families in the upper two quintiles of the income distribution. Adding to traditional remittance sources from India and Hong Kong recent Nepalese migration to the Middle East has swelled to flow of remittances to close to 20% of GDP and this flow of income could continue as more labor agreements have been signed with other countries. By 2009, remittances approached 22% of GDP in Nepal (World Bank, 2009i). Falling remittances as a result of the global recession adversely affected poverty levels in Nepal. Infrastructure bottlenecks including power shortages, slow growth in the irrigation network and high transportation costs as well as labor market rigidities and weak governance continue to constrain growth prospects in Nepal. Hence the manufacturing sector has been growing at a paltry 1% for 2008 and 2009. In addition, Nepal also failed to control the excess liquidity in the market which later led to a cash crunch in the banking sector. It has resulted in inflation shooting up to double-digit figures. Furthermore, pegging of the Nepali currency with the Indian currency has adversely affected its balance of payment. Nepal ranks next to last among the South Asian economies in Human Development (see Dowling and Yap, 2009, Table 6.8). Its spending on social protection is low and nearly half of its children under five years of age are underweight (see Table 9.5). The global economic recession is unlikely to have much of an impact on other aspects of Nepal's economic performance as the fiscal deficit is projected to stay in the range of 2% of GDP. Although the trade deficit will continue, exports are a small fraction of GDP and not likely to be reduced significantly as a result of the global recession. Lower oil prices should provide some offset to the trade deficit as well as tourism receipts and remittances. Increased labor productivity is critical if the rate of economic growth is to be raised and poverty further reduced. There are several components to such efforts (see ADB, DFID and ILO, 2009). These include: (i) upgrading the transportation network, particularly for new road rural construction and better maintenance; (ii) improving the industrial relations climate including strike reduction and relaxation of labor market restrictions on hiring and firing; (iii) reduction in discrimination against minorities; and (iv) provision of a more comprehensive social safety net and better distribution of benefits to poorer segments of society from infrastructure projects and from opportunities for migration and remittance. Many of these investments would have to be made in partnership with donor agencies.

Nepal has been identified as one of six countries (see Table 9.2) where poverty and hunger issues are likely to be exacerbated by the global crisis and are unable to marshal enough domestic resources to provide support. As noted they all have global hunger indices over 20, placing them in the alarming category by the United Nations. Its ability to address poverty issues are limited and it is one of three countries (Bangladesh and India are the others) identified by Dowling and Yap (2009) that do not have enough domestic resources to lift the chronically poor out of poverty even if they devoted 3% of their government budget to poverty reduction. There are around 14 million people in Nepal living on less than US$1.25 per day and more than half of its population is poor (CPRC, 2008). Vulnerable groups include farmers, women and ethnic groups that are subjected to discrimination. Poor households had suffered a fall of 13.5% in purchasing power during the 2006–2007 rising food prices period (Chhibber et al, 2009). With the aid of World Bank, Nepal implemented a food price crisis program in 2008 to provide assistance for poor households in food insecure households and long-term initiatives to increase agricultural productivity. More remains to be done by the government and the challenge lies in balancing economic growth and sharing the fruits of the growth with the population.

Pakistan

Economic growth in Pakistan was estimated at 3.7% in 2009 with a slowdown to 3% in 2010 expected as political uncertainty and fighting continue to disrupt economic recovery. The global economic crisis has come at an unfortunate time when Pakistan has been battling a series of domestic challenges that threaten to derail economic growth and serious implications for political and social stability. After four years of strong economic growth that averaged over 7% per annum, external imbalance began to multiply in 2008 as import growth outstripped exports as a result of sharply higher oil and food import costs. As a result the current account balance deteriorated, inflation accelerated, the currency depreciated, the government deficit increased and there was a run-down in foreign exchange reserves. A reversal of capital inflows and slow exchange rate adjustments added to the pressure on foreign exchange reserves which fell from over $15 billion to $8.6 billion between October 2007 and June 2008. To stem the tide of red ink the IMF provided foreign exchange support by way of a $7.6 billion loan in 2008 and the government sought an additional $4.5 billion in 2009. The third review of Pakistan's stand-by arrangement with the IMF took place in November 2009. By late December, the fourth tranche of US$1.2 billion was released. In part the difficulties were created by the efforts of the government to protect consumers from higher oil prices by increases in subsidies for oil products and electricity as well as increased subsidies for wheat and fertilizers. To correct the imbalances that led to the foreign exchange crisis the government has, with the help of the IMF, forged a framework that includes tighter monetary and fiscal policy to bring down inflation, reduction in the fiscal deficit by a combination of expenditure cuts, primarily in fuel and power subsidies and some cuts in development spending along with some measures to increase revenue. The import bill is expected to fall with commodity and oil price declines. Remittance income has also provided support to the balance of payments and this is expected to continue as most international migrants from Pakistan go to the Middle East which is relatively less affected by the global recession. Workers' remittances by end of 2009 were estimated to be around US$700 million. The recent run-up in oil prices combined with continued slow export demand in industrial countries will create some difficulties in achieving the projected turnaround in the balance of trade and payments. However by early 2010, Pakistan had met most of its targets under the two-year IMF program with the exception of the budget deficit target. The currency had stabilized and its external position had shown an improvement.

While the World Bank reported in April 2009 that fiscal consolidation was on track at the end of December 2008 it recognized that further fiscal adjustments may be required going forward. World Bank (2010a) estimates the fiscal deficit to be 8.6% of GDP in 2010. There are several positive signs including some reduction in inflation, which still remains high, and optimism that agricultural sector output will recover from disruptions in power and lower private sector credit growth. Investments in power generation to relieve outages that reduce industrial output and efficiency as well as medium-term recovery in exports and implementation of key revenue measures including a value-added tax are critical to the achievement of more rapid growth in the medium term. Measures to ease entry and exit into the industrial sector as well as labor market flexibility are also needed. The ADB suggests an interrelated set of challenges that need to be faced. These include generating exports with a higher world income elasticity of demand. This requires improved productivity and moving to diversify exports away from low-end textile and apparel products. It also includes improving agricultural productivity along with more rapid growth in industry and services sectors to be able to absorb migrants from agriculture. Infrastructure improvements, particularly power have already been mentioned and is another key component in the development agenda.

Finally, poverty needs to be squarely addressed, particularly in the in Northwest Frontier and Federally Administered Tribal Areas (FATA). However, the reform agenda is complicated by political difficulties with Taliban insurgence, refugees fleeing fighting in the Swat valley and high existing levels of poverty in these two regions. The budget deficit is likely to be widened in 2010 with the increase in military spending. The Chronic Poverty Research Center and a book by one of the authors of this manuscript (Dowling and Yap, 2009) suggest that Pakistan has relied too heavily on voluntary contributions (*zakat*) to address poverty issues in the past. Pakistan has the smallest percentage of the poor covered by social protection schemes and social protection as a share of GDP of all the countries in East Asia, Southeast Asia and South Asia). Only 8% of the poor receive assistance and it amounts to 3% of GDP (see Table 9.6). Pakistan also has a high rate of stunted growth, high infant mortality and low life expectancy. Much of this poor performance is because membership in the main social protection schemes is confined to government and formal sector employees. There are some programs to provide subsidized food or to reduce the costs of education and health coverage for the poor but they are not comprehensive. There are broadly based subsidies to lower costs of fuel and basic food stuffs. These are available to everyone and not targeted to the poor. They are expensive and can create fiscal stress as we have noted above. A more focused program to assist the poor is needed, particularly at the present time when refugees are fleeing the Swat valley. The stress on the poor also increased dramatically in 2008 as food and fuel prices increased. A UN interagency study in 2008 found that over half of Pakistan's population did not have enough to eat as a result of the price hikes (quoted in Reuters alert news; http://www.alertnet.org/thenews/newsdesk/UNICEF/5f43b8cb5b4c551df1187 dbb43d6febd.htm).

Sri Lanka

By 2010, GDP growth in Sri Lanka is forecasted to increase by a firm 6.2% due to the end of the civil war. The main engine of growth will be the services sector led by telecommunications and tourism. Sri Lanka faced a series of daunting challenges in 2009. Having successfully completed its military campaign against the LTTE it had to heal wounds with the Tamil community and undertake resettlement and rehabilitation of the war-torn areas in the Eastern and Northern parts of the country. This placed pressure on a government budget already stretched by past defense expenditures and a global economic recession that has had an adverse impact on economic growth, the government budget, exports, foreign direct investment, stock market prices, the value of the currency and remittance income. Growth in 2008 fell to 6% from 7% in 2007. Export earnings growth declined from 11% in 2007 to 6.5% in 2008 as the exchange rate deteriorated. The fiscal deficit increased as tax revenues declined and expenditures, partly related to the conflict with the LTTE, escalated. Attempts to shore up the exchange rate resulted in a precipitous loss in foreign exchange reserves which was stopped only when these efforts ceased and the currency was allowed to float and then depreciate.

The government applied for a stand-by loan from the IMF of $1.9 billion which was approved in mid-2009. This has reduced the risk of the currency crisis in Sri Lanka. The central bank floated the currency in late March 2009 and reserves have increased. Recently the government also has been able to borrow on capital markets. However significant challenges remain. Agriculture, which did very well in 2008, growing at a record 7.5% cannot be expected to match this performance in 2009, although rice and tea production should benefit from expansion in cultivated area last year. A vibrant agriculture should also provide support for the rural community and poverty reduction which will be needed as refugees return to their villages and rehabilitation begins. Export demand is likely to be weak. The Asian Development Bank (2009) forecasts negative export growth of 22% as apparel exports are expected to fall despite extension of the Generalized System of Preferences and concessions from the European Union. The budget deficit is expected to increase to around 8% in 2009, up slightly from 6.8% in 2008. Pressure from high defense spending and interest payment on the debt continue and revenue from value-added taxes and income taxes will remain soft as economic growth is expected to moderate to 4% from 6% in 2008. The government is aggressively boosting international reserves by promoting investment in government securities with overseas Sri Lankans and offering bonuses on foreign currency deposits by both non-resident and resident foreign currency deposits. The government is also negotiating an IMF Standby Facility of $1.9 billion. These measures should provide currency support and also increase investor confidence. Tax reform is another initiative that has drawn praise from observers. Whether a task force charged with simplifying the tax system and broadening the tax base can accomplish such needed reform is another matter. The commissioning of new power stations will also contribute to industrial output growth. In addition, Sri Lanka has also entered into long-term strategic partnerships with mid- to high-end retailers in the United States and the European Union such as Diesel and Nike (World Bank, 2010a). Amidst rising consumer and investors confidence, Sri Lanka's equity market has also recovered to pre-crisis highs of 2007. Capital inflows are also on the rise. Generally the economic outlook is positive in 2010. However there are concerns that the persistent fiscal deficit could aggravate ties with IMF whose financial support is key to the economic growth of Sri Lanka.

Poverty is likely to be adversely affected by the global recession and its impact on the Sri Lankan economy both in terms of lost jobs and income and the limited ability of the government to provide substantial fiscal stimulus because of the tight budget situation. In terms of human resource development Sri Lanka is a bit of a puzzle. There have been remarkable improvements in its health and literacy indicators yet progress in poverty reduction is somewhat lethargic. Sri Lanka enjoys near universal primary enrollment, literacy rates and good health services yet it has made slow progress on poverty reduction. Economic growth in Sri Lanka does not seem to be having the salutary impact on poverty that it has had in other Asian economies. According to the World Bank a 1% increase in the growth of GDP per capita income leads to 0.5% decline in the poverty headcount ratio in Sri Lanka whereas a similar increase in the pace of growth in GDP per capita in three other Asian countries led to a 0.9% decrease in poverty in South Korea, a 1.4% decrease in poverty in Vietnam and a 2.6% decrease in poverty in Thailand (World Bank, 2007). From 1991 to 2002, Sri Lanka's per capita GDP grew by 40% yet rural poverty declined by less then 5 percentage points. Poverty reduction has been fastest in districts where the incidence of poverty was already low like Colombo and Gampaha in the Western Province, whereas poverty increased in the poorest districts. As a result income inequality has been on the rise. Average per capita consumption grew by 50% for the rich income groups whereas it grew by only 2% for the poorest group. This failure to address poverty concerns of the poorest can be partly attributed to historical tension between the Singalese majority and the Tamil minority. Not surprisingly, the poorest groups are located in rural areas. The rural sector accounts for less than one-fifth of the country's economic growth rate yet houses 88% of the population and about 3.5 million poor (World Bank, 2007). About one quarter of all rural households are poor. In the poorest district of Uva, the poverty rate for agricultural households is about 34.3%. This is nearly double the rate of poverty for non-agricultural households. Agricultural productivity has also grown slowly and is much lower than its other Asian counterparts (see Table 10.3). India enjoys almost double the rate of agricultural sector productivity growth of Sri Lanka and agricultural sector productivity growth rates are even higher in Pakistan, Vietnam, China and South Korea.

Other than the lack of economic growth outside the Western province and the stagnant agricultural sector, the World Bank (2007) reports poverty is due to inadequate infrastructure, restrictive labor practices and civil conflict in the North and East that has hampered the growth of the non-rural sector. Installed infrastructure in Sri Lanka deteriorates the further the distance from Colombo. Access to electricity generally

Table 10.3   Agricultural productivity growth in selected Asian countries, 1990–2000

Country	Agricultural productivity growth (%)
Sri Lanka	0.65
India	1.13
Thailand	1.35
Malaysia	1.62
Pakistan	2.56
Vietnam	2.80
China	3.51
South Korea	5.89

Source: World Bank, 2007 (p. 4, Table 1.1)

lags behind all East Asian countries with the exception of Vietnam and installed electricity capacity is heavily concentrated in the Western province which has over 80% coverage while rural areas like Uva province have less than half the coverage. Under the Mahinda Chintana (President Mahinda's vision), the government recently announced plans to further develop regional urban growth centers and towns and to integrate them with rural hinterlands over the next ten years. The government also pledged to increase spending on infrastructure like rural roads and highways. This is especially important as only the Colombo district in Western Province and its surrounding areas are well-connected to markets. It has been found that the further the distance from Colombo, the lower is the accessibility index, the higher the probability of poverty. The index is defined and constructed as the reciprocal of the road network travel time to nearby town. In addition, the government has recently announced the allocation of funds for the rehabilitation and rebuilding of Northern Province from 2010 to 2012. It will focus on a number of sectors such as health, education, housing, electricity, water and sanitation, agriculture, and manufacturing. Loans will be given to small and medium enterprises within the Northern province to stimulate entrepreneurship and economic growth.

Pro-poor schemes to help the vulnerable groups in Sri Lanka include the Samurdhi (Prosperity) program which consists of income transfers and small-scale rural infrastructure works and micro-credit schemes; payouts to soldiers injured in the conflict and their families; nutrition supplements to poor mothers and children; Public Assistance program with monthly payouts to specific vulnerable individuals like poor, elderly, disabled and families without breadwinners. The Samurdhi program is the largest social assistance scheme in Sri Lanka and covers up to 45% of the population. However there are criticisms of leakage to the non-poor with party affiliation and the need to be better targeted. The

Samurdhi system is a good start to increase access to micro-credit and could be further improved. More also needs to be done for those living in conflict-stridden areas like the North and East and particularly so for the internally displaced persons who do not have identification documents like birth certificates and national identification cards and hence are unable to access government assistance and resettlement in Southern Sri Lanka (Gunatilaka et al, 2009). The government could provide schemes to better ease the migrants to working in Southern Sri Lanka like language training (Sinhala is the *lingua franca*) and set up job centers to match job opportunities. It remains to be seen if the welfare of the poor is improved. There is also a pressing need to revamp the public sector as it is too big and lacks accountability especially for the effective implementation of pro-poor development policies and programs. Sri Lanka currently has 56 ministries with considerable overlaps in functions and employs more than 1 million workers (ADB, 2009). See Dowling and Yap (2009) and ADB (2009) for more details.

Final thoughts and a summing up

Much of the rhetoric concerning the global recession has been carried out against a backdrop of a return to a stable growth path either late in 2009 or early 2010. The optimistic scenario suggested by Robert Gordon puts the bottom of the recession in the United States in Q2 2009. First Q 2009 or 2010 GDP results in OECD countries and partial results for Asian economies suggest that this might be premature. While it is true that the large economies of the region which have large domestic demand (China, India and Indonesia) continued to grow although at a somewhat slower rate, the smaller economies with greater export dependence continued to struggle to recover from sharply negative exports and poor stock market and investment performance. Among these economies only South Korea has been able to recover quickly enough to record positive growth. Nevertheless, by the middle of June 2010 the outlook for developing Asia was quite strong. Stimulus measures were largely responsible aided by stronger international trade and a resumption of capital inflows (see Table 10.4). The impact of the stimulus measures will abate somewhat toward the end of 2010. As a result growth projections for 2011 are somewhat weaker in some countries. The drag of financial restructuring on the US and European economies continues to pull down these economies and this is reflected in slower export growth, negative expectations and meager evidence that fiscal stimulus measures and looser monetary policy are having a tangible upside impact. Time will tell whether the recovery will be more evident. The negative impact of potentially higher interest rates arising from the massive fiscal stimulus measures in many OECD countries have also raised concerns that the recovery will be attenuated both in OECD countries and in Asia. The

Table 10.4   Asian GDP growth forecasts 2010 and 2011

Country	2010 GDP growth	2011 GDP growth
China	9.9	8.1
Hong Kong	5.6	4.4
India	7.7	8.0
Indonesia	5.6	5.8
Malaysia	7.1	4.0
Pakistan	2.8	3.9
Singapore	8.0	4.6
South Korea	5.9	4.3
Taiwan	5.6	4.2
Thailand	3.2	4.2

Source: EIU, June 2010

growing possibility that the global recession will be less V-shaped and more U-shaped, makes greater focus on the needs of the poor even more pressing. Stimulus measures already adopted and summarized in Table 6.2 have been targeted to address a variety of different challenges including boosting aggregate demand, particularly consumption. This has been done either by spending on a variety of "shovel ready" projects, tax breaks and investment incentives. There are only a few countries that have even mentioned assistance to those in poverty and these programs are tangential to the major thrust of the stimulus packages, which is to help the industrial and export sectors recover and move to a higher-growth platform. There is a preoccupation with restoring aggregate demand, keeping budget deficits in check while at the same time providing appropriate fiscal stimulus. The impacts of budget deficits on possible currency depreciation as well as other macroeconomic and trade issues are also being considered. Other issues including poverty are hardly mentioned. Governments must also address the needs of the poor in order to avert a sharp increase in poverty, sacrificing the gains of the past decade. It means mobilizing resources to address the plight of the poor in case the economies of the region are slow to recover and move to a sustained growth trajectory. Such an effort will allow them to address poverty concerns within the context of slow economic growth which might persist for some time. The most important component of this agenda is to keep a safety net in place to provide assistance for the chronically poor. Such a program is even more crucial now than it will be once economic growth has resumed.

While poverty incidence is not perfectly correlated with the unemployment rate, particularly in developing countries where unemployment statistics are compiled for a small part of the labor force, it is useful to remember that in industrial countries the time from peak to trough in the unemployment rate is much longer than the trough to peak. This is obvious from looking at the time profile of US unemployment in the postwar era, particularly since the mid-1980s when the rate hit a high of 10.8 at the end of 1982. It would take six years and three months for the unemployment rate to fall to its next cyclical low of 5% in March 1989 (see Chart 7.4).

The next trough to peak in unemployment took only three years and three months for unemployment to rise to the 7.8% in mid-1992 while the next secular acceleration in economic activity was seven years and nine months, taking the unemployment to a 3.8% in April of 2000, a level that had not been reached since early 1966, a period of over 34 years. In previous recessions, the unemployment rate has receded somewhat quickly from its peak. In the 1983 recession, the unemployment fell from 10.8% to just over 7% in a year and a half and from 9% to 7% in two years following peak unemployment rate of 9% in May 1975. Of course "quickly" means something different if you are among the unemployed. There is no getting around the fact that this recession is exacting, and will continue to exact a toll on the labor market not only in the US but elsewhere in industrial and developing countries.

Is the past prologue? It is difficult to predict the evolution of unemployment and GDP in the US or the global economy. In Europe where people are used to higher unemployment rates because of more generous and comprehensive unemployment schemes, the rate has risen to about the same as the current rate in the US. Will it recede slowly as the global economy recovers? And how will this impact emerging economies in Asia? It is important to take steps to insure the poor in Asia and elsewhere, should such a recovery scenario come to pass.

11
Economic Integration in Asia: Trends and Policies

Introduction

While the dynamism of East Asia and the emergence of China and India as major players in the global economy are frequently discussed and debated in academic literature and popular press, much less attention has been placed on Asian economic integration and the rapid increase in Pan-Asian[1] trade and investment.[2] Unlike in Europe, this process is being led mainly by market forces (which enhance efficiency in production and augment dynamic gains through trade) with government-related regional cooperation policies also starting to play a role more recently. The rapid increase in Pan-Asian trade has made growth and development in Asia more dynamic and self-sustained. A regionally integrated but globally connected Asia is starting to emerge. As the experience with the ongoing global economic crisis has shown, Asia has not yet "de-coupled" completely from the OECD. Asian countries are, however, becoming more symmetric and business cycles are becoming more synchronized.

Unlike in the other regions of the world – such as Africa and Latin America – regionalism (or the adoption of regional cooperation policies) is a relatively new phenomenon in Asia.[3] Aside from the establishment of the Association of Southeast Asian Nations (ASEAN) in 1967 and the South Asian Association for Regional Cooperation (SAARC) in 1985 and several efforts to promote intra-regional trade, few policy actions were taken by the Asian countries to promote regional cooperation with each other until the mid-1990s. During much of the colonial period in the 19th and the 20th centuries, South Asia was relatively isolated from East Asia (defined as ASEAN+3). South Asian countries also isolated themselves from each other behind high tariff and non-tariff barriers, and during the mid-1960s, the level of intraregional trade among them was only about 2% of their total trade. This policy started to change after the implementation of the "Look East" policy in India.

The Asian financial crisis of 1997–1998 was a watershed as it focused the region's attention on growing interdependence and shared interests and

East Asian policymakers became keen on supporting market-led integration with various regional cooperation efforts. This sentiment was the strongest in East Asia where the adverse impacts of the crisis and the contagion were the most significant. South Asia has also joined the bandwagon after the 1980s and 1990s when it initiated its economic reform program and it started to implement "Look East" policies. The major factor that ignited the interest of East Asian countries towards regional monetary and financial integration was the virulent contagion of the East Asian financial crisis and the policy mistakes made by the IMF in managing it.[4] It was also felt that the resources of the IMF were limited and that it might not have adequate resources to handle a capital-account crisis associated with large surges and outflows of short-term private capital. Slow progress in the Doha Round under the auspices of the WTO and the popularity of regionalism elsewhere (e.g. EU and NAFTA) also encouraged East Asian countries to promote regionalism in trade. Additional factors were the desire to internalize the benefits of growing interdependence and the realization that regionalism could help maximize the benefits of globalization and minimize the costs. In the post-crisis period, East Asia realized that it needed to be more self-reliant and gain fuller control of its destiny (MAS, 2007).

The ongoing global economic crisis has further enhanced the case for Asian regionalism for a number of reasons. First, the crisis has strengthened the case for rebalancing growth not only at the national level but also by finding economies of scale at the regional level. Second, the global crisis and the high and growing level of economic interdependence among Asian countries have increased the need for policy coordination at the regional level to take into account the spillover effects. Third, the global economic crisis has highlighted the need for joint policy statements and show of force to reverse the flight to quality and loss of investor confidence in the region. Fourth, the global crisis has once again revived interest in the reform of the international financial architecture and the G20 has been given the lead role in spearheading discussions on these issues. Asian countries should, therefore, coordinate their views and positions and make effective representation and make their voice heard at the G20.

Reflecting market policies and government efforts, Pan-Asian trade – comprising intraregional trade between East Asian countries, intraregional trade between the South Asian countries, and interregional trade between South Asia and East Asia – has been surging rapidly, albeit from a low base, especially after 2000. It tripled during the period 1990 to 2000 and has since nearly tripled again to $2.2 trillion in the next seven years. Intraregional trade among the East Asian countries has grown the fastest and presently accounts for about 94% of total Pan-Asian trade, with East Asia-South Asia trade accounting for 5% and intra-South Asian trade a mere 1% (Francois, Rana and Wignaraja, 2009).

The objectives of this chapter are to: (i) review steps taken and progress made in Asian economic integration at the three sub-regional levels; and (ii) recommend actions to promote Asian economic integration including South Asian integration which has been stuck at a low level.

The next Section of the chapter focuses on East Asian integration, while the following Section focuses on growing economic linkages between South Asia and East Asia. The chapter concludes with a discussion of South Asian integration.

Trade and financial integration and macroeconomic policy coordination in East Asia

Trade integration

On trade integration, East Asia has made encouraging progress with intra-regional trade reaching 57% of total trade (up from 43% in 1990), which is higher than the level for NAFTA (North American Free Trade Agreement, 46%) but lower than that for the EU (67%). Much of this expansion has been driven by market forces especially the establishment of production networks in East Asia. The traditional production networks were triangular whereby Japan and the NIEs exported parts for electrical appliances, office and telecommunication equipment and textiles and garments to China and the third generation countries (Indonesia, Malaysia, the Philippines and Thailand). These countries in turn completed the processing and exported the final product to markets in the US and Europe. Since the mid-1990s, more sophisticated and complex production networks have emerged which involve the transshipment of components – back and forth trade in parts and components across Asian countries (Gill and Kharas, 2007). With the rapid emergence of China these networks in the so-called "factory Asia" model are being increasingly centered in China.

East Asian governments began to use FTAs as instruments of trade policy in the late 1990s. In 2000, only three FTAs were in effect, but today there are 47 bilateral and plurilateral FTAs in effect, with another 64 in the pipeline.[5] FTAs will no doubt proliferate further if the Doha Round continues to falter. If they are designed properly, FTAs can help countries reap the benefits of their comparative advantage. That is why FTAs are allowed as exceptions to the anti-discrimination rules of the GATT/WTO. But there is a risk that the proliferation of FTAs could come at the expense of trade with non-members, known as trade diversion. It could also create an "Asian noodle bowl" effect and raise administrative costs of trade especially to small and medium-scale enterprise. The multiplicity of bilateral and plurilateral deals could also hinder the push toward a global trade agreement.

A recent firm level survey study by the ADB found that many businesses view FTAs as a benefit rather than a burden and use them to expand trade to a far greater degree than had been previously thought. "The benefits of

FTAs include wider market access and preferential tariffs that make it easier to import intermediate materials needed for finished goods. Multiple country rules of origin (ROOs), which determine where goods originate from for a variety of purposes, including quotas and labeling, may add some administrative and transaction costs. But the large majority of exporters do not view ROOs as a significant hindrance to business activity. In addition, bilateral and plurilateral FTAs counter protectionist tendencies amid the current economic uncertainty. They provide a valuable stepping stone toward broader trade liberalization in support of economic recovery (Kawai and Wignaraja, 2009).

Financial integration

Lack of data makes it difficult to measure the level of financial integration in East Asia, but those that are available suggest that it is now starting to increase, albeit from low levels (MAS, 2007; Rana, 2007). East Asian countries have taken collective actions to develop local currency bond markets as these markets will reduce the "double mismatch" problem, which was at the heart of the crisis, and overcome the so-called "original sin" problem.[6] The basic idea is to mobilize the region's vast pool of savings to be intermediated directly to the region's long-term investment, without going through financial intermediaries outside of the region. Regional financial intermediation through bond markets would diversify the modes of financing in the region and reduce the double mismatch. The initiatives include the EMEAP Asian Bond Fund (ABF) Initiative and the ASEAN+3 Asian Bond Markets Initiative (ABMI).

EMEAP introduced the ABF in June 2003. The idea was to help expand the bond market through demand-side stimulus from purchases by central banks of sovereign and quasi-sovereign bonds issued by 8 EMEAP emerging members (including China, Hong Kong, Indonesia, South Korea, Malaysia, the Philippines, Singapore and Thailand) using all 11 members' foreign exchange reserves. The initial attempt was to purchase US$1 billion of US dollar-denominated bonds (ABF-1). Given the recognition that local-currency denominated bonds need to be promoted in order to address the "double mismatch" problem, the central bankers introduced ABF-2 in December 2004, involving purchases of US$2 billion equivalent of sovereign and quasi-sovereign local currency-denominated bonds.

ABF-2 consists of two components, a Pan-Asian Bond Index Fund (PAIF) and a Fund of Bond Funds (FoBF). PAIF is a single bond fund index investing in local currency bonds, issued in eight economies. A FoBF has a two-tiered structure with a parent fund investing in eight sub-funds, each of which invests in local currency sovereign and quasi-sovereign bonds issued in their respective markets. PAIF and the eight sub-funds are passively managed by private fund managers against a Pan-Asian bond index and predetermined benchmark indexes in local markets. ABF-2 is designed to facilitate investment by public and private sector entities, through the listing of local currency exchange-traded bond funds (ETF) – already listed in Hong Kong, Malaysia and Singapore.

The ASEAN+3 Finance Ministers' process launched ABMI in August 2003. The ABMI aims to focus on facilitating market access to a diverse issuer and investor base and on enhancing a market infrastructure for bond market development, thereby creating robust primary and secondary bond markets in the region. The ABMI initially created six working groups and later reorganized these into four working groups and two support teams (Ad Hoc Support Group and Technical Assistance Coordination Group). Currently the four working groups are focusing on: (i) issuance of new securitized debt instruments; (ii) establishment of a regional credit guarantee agency to help mitigate risks through credit enhancement; (iii) exploration of possible establishment of a regional clearance and settlement system to facilitate cross-border bond transactions without facing the Herstatt risk (i.e. the risk of being in a different time zone); and (iv) strengthening of regional rating agencies and harmonization of rating standards.

ADB launched the AsianBondsOnline website in May 2005,[7] which has become a popular one-stop clearinghouse of information on sovereign and corporate bonds issued in ASEAN+3 countries. In May 2009, the ASEAN+3 Ministers endorsed the establishment of the Credit Guarantee and Investment Mechanism (CGIM) as a trust fund of the ADB with an initial capital of $500 million. Issues relating to the establishment of the CGIM are to be discussed at the working level and the decision taken in May 2010.

Macroeconomic policy coordination

Macroeconomic policy coordination is essentially a post-crisis phenomenon in East Asia. There is an ascending order of intensity of these efforts in the sense that they involve progressively increasing constraints on the amount of discretion that individual countries can exercise in the design of macroeconomic policies. By level of intensity, these efforts have ranged from economic review and policy dialogue to establishing regional financing arrangements and eventually toward coordinating exchange rate policies.

Economic review and policy dialogue. In the area of economic review and policy dialogue, there are three major ongoing initiatives. First, the ASEAN Surveillance Process was established in October 1998 to strengthen the policy-making capacity within the group. Based on the principles of peer review and mutual interest, this process reviews global regional, and individual country developments, and monitors exchange rate and macroeconomic aggregates, as well as sectoral and social policies. Under this Process, the ASEAN Finance Ministers meet annually and the ministries of finance and central bank deputies meet semi-annually to discuss issues of common interest.

Second, with the formation of the ASEAN+3 Finance Ministers Process in November 1999, the ASEAN+3 Economic Review and Policy Dialogue (ERPD) process was introduced in May 2000. Under the ERPD, ASEAN+3 Finance Ministers meet annually and their deputies meet semi-annually. Initially, Deputies would meet for a couple of hours but now their meeting lasts for two days and discussions focus on: (i) assessing global, regional and national conditions and risks; (ii) reviewing financial sector (including bond market) developments and vulnerabilities; and (iii) other topics of interest. The value-added of regional surveillance is that countries tend to be more frank with each other in a regional forum as they focus on issues of common interest (such as high oil prices, avian flu, global payments imbalances and capital inflows). However, so far, the ERPD is in transition from the simple "information sharing" stage to "peer reviews" among the member countries. Currently the ADB and more recently the IMF provide assessments of regional economic and financial conditions and risks and individual countries provide self-assessments of their respective economic situations. With a move toward "peer reviews" the participating members are expected to conduct more active discussions of other countries' policy-making.

Steps have been taken to monitor short-term capital flows and to develop early warning systems of currency and banking crises. National Surveillance Units have been established in many ASEAN+3 countries for economic and financial monitoring and operating the early warning system with ADB support and so has a Technical Working Group on Economic and Financial Monitoring. A Group of Experts has also been appointed. But the ASEAN+3 does not have a technical secretariat which prepares a comprehensive assessment of member countries' economic and financial outlook and risks.

Third, central bank governors in the region have also developed their own forums for regional economic information exchange, analysis and policy dialogues, including the Executives' Meeting of East Asia Pacific Central Banks (EMEAP), South East Asian Central Banks (SEACEN), South East Asia, New Zealand and Australia (SEANZA). EMEAP is the most prominent group and was organized in February 1991 with the leadership of the Bank of Japan and the Reserve Bank of Australia. Its major objectives include enhanced regional surveillance, exchanges of information and views, and the promotion of financial market development. Its activities include annual meetings of EMEAP central bank governors, semi-annual meetings of the deputy governors, and three working groups concerned with bank supervision, financial markets, and payments and settlement systems. Like the ASEAN+3 finance ministers' process, EMEAP has no secretariat.

Until its dissolution in December 2005, the Manila Framework Group was another forum that brought together deputies from a wider range of countries for policy dialogue. There are trans-regional forums such as the

Asia-Pacific Economic Cooperation (APEC) finance ministers and the Asia-Europe Meeting (ASEM) finance ministers for trans-regional processes.

Regional financing arrangement. Progress has also been made in establishing regional financing arrangements. They are designed to address short-term liquidity needs in the event of a crisis or contagion, and to supplement the existing international financial arrangements. At their May 2000 meeting in Chiang Mai, the ASEAN+3 Finance Ministers agreed on the Chiang Mai Initiative (CMI) to expand the ASEAN Swap Arrangement (ASA) to all ASEAN members, and to set up a network of bilateral swap arrangements (BSAs) among ASEAN+3 countries. The ASA expansion was done in November 2000, and its size increased from $200 million to $1 billion. In April 2005, the ASA size was again increased to $2 billion. A network of BSAs has been signed among the plus-3 countries (China, Japan and South Korea) and between a plus-3 country and a selected ASEAN country. To date, eight ASEAN+3 members have signed 16 BSAs amounting to $84 billion.

One of the important features of CMI BSA is that members requesting liquidity support can immediately obtain short-term financial assistance for the first 20% (originally 10%) of the committed amount. The remaining 80% is provided to the requesting member under an IMF program. Linking the CMI liquidity facility to an IMF program – and hence its conditionality – is designed to address the concern that the liquidity shortage of a requesting country may be due to fundamental problems, rather than mere panic and herd behavior by investors, and that the potential moral hazard problem could be non-negligible in the absence of tough IMF conditionality. The general view is that, with the region's currently limited capacity to produce and enforce effective adjustment programs in times of crisis, linking CMI to IMF programs is prudent, at least for the time being.

Substantial progress has been made on CMI multilateralization (CMIM) since its launch. Some of the major developments over the last few years include:

- Integration and enhancement of ASEAN+3 ERPD into the CMI framework (May 2005);
- Increasing the ceiling for withdrawal without an IMF program in place from 10% to 20% of the total (May 2005);
- Adoption of the collective decision-making procedure for CMI swap activation, as a step toward multilateralizing the CMI (May 2006);
- Agreement in principle on a self-managed reserve pooling arrangement governed by a single contractual agreement as an appropriate form of CMI multilateralization (May 2007).
- Agreement that the total size of the multilateralized CMI would be at least $80 billion (May 2008);

- The size of the multilateralized CMI increased to $120 billion (February 2009);
- CMIM was implemented on 24 March 2010.

On CMIM, at their meeting in Hyderabad in 2006, the ASEAN+3 Finance Ministers decided that "all swap providing countries can simultaneously and promptly provide liquidity support to any parties involved in bilateral swap arrangements at times of emergency." At their Kyoto meeting in 2007, the Ministers decided to establish a "self-managed reserve pooling arrangement". At their May 2008 meeting in Madrid, the Ministers "agreed that the total size of the multilateralized CMI would be at least $80 billion". In response to the global economic crisis, at the Special ASEAN+3 Finance Ministers meeting in Phuket in February 2009, the amount was subsequently increased to $120 billion.[8] At their May 2009 meeting, the Ministers announced that they had agreed to implement CMIM before the end of this year. They also announced an agreement to establish an independent surveillance unit to monitor and analyze regional economies and support CMIM decision-making. As a start, they agreed to establish an advisory panel of experts to work closely with the ADB and the ASEAN Secretariat to enhance the current surveillance mechanism. The Ministers also welcomed Hong Kong to participate in the CMIM.

The ASEAN+3 independent surveillance unit is not intended as a substitute for the IMF. It is intended to enhance objective monitoring by supplementing the IMF especially its new Short-term Liquidity Facility, which enables certain countries to borrow without conditions.

Exchange rate issues.   Despite the close and rising interdependence of East Asian economies through trade, investment and finance, there has been no exchange rate policy coordination in place in East Asia. Moreover, the region's exchange rate regimes are in serious disarray. In contrast to the pre-crisis period where many emerging market economies in East Asia maintained *de jure* or *de facto* US dollar pegged regimes, the post-crisis period exhibits a greater diversity in exchange rate regimes. The two giant economies in the region, Japan and China, adopt different exchange rate regimes – Japan a free float and China a heavily managed regime targeted at the US dollar.

So far, only some research has been conducted, under various forums such as the ASEAN Currency and Exchange Rate Mechanism Task Force, the ASEM Kobe Research Project, and the ASEAN+3 Research Group. This will, however, undoubtedly change as the integration process moves forward, business cycles become more synchronized, and macroeconomic policy interdependence becomes even stronger. In fact, at the May 2006 meeting, the ASEAN+3 finance ministers endorsed a study on "regional monetary units," or Asian currency units.

Next steps

East Asia's market-led integration, which now is also being driven by various policy actions, is expected to deepen further. One reason for optimism is that the increasing level of trade integration and bilateral trade intensity has led to a greater synchronization of output and business cycles in the region. This means that symmetric shocks are expected to prevail enhancing the case for cooperation and coordination of policies (Rana, 2008) perhaps more than in Europe where the level of vertical integration is lower (Rana, Chen and Chia, 2009).

Going forward, Asian economic integration is expected to follow what Senior Minister Goh Chok Tong (2006) once referred to as the "variable geometry, flexible borders" approach. The process will be multi-track with a trade (including infrastructure), finance, and monetary track with new members coming on board when they feel that they are ready. The CMIM has set the stage for institutionalizing East Asia regionalism. Hence new institutions to support Asian integration are also expected to emerge. The "bottom-up" integration in East Asia is starting to be "top-down" as well following the European approach.

On the trade track, effort should be put in to: (i) make the FTAs compatible with each other (by having similar rules of origin as in Europe); and (ii) consolidate the proliferation of FTAs into a deeper and wider FTA such as the East Asian FTA (including India). Kawai and Wignaraja (2007) have shown that an ASEAN+6 FTA would provide more gains than an ASEAN+3 FTA. Connectivity issues including infrastructure development and trade facilitation are also being addressed.

On the finance track, Asian bond markets should be developed further. Regional institutions to deepen local-currency bond markets – such as a regional settlement agency – need to be established. With the progress in reforming market infrastructure at the national levels, a regional regulatory agency that promotes coordination of capital market rules and regulations (micro-prudential supervision) and monitors the stability of the financial system throughout the region through early warning systems (macro-prudential monitoring) such as an Asian Financial Stability Dialogue could be established.[9]

On the macroeconomic policy track many of the decisions of the Ministers in relation to the CMIM must be implemented as scheduled by the end of this year. It is understood that the details on contributions, voting rights, decision-making rules, and other operational aspects have already been reached. The ERPD should also be strengthened beyond "information sharing" to "peer review" and ultimately to "due diligence".

The deepening regional and financial integration in the region together the synchronization of business cycles suggests that East Asia should initiate actions to coordinate exchange rate policies using a step-by-step approach. The first step could be to promote greater exchange rate flexibility while maintaining a certain amount of intraregional stability by monitoring deviations from an Asian Currency Unit (ACU) basket (Kawai and Rana, 2009).

Some commentators see recent trends in the region as heralding the eventual adoption of a single currency or the establishment of an East Asian monetary union. Europe's experience shows that a monetary union imposes stringent demands on policy coordination and institution building that needs strong political will and a strong sense of common purpose which East Asia lacks at the present (Monetary Authority of Singapore, 2007).

In addition to being multi-track, East Asian regionalism is also expected to be multi-speed – with the pace of progress for different aspects of regional cooperation and integration varying and with members, from other Asian regions as well, joining as and when they feel that they are ready to do so.

Regionalism in East Asia is expected to improve the medium and long-term economic outlook for the region and enhance the region's resilience to external shocks through the expansion of trade and investment based on comparative advantages of member countries; lead to greater monetary and financial stability and prevent financial crises; and provide cross-border connectivity which is essential for the movement of goods, services, labor and information across countries. Competitiveness, industrial production and productivity of East Asian countries are expected to increase.

Economic relations between South Asia and East Asia[10]

Prior to 1990, South Asian and East Asian countries were relatively isolated from one another. The only trade agreement that covered the two sub-regions was the Bangkok Agreement signed in 1975 (now called the Asia-Pacific trade agreement). The adoption of the "Look East" policy in India in 1991 and similar policies in other South Asian countries together with the economic dynamism of India and China, has now heightened the interest on the evolving economic relationships between the two sub-regions. Some landmarks in South Asia–East Asia economic relations are presented in Table 11.1.

South Asia's total merchandise trade with East Asia has grown significantly in absolute terms albeit from a low base. It increased 12-fold during 1990–2009, from $12.4 billion to $174 billion. The annual growth rate was relatively moderate until 2000, but it has surged after that growing by over 25% per annum. As expected, a large part of the increase (roughly one-third) in South Asia-East Asia trade is accounted by the bilateral trade between the two giant economies of India and China.

In relative terms, however, the level of South Asia-East Asia trade accounted for 18.9% of South Asia's total trade in 1990 and is now about 25%. On the other hand, South Asia accounted for a mere 1.3% of East Asia's trade and a slightly higher 2.5% in 2009. Hence, East Asia is a more important trading partner for South Asia than vice versa.

Table 11.1   South Asia–East Asia economic relations: some landmarks

1975	• Signing of Bangkok Agreement by Bangladesh, India, Lao People's Democratic Republic (Lao PDR), Republic of Korea, Sri Lanka and People's Republic of China (PRC).
1985	• Formation of the South Asian Association for Regional Cooperation (SAARC) by Bangladesh, Bhutan, India, Maldives, Nepal, Pakistan and Sri Lanka. Afghanistan joined in 2007.
1991	• India adopted "Look East" Policy to strengthen economic relationships with East Asian countries.
1992	• Signing of the Association of Southeast Asian Nations (ASEAN) Free Trade Area (AFTA) by Brunei Darussalam, Indonesia, Malaysia, Philippines, Singapore and Thailand. Other Southeast Asian countries joined later: Vietnam (1995), Lao PDR and Myanmar (1997), and Cambodia (1999). AFTA became fully operational in 2003.
	• India became a sectoral dialogue partner of ASEAN.
1993	• Signing of Agreement on SAARC Preferential Trading Arrangement (SAPTA) by eight SAARC members. SAPTA entered into force in 1997.
1996	• India became a full dialogue partner of ASEAN.
1997	• East Asian financial crisis, which highlighted the importance of regional cooperation among East Asian economies.
1998	• Signing of Indo-Sri Lanka Free Trade Agreement, which came into force in 2000.
2000	• The PRC joined the World Trade Organization (WTO), starting with an early harvest program that liberalised 600 farm products. An agreement to trade in goods was signed in 2005, liberalising 7,000 trading goods.
2002	• India-ASEAN partnership was upgraded to summit-level dialogue.
	• Signing of Framework Agreement between the PRC and ASEAN. Early Harvest Scheme came into force in 2005.
2003	• Signing of a Framework Agreement on Comprehensive Economic Cooperation between India and ASEAN, incorporating free trade agreement (FTA), at the Bali Summit.
2004	• Signing of an Agreement on South Asian Free Trade Area (SAFTA) during the 12th SAARC Summit in Islamabad. SAFTA came into force in 2006.
	• Signing of a Long-Term Partnership for Peace, Progress and Shared Prosperity by India and ASEAN at the Lao PDR Summit.
	• Signing of Early Harvest Scheme for the India-Thailand Free Trade Framework Agreement under which preferential concessions have been exchanged on a specified set of commodities.
	• Signing of a Framework Agreement under the Bay of Bengal Initiative for Multi-Sectoral Technical and Economic Cooperation (BIMSTEC) by Bangladesh, Bhutan, India, Myanmar, Nepal, Sri Lanka and Thailand.
2005	• Signing of a Comprehensive Economic Cooperation Agreement (CECA) between India and Singapore.
	• Renaming of the Bangkok Agreement as the Asia-Pacific Trade Agreement (APTA), which would offer up to 4,000 tariff concessions among members.
	• Signing of a Comprehensive Economic Framework Agreement between Pakistan and Indonesia.
2006	• PRC became an observer of SAARC.
	• Ongoing Japanese proposal for a comprehensive agreement covering ASEAN+3, Australia, India, and New Zealand.
	• Signing of an FTA between the PRC and Pakistan.
2007	• Signing of Pakistan-Malaysia Free Trade Agreement – Pakistan's first comprehensive FTA and Malaysia's first bilateral FTA with a South Asian country.
2009	• Signing of the ASEAN-India FTA in August 2009.
	• Signing of the India-South Korea Comprehensive Economic Partnership Agreement in August 2009.

Source: Francois, Rana and Wignaraja, 2009

The absence of comparable data on FDI by source limits an analysis of investment relationships between South and East Asia. The data that are available from national sources and the ASEAN Secretariat show that investment relations between the two regions, although starting to increase in recent years is still limited.

Calculation of revealed comparative advantage indices shows that there is potential for enhancing trade between the two regions. South Asia has comparative advantage mainly in primary goods and labor-intensive manufactures and IT services, while East Asia has comparative advantage across a much wider range of products. These include primary goods such as crude

Table 11.2   FTAs involving South and East Asian countries

FTAs in effect
- Asia-Pacific Trade Agreement (APTA, formerly known as the Bangkok Agreement), signed in 1975 and in effect since 1976
- India-Singapore Comprehensive Economic Cooperation Agreement (CECA), signed in June 2005 and effective since August 2005
- Preferential Tariff Arrangement-Group of Eight Developing Countries (D-8 PTA),[11] signed in 2006
- People's Republic of China (PRC)-Pakistan Free Trade Agreement, signed on 24 November 2006 and in effect as of 1 July 2007 [agreement on Early Harvest Program (EHP) was also signed]
- Malaysia-Pakistan Closer Economic Partnership, signed in November 2007 and took effect in January 2008
- Association of Southeast Asian Nations (ASEAN)-India Free Trade Agreement, signed in August 2009
- India-Korea Comprehensive Economic Partnership Agreement (CEPA), signed in August 2009

FTAs under negotiation
- India-Thailand Free Trade Area
- Bay of Bengal Initiative for Multi-Sectoral Technical and Economic Cooperation (BIMSTEC) Free Trade Area
- Pakistan-Singapore Free Trade Agreement
- Pakistan-Indonesia Free Trade Agreement
- Trade Preferential System of the Organization of the Islamic Conference (TPS-OIC)

FTAs proposed
- Pakistan-Brunei Darussalam Free Trade Agreement
- China-India Regional Trading Arrangement
- India-Indonesia Comprehensive Economic Cooperation Arrangement
- Japan-India Economic Partnership Agreement
- Pakistan-Philippines Free Trade Agreement
- Pakistan-Thailand Free Trade Agreement
- Singapore-Sri Lanka Comprehensive Economic Partnership Agreement

---

Source: ADB FTA Database (ww.aric.adb.org)

rubber and fish, labor-intensive manufactures such as textiles, travel goods and footwear, and more capital- and knowledge-intensive items such as office machines and telecommunications equipment.

More recently, as in other parts of the world, there has been a proliferation of FTAs between South Asia and East Asia. In 1975, there was only the Bangkok Agreement. Now seven FTAs are already in effect, and 12 are either under negotiation or have been proposed (Table 11.2). The most significant of these, so far, is the signing of the India-Singapore Comprehensive Economic Cooperation Agreement (CECA) on June 2005. The CECA became effective in August 2005 and covers not only trade in goods but also services, investments and cooperation in technology, education, air services, and human resources. The Asia Pacific Trade Agreement went into effect in 1976, the Group of Eight FTA in 2006, the China-Pakistan FTA in 2007 and the Malaysia-Pakistan FTA – Malaysia's first with a South Asian country – in 2008. Last year, the India-ASEAN and the India-South Korea FTAs became effective. Although comprehensive in terms of trade liberalization, the former allows India to protect its agriculture and services sector for some time. The India-FTA has the potential of attracting South Korean investment into India for export to third country markets.

Looking forward, a number of policy actions could be taken to increase the level of South Asia-East Asia integration. First, the levels of tariffs and NTBs are already low in many East Asian countries and since the 1990s South Asia has made encouraging progress in the same direction. However, there is room for further reductions in tariffs and NTBs in both regions (especially NTBs in East Asia because tariffs are already low). Second, in addition to reducing tariffs and NTBs, South Asian countries and several East Asian countries also need to make progress in implementing the remaining reform agenda – namely, developing the social (e.g. schools, hospitals, rural medical centers) and physical (power, water, roads, railways) infrastructure and implementing the so-called second generation reforms to enhance transparency, good governance, and the quality of fiscal adjustment. These include, among others, reforms of civil service and of delivery of public goods, creating an environment that is conducive to private sector opportunities (greater competition, better regulations, and stronger property rights), and reforms of institutions that create human capital (e.g. health and education).

Third, South and East Asian countries need to consolidate their FTAs. Quantitative estimates using the computable general equilibrium (CGE) model and the Global Trade Analysis Project (GTAP) database suggest that a broader regional approach will have large beneficial impact. The estimated impact on national income of an ASEAN+3 and South Asia FTA is much higher than that of an ASEAN+3 and India FTA, which in turn is higher than that of an ASEAN FTA. While India benefits from an ASEAN+3 and India FTA, other South Asian countries lose. However, a broader

ASEAN+3 and South Asian FTA is a win-win for all. Countries should also deepen FTAs – extend coverage beyond trade in good into services, investment, technology etc. The Comprehensive Economic Partnership Agreement for East Asia, which is an FTA that includes all East Asia Summit countries, is being established and the Economic Research Institute for ASEAN and East Asia has been established to sensitize and support the process.

The fourth measure that could impact significantly on the level of trade between South Asia and East Asia is the reduction of trading costs. This could be brought about through: (i) investment in trade-related infrastructure; and (ii) streamlining of cross-border procedures (including customs procedures and logistic costs). Most cargo between South Asia and East Asia moves by water and air as there is no land transport services that are operational at the present time. Rapid growth in trade has been accommodated through the introduction of larger container ships.

The expansion and diversification of feeder services and bottlenecks, primarily in public ports, remain to be addressed. For instance, land transit through Myanmar is not possible at the present time. Additional corridors between India and China with Bangladesh, Bhutan and Nepal as "land bridges" will have to be developed. China has plans to extend the recently-opened Qinghai-Tibet railway to Nepal and India. The proposed Asian Highway and Asian railway have missing links that are not fully operational. The proposal to establish an Asian Infrastructure Fund with financing from various multilateral agencies and private-public partnership is making progress. The Pan-Asian Infrastructure Forum to sensitize issues related to promoting greater connectivity in Asia is in the process of being established. The ADB has identified 21 high-ticket infrastructure projects to connect Asia.

Finally, countries should make efforts to reduce transport and logistic constraints to facilitate movement of goods between the two regions. These include delays in customs inspection, cargo handling and transfer, and processing of documents. Customs procedures could be modernized by: (i) aligning the customs code to international standards; (ii) simplifying and harmonizing procedures; (iii) making tariff structures consistent with the international harmonized tariff classification; and (iv) adopting and implementing the WTO Customs Valuation Agreement. South Asian and East Asian countries have made progress in implementing many of these procedures but much more remains to be done.

Economic integration in South Asia

The World Bank (2004) has estimated that the volume of trade among South Asian countries before the Partition of India and Pakistan in 1947 was around 20% of their total trade. This fell to about 4% by the 1950s and to 2% in 1967 mainly because of mutual mistrusts and political conflicts in the region. Also for four decades after independence, South Asian countries had adopted inward-looking development strategies with high barriers to trade and investment. The two landlocked countries, Nepal and Bhutan, had maintained close trade links with India but not with other South Asian countries and the rest of the world.

This trend of declining intraregional trade in South Asia started to reverse only in the late 1980s and 1990s when South Asia abandoned import-substituting policies and began to adopt market-oriented reforms including trade liberalization. Nevertheless, the level of intraregional trade presently stands at only a dismal 5% of total trade. The comparative figures for East Asia are about 25% in the case of ASEAN and 55% in the case of ASEAN+3.

The lackluster performance of South Asian integration can be explained by several factors. First, the deep mistrusts and political conflicts of the past continue. Second, the presence of India as a large country arouses fear of hegemony and economic dominance among the smaller neighboring countries. Third, complementarities that existed in the 1940s may have lessened considerably as countries have developed similar types of industries. A recent ADB/UNCTAD (2008) study, however, finds enormous potential for intraregional trade among the South Asian countries.

With the view of promoting intraregional trade, the South Asian Association for Regional Cooperation (SAARC) initiated the South Asian Preferential Trading Arrangement (SAPTA) in 1995. But SAPTA's progress was painstakingly slow because of the product by product approach to tariff concessions, low product coverage, and stringent rules of origin. One study found that many trade restrictions maintained by South Asian countries were designed not to restrict imports from outside the region but to keep out exports of neighboring countries, particularly from India (Weerakoon, 2008).

In certain ways, the South Asian Free Trade Area (SAFTA) of 2004 was a leap forward. It was formally launched on 1 July 2006, six months late because of Pakistan's failure to ratify it on time. Unfortunately, the SAFTA also had its own weaknesses. Among others, services trade, which is emerging as a major export item from South Asia especially India, was excluded. So was the issue of non-tariff barriers. Despite this, a recent model-based study by the ADB/UNCTAD (2008) finds that the successful implementation of the SAFTA would provide significant trade and income gains for both the larger and the smaller countries in the region.

On money and finance, the SAARC Finance, which is a network of central bank governors and finance secretaries set up following the 1998 Colombo SAARC Summit, has achieved some success in forging closer cooperation on macroeconomic policies. The SAARC has also decided to hold regular meetings of the South Asian Finance Ministers modeled after the ASEAN and ASEAN+3 Finance Ministers meetings. The more recently announced goal of attaining a South Asian Economic Union and the expressed desire of a common currency will, however, have to wait for some time in the future as they can be feasible only in the longer term as economic convergence is achieved in the region.

In the area of cross-border infrastructure development, the South Asia Subregional Economic Cooperation (SASEC) program initiated by four members of the SAARC (Bangladesh, Bhutan, India and Nepal) has made notable progress in identifying projects in the six priority sectors (transport, energy and power, tourism, environment, trade and investment, private sector cooperation). However, the implementation of the SASEC initiatives has been modest.

More recently, there have been signs which suggest that South Asia's mindset on regional integration agenda is perhaps starting to change somewhat. The recent elections in Bangladesh, Pakistan and India and decision by Sri Lanka and Pakistan to deal with insurgencies may have created an environment which is more favorable to inter-country cooperation. India, in particular, appears to have adopted a more positive stance on South Asia befitting its rapid emergence in the global economy. India's relations with Bangladesh have also improved somewhat. The Asian Development Bank's India 2039 study notes that India has the potential of achieving an average of 9.5% growth per annum over the next 30 years provided it continues its economic reform programs.[12] By that time, India could be the second largest in the world, second only to China surpassing the US. A prosperous South Asia would be beneficial for all. In 2008, India announced that it would provide free market access to imports from its least developed neighbors and signed a FTA with Sri Lanka. It also made commitments to reduce its negative list and to promote regional connectivity. More recently, India has also proposed a Dhaka-Delhi-Lahore railway line to connect to the proposed Islamabad-Tehran-Istanbul service.

Positive signs are not confined to India alone. Despite the terrorist attacks, India-Pakistan relations appear to have thawed a bit. Pakistan has also increased the list of items in its positive list resulting in rapid growth of its imports from India. The new regime in Nepal has made progress in advancing discussions on a number of hydroelectric projects.

In this changing context and based on East Asia's successful experience with regional integration, South Asia needs to learn lessons from East Asia's successful experience with economic integration. The need for further cooperation in South Asia is clear. Burki (2009) argues "South Asia has two options – it could pursue national interests or it could work as a region with the countries in the area prepared to step back a little from including only national interests in their economic strategies (in addressing regional and global issues). South Asia could do so much better by adopting a regional approach". Three lessons are particularly relevant for South Asia.

The first is for South Asia to take advantage of the recent positive signs and promote integration within itself by giving primacy to economic issues and not allowing political differences to stand in the way of regional integration efforts. The East Asian countries have not been immune to political conflicts. Despite these problems, however, the East Asian leaders have pressed ahead and agreed to keep their political differences aside on the regional cooperation agenda. It is now time for South Asia leaders to also follow suit and implement ongoing integration schemes effectively and deepen them further.

The second is for the South Asian leaders to adopt the East Asian concept of "open regionalism" rather than the failed concept of "closed regionalism". This means extending any preferences granted by a country to neighbors and eventually to the rest of the world as well or "multilateralizing regionalism". Successful implementation of "open regionalism" in East Asia has contributed to the establishment of regional production networks and increased intraregional trade without trade being diverted from the rest of the world. In fact, East Asia's trade with its three main partner groups (the EU, the US, and the rest of the world) has increased. This, in turn, has had favorable spillover effects on East Asian intraregional trade and investment. South Asia could also "multilateralize regionalism" by promoting trade with the rest of the world, including East Asia. This would be good for South Asian integration as well.

The third is for South Asia to adopt the East Asian approach to sequencing integration and not the European one. When the Europeans initiated the integration process in the post-World War II period there was a strong political will to cooperate and promote peace in order to avoid wars in the future. That is the reason why they went for a customs union and an economic union. Efforts to promote monetary integration began only later in 1979 when the European Monetary System (EMS) was established. The East Asian sequence was different. Given the weakness in the global financial architecture, East Asia initiated cooperation by establishing the ASEAN and the ASEAN+3 Finance Ministers Process. Efforts to promote trade integration started later after 2000 when countries started to promote FTAs. For South Asia too, given the lack of political will, it might be advisable to build up on the various activities of SAARC Finance, and maybe even establish a European Monetary System (EMS) type system of fixed but adjustable exchange rates before trade integration. The increased level of intraregional trade brought by such an exchange rate regime could play a catalytic role in encouraging cooperation on trade.

12
Reform of International Financial Architecture: Progress and Remaining Agenda

Introduction

For roughly three decades after the creation of the IMF in 1944, issues related to the international monetary system focused on exchange rate policies, international reserve management, and balance of payment positions of the major industrial countries. With financial globalization and increased cross-border capital flows and crises in emerging markets (see Chapter 1), the attention of academics and policymakers has shifted to crisis prevention and crisis management. The subject of "international monetary reform" has now been renamed "international financial architecture reform (IFA)" by most writers on the subject.

IFA refers to the institutions, policies and practices associated with the promotion of global financial stability and prevention and management/ resolution of financial crisis. Many institutions are involved including the IMF, the World Bank, and the more technical entities such as the newly-constituted Financial Stability Board and the Basel Committee on Banking Supervision. It also includes the various inter-governmental groups such as the G7/G8 and the G20 which oversee the activities of various institutions. Several aspects of crisis prevention and crisis management/resolution deal with weaknesses in the global financial system and require collective actions at the international level. But global financial stability also rests on robust national financial systems and hence requires actions at the country level as well.

The Asian financial crisis (AFC) of 1997–98 had heightened the call for the reform of the IFA. The AFC was triggered primarily by capital account factors associated with financial globalization – such as large inflows of foreign private capital and their sudden reversals – as opposed to current account problems.[1] It was felt by academics and policymakers that the IMF might not have adequate resources especially compared with the scale of cross-border capital flows. It was also felt by them that several of the policy recommendations made by the IMF in managing the Asian financial crisis were not appropriate. With the V-shaped recovery from the AFC, complacency had set in and the reform measures were quickly forgotten (Kawai and Rana, 2009). This partially set the stage for the present crisis. At the global level, several institutions continued to recommend financial deregulation and capital account liberalization even though they were recognized as having contributed to the crisis (UN, 2009a). Also many surplus countries started to accumulate international reserves to "self-insure" themselves and this led to the widening of global imbalances which added further fuel to the credit boom in the US and thereby contributed to the present economic crisis.

The inadequacies of the responses of international financial institutions to the ongoing global economic crisis (GEC) and their failure to take effective actions to prevent it, has once again ignited interest in IFA reforms. It would be a pity if complacency sets in yet once again because of the faster than expected recovery from the crisis and the seeds of a future crisis sewn. A big opportunity to reform the IFA would have been missed and, as before, vulnerabilities of countries to future crises would remain.

The objectives of this chapter are threefold, to: (i) discuss IFA reforms that were implemented during the post-AFC period; (ii) review the reforms that are now being considered and implemented in response of the GEC mainly under the auspices of the G20; and (iii) outline several longer-term agenda in reforming the IFA which will require the attention of the G20. These together will determine how the future IFA may look like.

Post-Asian financial crisis reforms of IFA

After the AFC, several academics had put forward radical reform plans ranging from abolishing the IMF to transforming it into the international lender of last resort, or an international bankruptcy organization. Actual changes were more modest partly because the crisis turned out to be short-lived. Nevertheless, as a response to the AFC, under the auspices of the G7/G8, various organizations such as the IMF, World Bank, and the Bank for International Settlement (BIS) undertook important efforts to reform the IFA. These efforts focused in the areas of crisis prevention, crisis management/resolution, and IMF governance reforms. While some of these efforts have been completed, others continue, and several new issues have also emerged after the GEC. The reforms implemented in the post-AFC period are summarized in Table 12.1.

Crisis prevention

Standards and codes. Standards and codes refer to provisions relating to the institutional environment or "rules of the game" within which economic and financial policies are devised and implemented. The development, dissemination, and adoption by countries of international standards is expected to assist countries in strengthening their economic institutions,

Table 12.1   IFA reforms: post-Asian financial crisis efforts

Crisis prevention

Standards and codes
- The IMF, World Bank, and BIS established international standards in 12 areas, which are broadly categorized into three groups: (i) policy transparency; (ii) financial sector regulation and supervision; and (iii) market integrity. Standards in policy transparency include data transparency, fiscal transparency, and monetary and financial policy transparency. Standards on financial regulation and supervision cover five areas: banking supervision, securities, insurance, payments systems, and anti-money laundering and combating the financing of terrorism. Standards of market integrity include corporate governance, accounting, auditing, and insolvency and creditor rights.
- A country's observance of standards in each of the 12 areas is assessed at the request of a member country by the IMF and the World Bank; the results of these assessments are then summarized in a Report on the Observance of Standards and Codes (ROSCs).
- Some of these standards (especially those related to the quantity and quality of bank capital and compensation practices) are now undergoing revisions.

Data transparency
- The IMF took steps to enhance information transparency and openness, including the establishment and strengthening of data dissemination standards to help countries prevent future crises and diminish the effect of unavoidable ones. The standards for data dissemination comprise two tiers. The first, called the Special Data Dissemination Standards (SDDS), was established in 1996 to guide countries that have, or might seek, access to international capital markets. The second tier, the General Data Dissemination System (GDDS), was established in 1997 to help countries provide more reliable data. The GDDS focuses on improving statistical systems, while the SDDS focuses on commitments to data dissemination standards in countries that already meet high data quality standards.
- On the other hand, information disclosure of highly leveraged institutions (HLIs) – including hedge funds – was not strengthened. This issue is now being addressed under the auspices of the G20.

Financial system soundness
- The Financial Sector Assessment Program (FSAP) was launched jointly by the IMF and the World Bank in 1999. It provides member countries with a comprehensive evaluation of their financial systems, with a view to alerting national authorities on vulnerabilities in their financial sectors and assisting them in designing measures to reduce weaknesses. FSAP reports are designed to assess the stability of the financial system as a whole rather than as individual institutions.
- More recently, the G20 has requested the Financial Stability Board to monitor the progress in the implementation of regulatory and supervisory reforms and it together with the IMF to undertake "macro-prudential" monitoring to provide early warnings of systemic risks.

Crisis management

New financing instruments and credit lines at the IMF
- A New Arrangements to Borrow (NAB) was established in November 1998 doubling the resources of IMF. Under the auspices of the G20, the NAB has been increased by a further $500 billion.

Table 12.1   IFA reforms: post-Asian financial crisis efforts – *continued*

- The Contingent Credit Line (CCL) was introduced in 1999 as part of the IMF's efforts to strengthen member countries' defences against financial crises. This facility was never used and, in November 2003, the CCL was allowed to expire.
- In March 2009, IMF introduced the Flexible Credit Line to countries that meet pre-set qualification criteria. This Line replaces the earlier Short-Term Liquidity Facility, has no limit and is, therefore, particularly well-suited for crisis prevention. Columbia, Mexico, and Poland have been provided credits totalling $78 billion.

IMF conditionality
- The IMF initiated actions to limit structural conditions to a core set of essential features that are macro-relevant and in the IMF's core area of responsibility, with a broader approach requiring justification based upon the specific country situation.
- Starting May 2009, structural performance criteria have been discontinued for all IMF loans except when they are critical.
- IMF-supported programs now appear to have been tailored to individual country circumstances. Recent programs for Iceland, Costa Rica, Hungary and Guatemala allow for fiscal stimulus and deficits, and exchange rate stabilization.
- Bailing in private sector: Two methods were discussed: a contractual approach and a statutory approach. The former approach was adopted while a more comprehensive statutory approach was on hold.

Reform of IMF governance
- IMF has made efforts to increase quotas of emerging markets in phases. The first phase, where the total share of emerging markets is to be increased by 2.7 percentage points, with 54 members getting a small increase, was approved in April 2008. But the agreement has yet to be implemented.

Source: Kawai and Rana, 2009 and http://www.imf.org

inform market participants to allow for more effective market discipline, and inform IMF surveillance and World Bank country assistance strategies.

The IMF, World Bank, OECD, IOSCO, and BIS have established international standards in 12 areas to prevent a crisis, which are broadly categorized into three groups: (i) policy transparency; (ii) financial sector regulation and supervision; and (iii) market integrity. Standards in policy transparency include data transparency, fiscal transparency, and monetary and financial policy transparency. Standards on financial regulation and supervision cover five areas: banking supervision, securities, insurance, payments systems, and anti-money laundering and combating the financing of terrorism. Standards of market integrity include corporate governance, accounting, auditing, and insolvency and creditor rights. A number of these standards are now being revised because they turned out to be "pro-cyclical".[2]

A country's observance of standards in each of the 12 areas is assessed at the request of a member country, the IMF, or World Bank; the results of these assessments are then summarized in a Report on the Observance of Standards and Codes (ROSC). The report is the principal tool for assessing members' implementation of these standards and codes and in promoting global financial stability. Publication of these assessments by member countries is voluntary, although the IMF and World Bank encourage their publication.

Data transparency.   Data dissemination standards help to enhance the availability of timely and comprehensive statistics, which in turn contributes to designing sound macroeconomic policies. The IMF took several steps to enhance information transparency and openness, including the establishment and strengthening of data dissemination standards to help countries prevent future crises and diminish the effect of unavoidable ones.

The standards for data dissemination consist of two tiers. The first, called the Special Data Dissemination Standard (SDDS), was established in 1996 to guide countries that have, or might seek, access to international capital markets. The second tier, the General Data Dissemination System (GDDS), was established in 1997 to help countries provide more reliable data. The GDDS is focused on improving statistical systems, while the SDDS focuses on commitments to data dissemination standards in countries that already meet high data quality standards. Both are voluntary. Countries must also agree to post information about their data dissemination practices on the IMF's external website on Dissemination Standards Bulletin Board (DSBB), and establish an Internet site containing the actual data, called a National Summary Data Page (NSDP), to which the DSBB is linked.

Financial system soundness and surveillance.   It was also realized that problems in the financial system can reduce the effectiveness of monetary policy, create large fiscal costs related to bailing out troubled financial institutions, trigger capital flight, and deepen economic recessions. Financial weaknesses in one country can also trigger contagion effects on others. A sound financial system is thus essential for supporting economic growth. It includes banks, securities exchanges, pension funds, insurers, the central bank and national regulators.

The IMF sought to strengthen its surveillance. Surveillance refers to the process of regular dialogue and policy advice provided to member countries. It covers macroeconomic and financial developments and policies. Under the new Mid-term Strategy endorsed in September 2005, IMF conducts multilateral consultations on common economic and financial issues with the first focusing on global payments imbalances. The first such surveillance involving several systemically important members – USA, China, the Euro area, Japan and Saudi Arabia – have not been very effective as the global imbalance problem was serious in the pre-GEC period and contributed to the GEC.

IMF surveillance was also fine-tuned to focus more systematically on regional developments, including through increased dialogue with regional institutions and think tanks. It also started to publish regional outlook reports for the major regions of the world. IMF-supported programs now include measures to strengthen financial systems, including financial assistance and assisting member countries in identifying and diagnosing financial system problems, designing strategies for systemic reforms and bank restructuring, and ensuring that these strategies are consistent with appropriate macroeconomic and structural policies.

A joint IMF-World Bank initiative, called the Financial Sector Assessment Program (FSAP), was launched in 1999. It provides member countries with a comprehensive evaluation of their financial systems, with a view to alerting national authorities on vulnerabilities in their financial sectors and assisting them in designing measures to reduce weaknesses. The FSAP also determines the development needs of the financial sector. Sectoral developments, risks and vulnerabilities are analyzed using a range of financial soundness indicators and macro-financial stress tests. Other areas of financial stability are also analyzed, including systemic liquidity arrangements, institutional framework for crisis management and loan recovery, transparency, accountability and governance. IMF had reportedly requested the US to undergo an FSAP prior to the outbreak of the subprime mortgage, but it was only at the end of 2007 that the US agreed.

In the aftermath of the AFC, two new institutions were established in 1999. These were the G20 process for finance ministers and central bank governors and the Financial Stability Forum (FSF) for financial authorities (finance ministers, central bankers and regulatory authorities). With the outbreak of the GEC, the G20 was upgraded to the Summit level or a leaders process and the FSF was upgraded to the Financial Stability Board (FSB) with a bigger mandate and a larger membership (all G20 members have now been included and the total membership is 25).

Capital account deregulation. Recent financial crises in emerging market economies have demonstrated that abrupt or improperly sequenced liberalization of capital account can generate vulnerabilities and a crisis. A sudden surge in capital inflows and a sudden stop or reversal of capital flows can occur precipitating a crisis. This was an important lesson learnt from the Asian financial crisis. Most important is the establishment of core institutional infrastructure – well-defined property and creditor rights, credible accounting standards, benchmark corporate governance, clear minority rights, and stringent prudential and regulatory regimes. However, the IMF continued to promote "financial, including capital market liberalization, although Articles of Agreement clearly allow governments to use capital controls" (UN, 2009). The need for a sequenced deregulation of the capital account is an important lesson from the GEC. Recently, Brazil introduced a 2% tax on foreign purchases of equity and debt. Other countries are also considering similar measures.

Crisis management

New financing instruments and credit lines. In order to play its role in safeguarding the international financial stability, in the immediate aftermath of the AFC, in November 1998 the IMF established a New Arrangements to Borrow (NAB), thereby, doubling its resources. Further increases were made in response to the GEC.

The Contingent Credit Line (CCL) was introduced in 1999 as part of the IMF's efforts to strengthen member countries' defenses against financial crisis. CCL was intended to be a precautionary line of defense to help protect countries pursuing strong policies in the event of a liquidity need arising from the spread of financial crises. For various reasons, however, the facility was never used and, in November 2003, the CCL was allowed to expire.

In 2008, in response to the GEC, the IMF reintroduced a contingent credit line: a new Short-term Liquidity Facility (SLF) to offer quick, large-scale financing without specific conditionality. But even the SLF proved inadequate. In March 2009, it was replaced by a Flexible Credit Line (FCL) which assures pre-qualified countries with large amounts of resources without ex-post conditions. The FCL also allows a longer repayment period of three and a quarter to five years.

IMF conditionality. At the time of the AFC, the IMF came in for harsh criticism for prescribing too many structural reforms. For example, the Indonesian program had over 100 conditions including the dismantling of the clove monopoly. Over time, the IMF has streamlined its programs to limit structural conditionality to a core set of essential features that are macro-relevant and in the IMF's core area of responsibility,[3] with a broader approach requiring justification based upon the specific country situation. More recent IMF-supported programs appear to have been tailored to individual country circumstances. To some extent, IMF now seems ready to move away from "one-size fits-all" approach to stabilization. Recent programs for Iceland, Costa Rica, Hungary and Guatemala allow for fiscal stimulus and deficits, and exchange rate stabilization. But how widely this flexibility is used remains to be seen.

Private sector involvement. In the post-AFC period, the international community started to explore possible mechanisms for official standstill provisions, or private sector involvement (PSI). It focused on the debt restructuring of international sovereign bonds with the recognition that, at the time of a liquidity crisis, holders of sovereign bonds, along with other creditors, would need to contribute to the resolution of such crises. Two methods were recommended: a contractual approach and a statutory approach. A contractual approach considers collective action clauses (CACs) in sovereign bond contracts as a device for orderly resolution of crises; their explicit inclusion in bond documentation would provide a degree of predictability to the restructuring process. A statutory approach, such as the Sovereign Debt Restructuring Mechanism (SDRM), attempts to create the legal basis – through universal treaty rather than through a set of national laws in a limited number of jurisdictions – for establishing adequate incentives for debtors and creditors to agree upon a prompt, orderly and predictable restructuring of unsustainable debt. The CACs approach was adopted while a more comprehensive statutory approach was put on hold. However, the lack of sovereign debt restructuring mechanism – a *de facto* international bankruptcy procedure – continues to make crisis resolution difficult (more recently, in Iceland and Baltic states)

Reform of IMF governance

Governance reforms at the IMF. These reforms refer to quotas and voting rights, executive board representation, and the management of the IMF. IMF quotas and voting rights must be substantially realigned to recognize better the economic and financial weight of emerging markets including those in Asia. Presently, the industrial countries as a group hold about 60% of the quotas and voting rights, with the emerging markets holding 20% and the rest of the developing countries holding the remaining 20%. These ratios have not changed significantly over time and do not reflect the growing size of emerging markets in the global economy. Since 85% of the votes are required for major decisions, the US which holds 17% of the quota is the only country that has a veto power at the IMF.

At the 2006 annual meeting of the IMF and the World Bank held in Singapore, a decision was taken to increase the quotas of China, Mexico, South Korea and Turkey by relatively small amounts. In April 2008, an agreement was reached to increase quotas of a larger number of countries (54) by also a small amount. But this agreement has yet to be implemented. Quota reform is a highly charged issue as it means a loss of power for countries that have a large voice at the IMF. At the Pittsburgh Summit, the leaders pledged to transfer at least 5% of the quota to emerging markets by January 2011.

Occupying eight of the 24 chairs and represented in another constituency at the IMF Board, there is a feeling among academics and policymakers that European countries are over-represented at the IMF. With the establishment of a monetary union, Europe should occupy fewer seats. Aside from the broad statements made, little concrete action has been taken so far.

Finally, as Mahbubani (2008) has pointed out, the rule that the head of the IMF should be a Western European automatically disqualifies 88% of world's population from leadership of this global economic institution. The choice of IMF head should be based on merit and qualifications and not on nationality. This issue has also not been addressed as yet.

One could sum up actions taken to reform the IFA in the immediate aftermath of the AFC as: while encouraging progress was made on crisis prevention efforts, and some progress was achieved on crisis management efforts, progress in reforming IMF governance was very limited. In view of the latter, many felt that the IMF had lost legitimacy in its operations and was sidelined. Its lending operation had declined significantly and it was also suffering from a precarious financial situation. IMF credit outstanding which had peaked at almost $100 billion at the end of 2005, had declined to about $10 billion by the end of September 2008. IMF's income, which is related to its lending operations, had dwindled and staff retrenchments had begun. But in the aftermath of the GEC, the IMF was called to assist more and more countries affected by crisis.

Post-global economic crisis reforms of IFA

The GEC has once again led to calls for the reform of the IFA for various reasons.[4] First, the GEC has illustrated clearly that the view that financial markets regulate themselves was not only wrong but could also be highly damaging. Supervisors failed to prevent excessive risk-taking and leveraging by financial institutions. Market failures, due in part to rapid financial innovation, discredited the regulatory model that relied on transparency, disclosure, and market discipline to curb inordinate risk-taking. There is now an emerging consensus on the changes that are to be made: higher capital requirements, particularly for trading; closer supervision of shadow banks and derivatives market; lighter liquidity controls; and restrictions on bankers' bonuses These changes need to be implemented both nationally as well as internationally.

Second, the crisis has also highlighted the need for a coordinated approach beyond national borders. This is because one of the factors of the rapid panic around the world was the lack of a clear mechanism for regulating, information sharing and monitoring international banks. Also the lack of clear rules for crisis resolution and burden sharing led authorities to ring-fence assets in their jurisdictions.[5] The Iceland example is good. We should have more examples and not just in the footnote.

Third, the GEC has also highlighted that a missing component in both global and domestic regulations was "macro-prudential supervision". Someone has to be looking not only at the risks run by specific institutions (micro-prudential monitoring) but also at the systemic risks that arise because of actions taken across groups of institutions. Such an analysis might have identified risks arising from widespread growth of shadow banks and dangerous asset bubbles that precipitated the GEC.[6]

Fourth, once again, global organizations such as the IMF, the World Bank, and the BIS were not effective in identifying systemic risks in the US, UK, and the EU. In its Article IV consultations with the US throughout 2005–2006, IMF staff was preoccupied with reducing fiscal and external deficits and maintaining control over inflation as the main policy challenge, while assuring that the "US financial sector has proven exceptionally resilient in recent years" (IMF, 2005; IMF, 2006). Even a month before the beginning of the credit crunch, IMF staff argued that "the most likely scenario is a soft landing as growth recovers and inflation falls, although both are subject to risks" (IMF, 2007).

There were calls from President Nicholas Sarkozy in September 2008 to revamp the international financial system to deal with the problem of unfettered capital movements: "We must rethink the financial system from scratch, as at Bretton Woods".[7] In a similar vein, Prime Minister Gordon Brown in October 2008 said " We must have a new Bretton Woods, building on a new international financial architecture for the years ahead".[8] European leaders were united in calling for a new "Bretton Woods II" to redesign the world's financial architecture.[9] President Bush was agreeable to the calls and organized the first Summit of the G20 in Washington DC in November 2008. Since then, the G20 has been tasked, among others, to oversee reforms of the international financial architecture. The first Summit set in a motion a number of "big picture" reforms,[10] but as expected it did not take any concrete steps as it was too early to do so. This Summit established four Working Groups to support the group.[11] The second G20 Summit in London in April 2009, came up with three concrete pledges to: (i) provide more resources ($1.1 trillion) to the IMF and other multilateral institutions; (ii) strengthen prudential regulation of the financial sector through various measures; and (iii) upgrade the Financial Stability Forum into a Financial Stability Board for global financial surveillance and with an expanded mandate and a larger membership comprising all G20 members. The Summit, however, could not reach a consensus on the need for fiscal stimulus and on how to resolve the "toxic" assets held by "zombie" banks – the heart of the GEC (see Chapter 1). While the latter two pledges sought to prevent crisis in the future, the first sought to resolve the GEC through the involvement of IFIs. The $1.1 trillion comprised: (i) $500 billion pledged to the IMF to triple its resources; (ii) a new SDR allocation of $250 billion; (iii) a $250 billion trade finance facility; and (iv) $100 billion of development assistance.

With the worst of the GEC over, the third G20 Summit held in Pittsburgh in September 2009, moved on to the next phase of action – implementing an ambitious framework designed to correct global imbalances and improve global policy coordination and to rebuild confidence in IFA. The Summit also firmly established the G20 as the "premier forum" for international economic cooperation replacing the G7/G8 which is to focus more on security and foreign policy issues. Table 12.2 summarizes the key reforms agreed upon at the recent third G20 Summit.

Crisis prevention

Framework for strong, sustainable and balanced growth. On crisis prevention, the G20 Leaders at the Pittsburgh summit agreed to initiate a peer

Table 12.2   IFA reforms: outcomes of the third G-20 Summit

Crisis prevention

Framework for strong, sustainable and balanced growth
- The Leaders pledged not to withdraw stimulus measures until a durable recovery was in place. They agreed to coordinate their exit strategies.
- They agreed to harmonize economic policies to avoid global "imbalances ... and destabilising booms and busts in asset and credit prices."
- They agreed to initiate "a cooperative process of mutual assessment of policy frameworks and the implications of those frameworks for the pattern and sustainability of global growth." Also, "G-20 members will set out medium-term policy frameworks and will work together to assess the collective implications of national policy frameworks for the level and pattern of global growth and identify potential risks to financial stability." The IMF will help "with its analysis of how respective national and regional policy frameworks fit together." The World Bank will advise on progress in promoting development and poverty reduction. The FSB will monitor progress in implementing regulatory and supervisory reforms and it, together with the IMF, will undertake "macro-prudential" monitoring to provide early warnings of systemic risks.

Strengthening international financial regulatory systems
- Internationally-agreed rules to improve quantity and quality of bank capital to mitigate pro-cyclicity are to be developed by the end of 2010 and implemented by the end of 2012. The Leaders supported the introduction of a leverage ratio as a supplementary measure to the Basel II Capital framework.
- On reforming compensation practices to support financial stability, the leaders endorsed the implementation of standards developed by the FSB. The FSB is to propose additional measures as required by March 2010.
- All standardized OTC derivative contracts should be traded as exchanges or electronic trading platforms by the end of 2012.
- International accounting bodies are to develop a single set of global accounting standards by June 2011.

Crisis management and resolution

Additional resources to the IMF
- The Leaders noted that they had delivered on their promise to treble the resources available to the IMF. They had committed over $500 billion to a renewed and expanded IMF New Agreement to Borrow (NAB). The IMF has made SDR allocations of $283 billion.

Introduction of flexible credit line
- The Leaders welcomed the introduction of the innovative Flexible Credit Line by the IMF.

Reform of IMF governance
- The Leaders also agreed to implement the package of IMF quota and voice the reforms agreed in April 2008.
- The Leaders committed to a shift in quota share to dynamic emerging markets and developing countries of at least 5% from over-represented to under-represented countries, by January 2011. A similar shift of 3% is to happen at the World Bank.

Table 12.2   IFA reforms: outcomes of the third G-20 Summit – *continued*

- As part of the quota review, the Leaders will work to start on a new quota formula by October 2009 and agreed that other critical issues such as the size and composition of the Executive Board, ways of enhancing the Board's effectiveness, and the Board of Governors' involvement in the strategic oversight of the IMF, needs to be addressed.
- The Leaders agreed that the heads and senior leadership of all international institutions should be appointed through an open, transparent and merit-based process.

Source: G20 Leaders Statement: Pittsburgh Summit, 24–25 September 2009

review process or "a cooperative process of mutual assessment of policy frameworks and the implications of those frameworks for the pattern and sustainability of global growth" (G20 Leaders Statement: Pittsburgh Summit, 2009). The Leaders went on to add that "G20 members will set out medium-term policy frameworks and will work together to assess the collective implications of national policy frameworks for the level and pattern of global growth and identify potential risks to financial stability." The IMF is to help "with its analysis of how respective national and regional policy frameworks fit together." The World Bank is to advise on progress in promoting development and poverty reduction. The FSB is to monitor progress in implementing regulatory and supervisory reforms and it, together with the IMF, is to undertake "macro-prudential" monitoring to provide early warnings of systemic risks.

Strengthening international regulatory systems.   At the Pittsburgh Summit, there was broad agreement on the need for tightening regulations both at the national and international level, but partly reflecting the complexity of the issues, views appear to have differed on how best to regulate and the degree of regulation. A few agreements were announced. The Leaders pledged to develop internationally-agreed rules to improve quantity and quality of bank capital by the end of 2010 and implement them by 2012. All standardized over-the-counter (OTC) derivatives contracts are to be traded on electronic trading platforms, where appropriate, and cleared through central clearinghouses by the end of 2012. They also endorsed guidelines for bankers' pay but mentioned that the FSB is to propose additional measures by March 2010. International accounting bodies are to develop a single set of global accounting standards by June 2011.

With financial globalization, the case for financial regulations being international is strong for a number of reasons. This means that national decisions must be made with domestic as well as external consequences in mind. First, to avoid adverse global spillovers, national regulation should be subject to multilateral discipline. Second, multilateral rules would level the playing field and prevent regulatory arbitrage – that is, institutions moving from tightly to lightly regulated countries. Third, multilateral rules would reduce the influence of politicians and give regulators more room for maneuver.

A supreme international body with full-fledged regulatory and supervisory powers over all financial institutions is not possible as countries are not willing to give up autonomy over national policies. Eichengreen (2009) has, therefore, recommended the establishment of the World Financial Organization, a WTO-type system for financial regulation where within binding multilateral agreements national authorities have some autonomy with global oversight and sanction (discussed later in the chapter).

The G20 has instead adopted a more network-based approach to financial regulation rather a rules-based one with sanctions. This means extending the mandates and improving the governance of existing bodies like the FSB, the Basel Committee on Banking Supervision and colleges of supervisors (as agreed to by the G7 in April 2008), the International Association of Insurance Supervisors, and the International Organization of Securities Commissions and encouraging a voluntary process of closer coordination among national regulators based on agreed multilateral frameworks without any sanction.

Introduction of the flexible credit line.   The G20 Leaders also welcomed the introduction of the innovative Flexible Credit Line by the IMF. Under this new facility, the IMF will provide funds with no hard cap on access limit to countries meeting pre-set qualification criteria. This Line is expected to be particularly useful for crisis prevention. Three countries – Colombia, Mexico and Poland – have been provided credits totaling $78 billion under this facility.

Crisis management and resolution

Additional resources to the IMF.   On crisis management and resolution, the G20 Leaders announced that they had delivered on their promise to triple the resources of the IMF. They had committed over $500 billion to a renewed and expanded NAB and the IMF had made a new SDR allocation of $283 billion. The latter was allocated among the IMF's members in line with existing patterns of quotas which means that the G7 members, which do not need liquidity support from the IMF, got a large chunk of it (45%).

Reform of IMF governance

IMF Reforms.   On the reform of IMF quota and voice, the Leaders pledged to implement the package agreed in April 2008. They also pledged to shift at least 5% of quota share to dynamic emerging markets and developing countries[12] by January 2011 under the present quota formula. Work is to start on a new IMF quota formula by October 2009. A shift of 3% in quota to emerging countries was also pledged at the World Bank.

On the size and composition of the Executive Board and leadership of the IMF and the World Bank, the Leaders agreed that the issues needed further review. But, no concrete actions and pledges were announced.

Longer-term issues in reforming of the IFA

In addition to the reforms that are now being discussed at the G20, there are several longer-term issues which need the attention of the G20 (UN, 2009; Eichengreen, 2009). The remaining issues in the area of crisis prevention are the establishment of a: Stable system of international reserves, review of need for a Global Glass-Steagall Act, Global systemic risk facility, and World Financial Organization. Also a Multilateral Insolvency Trust needs to be established for international banks when they fail.

Stable system of international reserves.   A reserve system based on a national currency as a means of international settlement and a reserve system suffers from a major dilemma. This was pointed out by Triffin (1960) almost half a century ago when he questioned the viability of the Bretton Woods system based on the US dollar. In a dollar-based system net holding of dollar assets by the rest of the world depends on the US running current account deficits. If the US stopped running deficits, the shortage of international liquidity would stifle global trade, investment and growth. If, on the other hand, the US runs global deficits and supplies adequate liquidity to the world, the accumulation of liabilities could undermine the confidence in the dollar. Restoring confidence in the dollar and overcoming inflationary pressure would then call for the US to tighten monetary and fiscal policy which would adversely affect growth. Therefore, while issuing a reserve currency gives a country an advantage in financing its deficits, it can also be problematical.

Indeed one of the important reasons for the collapse of the Bretton Woods system was that the post-World War II dollar shortage (until the 1960s) was transformed into a dollar glut with growing US deficits which made it impossible to maintain dollar convertibility at the fixed rate.[13] After the collapse of the Bretton Woods system it was expected that the need for dollar reserves would decline as countries responded to external deficits by adjusting exchange rates. On the contrary, demand for dollars increased. Japan and Germany were reluctant to "internationalize" their currencies. Also international capital flows increased the vulnerability of emerging markets to sudden stops and reversals in such flows and emerging markets, therefore, responded by self-insuring themselves by accumulating large amounts of reserves, mainly in US dollars.

Many believe that the problems of the current reserve system could be eliminated by creating a supra-national currency. The G20 has so far remained silent on this idea but it certainly is an idea whose time has come. One proposal discussed by the Stiglitz Commission (United Nations,

2009a), which has also been reiterated by several others (e.g. Bergsten, 2007; Zhou, 2009), is to establish a "substitution account" at the IMF. This idea was first discussed in the 1970s to facilitate diversification from dollars without creating a dollar crisis. The idea was giving central banks the possibility of depositing dollars in a special "substitution account" at the IMF to be denominated in SDRs. The SDRs could also be used to settle international payments. Since the SDRs is valued as the weighted average of the major currencies, its value is more stable than each of the constituent currencies. This does not mean that the exchange rate risk would disappear; it would simply be transferred to the IMF for which a solution would have to be found.

A more radical proposal of the Stiglitz Commission is to establish a "Global Reserve Bank" to issue an "artificial" reserve currency such as the "bancor" – a weighted average of 10 major currencies – suggested by Keynes in his Bretton Woods proposal for an International Clearing Union (ICU).[14] Every member country would have an overdraft facility on its bancor account at the ICU. Keynes proposed that any country having a large trade deficit would be charged an interest in its account and would be obliged to depreciate its currency. Similarly, any country that had a surplus would also be charged an interest and would be required to appreciate its currency. Adjustment policies would, therefore, be symmetrical. At the end of the year, any remaining surplus would be confiscated. This proposal was, however, rejected by his American counterparts who instead proposed the International Monetary Fund, which would place the entire burden of adjustment on the deficit countries.

As the Stiglitz Commission notes, "Existing regional agreements might provide an alternative way of evolving toward a Global Reserve System". Regional reserve pools could issue alternative reserve assets which could be attractive for countries to hold. For example, the Latin American Reserve Fund established in the 1980s was allowed to issue Andean pesos. This asset, which has never been used so far, was expected to be used in intraregional trade, with periodic clearing of those held by central banks. In Asia, the bilateral swaps under the Chiang Mai Initiative have been mutlilateralized to a crisis fund of $120 billion. Eventually, the fund could issue a regional unit of account that could be used in settling intraregional trade. The Stiglitz Commission notes that one possibility is that a reformed IMF could be a network of regional funds especially if the governance of the IMF cannot be reformed. Such a decentralized system would have many advantages, including the possibility of resolving crisis at the regional level. The proposal could also be attractive to larger countries which could have a stronger voice at the regional level. One way to link regional and global arrangements would be to make the contributions to regional arrangements one factor to take into account in determining SDR allocations.

Global Glass-Steagall Act. There is a conflict between banks' core functions of providing a safe repository for household savings and the payments system, on one hand, and the advantage of diversification into the originating, distributing, and investing in risky assets utilizing wholesale funding and leverage. The second strategy offers economies of scale and diversification but may undermine banks' ability to carry out their safe-repository and payments-system function. The repeal of the Glass-Steagall Act in the US in 1999 permitted banks to branch into these risky lines of credit which precipitated the crisis. The broken dealer institutions (the shadow banks) no longer able to make comfortable living by underwriting new issues, issued new kinds of derivative securities and leveraged their operations. One option to prevent crisis in the future would therefore be to reimpose Glass-Steagall-like restrictions dividing the banking and financial system into two components – the commercial banking system would focus on mobilizing household savings for relative safe investments, while the investment banks would be allowed to invest in riskier assets. To be effective, however, in a financial integrated world such reforms would be feasible only if coordinated internationally.

Global systemic risk facility. Kashyap, Rajan, and Stein (2008) and Nishimura (2008) have suggested protecting banks against systemic risk by requiring them to purchase capital insurance. Rather than holding additional capital at all points in time in order to protect against systemic shocks against which a bit of additional capital will be an inadequate buffer, they recommend that banks sell financial catastrophic (CAT) bonds, paying insurance premia whose cost is equivalent to a bit of additional capital in good times in return for a large payout in the event that systemic risk materializes. For this scheme to work, there would have to be a counterparty prepared to put its own capital at risk. Eichengreen (2009) recommends that the IMF play such a role by establishing a Global Systemic Risk Facility and provide insurance against systemic risks.

World Financial Organization. As outlined above, the G20's approach for reforming international financial regulation is a voluntary network-based approach rather than a rules-based one with sanctions. Given that recent experiences have shown that adverse international spillovers from financial policies in industrial countries can be much more serious and damaging to developing countries than trade shocks, Eichengren (2009) makes the case for establishing a World Financial Organization (WFO) analogous to the already-existing World Trade Organization (WTO). In the same way that the WTO establishes principles for trade policy without specifying outcomes, the WFO would establish principles for prudential supervision (capital and liquidity requirements, limits on portfolio concentrations and connected lending, adequacy of risk measurement systems and internal controls) without attempting to prescribe the structure of regulation in detail. The WFO would define obligations for its members; the latter would be obliged to meet international standards for supervision and regulation for their financial markets. Membership would be mandatory for all countries seeking access to foreign markets. The WFO would appoint independent panel of experts to determine whether countries were in compliance of those obligations failing which the authorities would be able to impose sanctions against countries that fail to comply. Eichengreen reiterates that the WFO would not dictate regulatory conditions on countries.

Multilateral Insolvency Trust.   An important gap in the IFA highlighted by the GEC is the absence of a regime to deal with the insolvency of a major bank or other institutions doing business in multiple countries. International insolvencies are managed by separate national insolvency regimes each of which appoints a fiduciary (or trustee or administrator) to assume control of the firm and its assets, value and prioritize creditor claim, and reorganize and liquidate firms. But fiduciaries of different nationalities see their priorities differently. Consistency through the establishment of a Multilateral Insolvency Trust could go a long way in ensuring orderly insolvencies of financial institutions.

Conclusions

An evaluation by Kawai and Rana (2009) of the immediate post-Asian Financial Crisis efforts to reform IFA had concluded that while encouraging progress had been made on crisis prevention efforts, and some progress had been achieved on crisis management and resolution efforts, progress in reforming IMF governance had been very limited. Hence the legitimacy and effectiveness of the IMF was strongly questioned. Although it is still too early to fully assess the impacts of the post-GEC efforts under the auspices of the G20, an early assessment in this paper has reached a similar conclusion.

There is once again the possibility that the faster than expected recovery from the GEC could lead to complacency. If so, vulnerability to future crises would remain. Hopefully, however, it will not happen this time around as the process is now being led by the G20 and developing countries are important stakeholders in this process. Post-AFC efforts were led by the G7/G8 and developing countries had no representation.

There are two ways of looking at the achievements of the G20 Summits so far. It looks like that the IMF is a clear winner. As mentioned above, in the immediate pre-crisis period the IMF was perceived by many as an institution which had lost legitimacy and was heading towards irrelevance. The crisis has elevated the IMF to an innovative crisis-responder. IMF's lending volume which had dwindled to $10 billion in 2007, has increased to

$160 billion (the peak was $150 in 2005). Its lending capacity has been tripled to $750 billion by the G20. The G20 has also given the IMF, together with the FBS, an important role in its newly established "peer review process". To its credit, the IMF has also re-invented itself to a large extent by streamlining conditionality and by introducing new credit lines. This turnaround of the IMF is to be applauded. Nevertheless, the institution continues to lack legitimacy and trust of many and is viewed as an agent of western countries. The lack of legitimacy stems from the limited progress made in reforming its governance as Western countries are reluctant to give up their political clout in dictating the direction and priorities of the IMF. Eventually the G20 must put its money where its mouth is and place reform of IMF governance on the top of its agenda otherwise all its other achievements will lack effectiveness. If so, as noted by the Stiglitz Commission, the future financial architecture could be a network of regional funds with the IMF in a coordinating role.

A broader view is that the developing world has also come out as a winner. At the Pittsburgh Summit, the Leaders designated the G20 as the "premier forum" for international economic cooperation replacing the G7/G8 which would focus more on security and foreign policies issues. As compared to the Western-dominated G7/G8, the G20 brings the main industrialized countries together with systemically important developing countries such as China, India and Brazil. This decision is historic because it recognizes the growing economic weight of developing countries in the world economy and represents the passing of the baton to them.

Another reason why the Pittsburgh Summit was historic is that it introduced a "peer review" system of each member's macroeconomic and financial policies.[15] This is because in a globalized world, policies spill over national boundaries. Under this framework, the IMF is to help G20 assess collective implications and potential risks of the sum of their disparate growth strategies. The World Bank is also to help in promoting development and poverty reduction as part of the rebalancing of global growth. And the FBS and IMF are to help jointly in "macro-prudential supervision" to help prevent credit and asset price cycles from becoming forces for destabilization.

The G20 Summit should be seen as a process and not an event. The first Summit was held in November 2008 and so far only three Summits have been held. One important issue is that of inclusiveness. The G20 represents 4.2 billion people of the world but the other 2.6 billion people are not represented. How can their views be incorporated? There is, of course, a trade-off between effectiveness and inclusiveness. A related issue is that of the G20 agenda. So far the focus has been on the continuation of stimulus packages which has brought about faster than expected recovery globally, coordination of exit strategies, and designing a new international financial regulatory framework. Issues of trade and IMF governance which are of relevance to developing countries have figured less prominently in the G20 discussions. For example, the Leaders' statement mentions "We are determined to seek an ambitious and balanced conclusion to the Doha Development Round in 2010". But no concrete actions are mentioned on how this important objective is to be achieved.

Now that they have been invited to participate in the discussions, the onus is on developing countries to make sure that they are heard effectively. One way is for them to form a coalition of the unrepresented, a group of their own. But even if developing countries were successful in establishing such a coalition, it is not clear how the coalition could obtain a seat at the G20 table. Otherwise such a grouping could simply add to the recent proliferation of groupings or to the so-called alphabet soup.

A second way would be to involve Chairs of various regional groupings in the G20 Summits. So far, the Chairs of the ASEAN (since the London Summit) and APEC (since the Pittsburgh Summit) are invited to the Summits.[16] This status needs to be regularized and Chairs of selected regional groupings from other parts of the world could also be invited as observers in future meetings.

Notes

Chapter 1 Introduction

1 These refer to Generation I models developed by Krugman and Generation II models developed by Krugman and Obsfeld.
2 Europe is in the process of setting up the European Systemic Risk Board as a macro-prudential monitor and the European System of Financial Supervisors for micro-prudential coordination.

Chapter 2 The Crisis and How it Unfolded in the Industrial Countries

1 The term shadow banking was coined by Paul McCulley of Pimco, a management consulting company.
2 Blanchard, 2008, p. 4.
3 Speech by Timothy Geithner titled "Reducing Systemic Risk in a Dynamic Financial System", June 2008. At the time Geithner was President and CEO of NY Federal Reserve Bank.
4 Investment banks issue and sell securities, insure bonds (credit default swap sales) and provide advice on mergers and acquisitions as well as trade of derivatives, fixed income, foreign exchange and commodities.
5 See Federal Reserve Bank of San Francisco Economic Letter, February 6, 2009 House Prices and Bank Loan Performance.
6 Definitions from Wikipedia website.
7 See Gillian Tell and Paul J. Davies "Out of the shadows: How banking's secrecy system broke down", *Financial Times* December 16, 2007.
8 Federal Home Loan Mortgage Corporation commonly known as Freddie Mac and Federal National Mortgage Association commonly know as Fannie Mae.
9 Center for Responsible Lending 2007, A Snapshot of the Subprime Market, accessed for website on 25 April 2009.
10 Blanchard op. cit., p. 7 for BIS data.
11 ibid p. 8.
12 Milkin Institute – Mortgage Crisis Overview, http://www.scribd.com/doc/6371820/Milken-Institute-Mortgage-Crisis-Overview accessed on 19 April 2009.
13 See United Nations, 2009 Global Outlook, Chapter 1.
14 ibid.
15 Milkin Institute, op. cit.
16 See C.J. Boggs, Credit Default Swaps: AIG's Unregulated Killer? MyNewMarkets.com at http://mynewmarkets.com
17 Adam Davidson, How AIG fell apart, Reuters, 18 September 2008 accessed at http://www.reuters.com/articlePrint?articleId=USMAR85972720080918
18 Key Development Data and Statistics, World Bank accessed from World Bank website on 11 April 2009.
19 Adam Davidson, op. cit.
20 ibid.
21 Charles W. Calomiris and Peter J. Wallison, "Blame Fannie Mae and Congress for the Credit Mess", *Wall Street Journal*, September 23 2008.

22 According to Credit Suisse and quoted in Center for Responsible Lending, 2007.
23 At the risk of showing prejudice we recommend two books by Nobel Prize winners and another by a student of a Nobel Prize winner. Paul Krugman (2009) *The Return of Depression Economics and the Crisis of 2008*, Norton, New York; George A. Akerlof and Robert J. Shiller (2009) *Animal Spirits – How Human Psychology Drives the Economy and Why it Matters for Global Capitalism*, Princeton University Press, New Haven; Mark Zandi (2009) *Financial Shock – Global Panic and Government Bailouts – How We Got Here and What Must be Done to Fix it*, FT Press, Upper Saddle River, New Jersey.

Chapter 4   Policy Responses – Industrial Countries

1 See CBO 2009 January 2009 Budget and Economic Outlook and also Menzie Chinn (2009, May 29) More Thoughts on Potential GDP and Output Gap, in Global Macro EconoMonitor accessed at http://www.rgemonitor,com/globalmacromonitor/256934/more_thoughts_on_potential_gdp_and_the_output_gap

Chapter 5   Impacts of the Global Crisis on Asia and Outlook

1 Asian Development Bank (2009) *Asian Economic Monitor*, July, Table 9, p. 24.

Chapter 6   Policy Responses – Asia

1 IMF World Economic Outlook (2009) Chapter 3, p. 132.
2 See A. Ghosh, M. Chamon, C. Crowe, Jun I Kim and J.D. Ostry (2009) Coping with the Crisis: Policy Options for Emerging Market Countries, IMF Staff Position Note, April 23 and the Federal Reserve's Term Asset-Backed Loan Facility (TALF).
3 The IMF definition of Asia-Pacific leave out some of the countries we have been focusing on and includes others, i.e. Japan.
4 In the IMF analysis fiscal space is a weighted average of seven indicators including saving investment gap, debt to GDP ratio, fiscal balance, inflation and current account balance, institutional constraints and capacity and efficiency of public spending constraints.
5 The stimulus in the United States, estimated to be 3% of GDP is about half the estimated gap for 2009 and 2010 (0.5). This is about the same order of magnitude as the average for Asian economies, which is calculated as 0.63 from the final column of Table 6.5. Preliminary analysis suggests that the greater stimulus in China and Indonesia resulted in acceleration in growth in 2009. Paul Krugman has argued that the US stimulus is too small and has resulted in stagnating growth and continuing high unemployment. This could be because the US recession, unlike Asian economies, had financial sector and real sector components not unlike Thailand, Indonesia and Malaysia. All of these economies suffered extensive declines in GDP during the Asian financial crisis. Yet the situation in the United States has an additional component of labor market stickiness that is keeping employers from adding new workers as the economy recovers.

Chapter 7   Where We Stand at the Beginning of 2010

1   See Chapter 1 for time line of policies in the US.

Chapter 10   Individual Country Responses and Prospects

1   Using PPP to value GDP, the figure would be more than double.
2   See the Center for Science and Environment (2008) for a comprehensive analysis of India's NREGA and suggested reforms needed.

Chapter 11   Economic Integration in Asia: Trends and Policies

1   Pan-Asia is defined as the South Asian and East Asian sub-regions of Asia. Other sub-regions of Asia are not considered.
2   The recent emergence and integration of Asia are not without historical precedence. During much of the first 18 centuries of human history, Asia not only dominated the world economy but was a well-connected and well-integrated region of the world (Rana, 2009).
3   Regionalism or regional cooperation policies refer to official activities that encourage regional integration and/or help to shape coordinated actions and responses to developments that affect the region. Regional integration is a process that leads to greater interdependence within a region. Regional integration may be market-driven or regional cooperation policy-led. Regional cooperation policies in Africa and Latin America were not successful because they sought to promote import-substitution policies at the regional level. Regionalism in Asia is, by contrast, open regionalism which sees regionalism as a stepping stone to multilateralism.
4   Given that the Asian financial crisis was a capital account crisis, the IMF should not have required Asian countries to tighten fiscal policy and raise interest rates. It should also not have gone overboard in requiring these countries to meet many structural conditions that were imposed in its program. Its approach to financial and corporate reforms was also inappropriate, at least, in Indonesia. Subsequently, the IMF accepted many of these criticisms (IMF, 2003).
5   ADB's database in www.aric.adb.org.
6   The "double mismatch" problem refers to borrowing unhedged foreign funds to lend long term in domestic currency and borrowing short term to lend long term. The "original sin" is a situation where emerging economy residents cannot borrow abroad in domestic currency nor borrow long term, even domestically. Hence domestic banks and corporations tend to face a currency or maturity mismatch or both, thus facing balance-sheet vulnerabilities to sharp changes in exchange rates and/or interest rates.
7   This website tracks developments in East Asia's local currency bond markets and provides detailed progress reports on the various ABMI initiatives, among others.
8   Japan and China are to contribute identical shares of the total reserve pool (32%) double of South Korea's share (16%). The remaining 20% will be covered by ASEAN. See www.aseansecretariat.org/22536.htm for other details.
9   These correspond to the newly-established European System of Financial Supervisors and the European Systemic Risk Council.
10 This section draws on Chapter 4 of Rana and Dowling (2009).

11 D-8 PTA members are Bangladesh, Egypt, Iran, Malaysia, Nigeria, Pakistan, Indonesia and Turkey.
12 This requires a formidable set of reforms to: (i) tackle disparities among various social groups; (ii) improve the environment; (iii) eliminate pervasive infrastructure bottlenecks; (iv) renew education, technological development and innovation; (v) transform the delivery of public services especially in cities (vi) revolutionize energy production and consumption; and (vi) foster a prosperous South Asia and become a responsible global power.

Chapter 12 Reform of International Financial Architecture: Progress and Remaining Agenda

1 Kawai (2010) notes that there were at least nine capital account crises in the 1990s: Mexico (February 1995), Argentina (April 1995; March 2000–January 2003), Thailand (August 1997), Indonesia (November 1997–January 1998–August 1998–February 2000), South Korea (December 1997), Russia (August 1998), Brazil (December 1998), and Turkey (December 1999–February 2002).
2 For example, several provisions in the Basel II framework encouraged banks to decrease the amount of capital they held during business cycle expansions and increase them during contractions.
3 The IMF's core areas of responsibility include: macroeconomic stabilization; monetary, fiscal and exchange rate policy, including the underlying institutional arrangements and closely related structural measures; and financial sector issues including the functioning of both domestic and international financial markets.
4 Old mindsets, lax supervision, greed and cronyism were the roots of both the Asian financial crisis and the global economic crisis.
5 For example, facing imminent collapse of Icelandic banks, UK supervisors ring-fenced Icelandic bank assets to assure that liabilities in the UK were met.
6 The Turner report for the UK and the Larosiere report for the European Union have highlighted the need for "macro prudential monitoring". The European Union has also set up the European Systemic Risks Board to conduct such an analysis.
7 "Senior figures call for a new Bretton Woods ahead of Bank/Fund meetings" http://www/eurodad.org/whatsnew/articles.asp?id=2988.
8 "World needs new Bretton Woods, says Brown" AFP 13 October 2008 (http://afp.google.com/article).
9 "European call for 'Bretton Woods II'", *Financial Times*, 16 October 2008.
10 These include – strengthening the derivatives market; reducing the pro-cyclicity of regulatory policies; reviewing global accounting standards; reviewing compensation practices of financial institutions; reviewing the mandates, governance, and resource requirements of international financial institutions; and broadening the membership of the Financial Stability Forum.
11 Working Group I, Enhancing Sound Regulation and Strengthening Transparency; Working Group II, Reinforcing International Cooperation and Promoting Integrity in Financial Markets; Working Group III, Reforming the IMF; Working Group IV, World Bank and other multilateral banks.
12 The amount requested by the BRICs was 7%.
13 Another reason for the collapse of the Bretton Woods system was the Impossible Trinity Theory under which one cannot have all three polices at once – capital mobility, monetary autonomy and pegged exchange rates. Under the

Bretton Woods system, pegged rates and monetary autonomy was selected together with capital controls. This system worked until the early 1970s when it collapsed because cross-border capital mobility had increased considerably.

14 Akyuz (2009) and Eichengreen (2009) have suggested that a "global reserve system" could also be established by expanding the scope of the existing system of SDRs. They make the case for "commercializing" the SDR. This means allowing other entities besides the IMF (such as governments and banks) to issue SDRs and allowing SDRs to be bought and sold freely.

15 This "peer review" process is historic because aside from the Trade Policy Review Body of the WTO where peer review of trade policies is conducted, there is no institution where representatives of both the industrial and the developing world sit across or around the table to conduct a peer review of macroeconomic or financial sector policies.

16 A third way that the G20 could be made more inclusive is through the involvement of the United Nations. The Sitglitz Commission notes that decisions concerning necessary reforms to the IFA must not be made by a self-selected group (such as the G7, G8, or the G20) but all countries of the world, working in concert. Better representation and democratic legitimacy would not require the presence of all countries in all deliberations. Working committees chosen by a democratic process could be limited to a size that ensures effective decision-making (UN, 2009). This proposal merits further consideration.

References

Abu-Qarn, A.S. and S. Abu-Bader. 2007. "Getting Income Shares Right: A Panel Data Investigation for OECD Countries", Discussion Paper No. 07-01, Monaster Center for Economic Research, Ben-Gurion University of the Negev, Israel.

Ahmed, Nazneen. 2006. "Bangladesh Institute of Development Studies (BIDS), Ad hoc Expert Meeting in preparation for the Mid-Term Review of the Programme of Action for the Least Developed Countries for the Decade 2001–2010", Geneva, 29–30 May 2006.

Akerlof, G.A. and R. Shiller. 2009. *Animal Spirits: How Human Psychology Drives the Economy, and Why it Matters for Global Capitalism*, Princeton University Press, Princeton, New Jersey and Oxford, UK.

Akyuz, Yilmaz. 2009. "Policy Responses to the Global Financial Crisis: Key Issues for Developing Countries", Conference Paper, ISEAS, Singapore.

Alesina, A.F. and S. Ardagna. 2009. "Large Changes in Fiscal Policy: Taxes versus Spending", NBER Working Paper 15438, October.

Asian Development Bank (ADB). 2008. *Asian Development Outlook 2008*, Manila.

Asian Development Bank (ADB). 2008a. "Food Prices and Inflation in Developing Asia: Is Poverty Reduction Coming to an End?", Manila.

Asian Development Bank (ADB) 2008b. Social Protection Index for Committed Poverty Reduction, Volume 2: Manila.

Asian Development Bank (ADB) 2008c. Food Price Increases and Poverty in the Philippines, Manila.

Asian Development Bank (ADB). 2009. *Asian Development Outlook*, Manila.

Asian Development Bank (ADB). 2009a. *Asian Development Outlook Update*, Manila.

Asian Development Bank (ADB). 2009b. *Nepal: Political and Economic Update*, October, Manila.

Asian Development Bank (ADB). 2009c. *India 2039*, Manila.

Asian Development Bank (ADB). 2009d. *Asian Economic Monitor*, July, Manila.

Asian Development Bank (ADB), Department for International Development (DFID) and International Labour Organization (ILO). 2009. *Country Diagnostics Studies Highlights*, Nepal: Critical Development Constraints, Manila.

Asian Development Bank (ADB), United Nations ESCAP (UNESCAP) and United Nations Development Program (UNDP). 2008. *A Future Within Reach*, Asian Development Bank and United Nations.

Asian Development Bank and United Nations Conference on Trade and Development (ADB/UNCTAD). 2008. *Quantification of Benefits from Economic Cooperation in South Asia*, Macmillan, New York.

Athukorala, Prema-chandra and Pang-long Tsai. 2003. "Determinants of Household Saving in Taiwan: Growth, Demography and Public Policy", *Journal of Development Studies*, 39(5): 65–88.

Balakrishnan, R., S. Danninger, S. Elekdag and I. Tytell. 2009. "The Transmission of Financial Stress from Advanced to Emerging Economies", IMF Working Paper WP/09/133.

Bauer, A. 2009. "The Social Impacts of the Global Economic Crisis on the Poor and Vulnerable People in Asia", Background paper for Policy Forum on Labor Market Policy Responses to the Global Financial and Economic Crisis with Special Reference to Developing Countries, Asian Development Bank.

Bauer, A., R. Hasan, R. Magsombol and G. Wan. 2008. "The World Bank's New Poverty Data: Implications for the Asian Development Bank", *ADB Sustainable Development World Paper Series* No. 2, Manila, ADB.

Baulch, Bob, Joe Wood and Axel Weber. 2006. "Developing a Social Protection Index for Asia", *Development Policy Review*, 24(1): 5–29.

deBeck, Reinout. 2010. "The Composition and Cyclical Behavior of Trade Flows in Emerging Economies", IMF Working Paper 10/46, International Monetary Fund, Washington DC.

Bergsten, C. 2007. "Toward a Free Trade Area of the Asia Pacific". Policy Briefs in International Economics 07-2, Peterson Institute for International Economics, Washington DC.

Blanchard, Oliver. 2008. "The Crisis: Basic Mechanisms and Appropriate Policies", IMF Working Paper 80.

Blanchard, Oliver. 2009. "Sustaining a Global Recovery", *Finance and Development*, September, World Bank.

Blanchard, O. and Giavanni, F. 2006. "Rebalancing Growth in China: A Three Handed Approach", *China and World Economy*, 14(4): 1–20.

Bloomberg News. February 6, 2010. "Group of Seven Vows to Keep Cash Flowing".

Bloomberg News. December 29, 2009.

Boggs, C.J. 2010. "Credit Default Swaps: AIG's Unregulated Killer?" MyNewMarkets. com at http://mynewmarkets.com

Buiter, W. 2009. "Buiter on Emerging Markets – Crisis Talk". Available at http://crisistalk.worldbank.org/2009/05/buiter-on-emerging-markets.html

Burki, Shahid Javed. 2009. "South Asia's Public Choices in a Fluid World". Institute of South Asian Studies, Working Paper No. 83.

Business Monitor Online. *Emerging Market Outlook* (online database). Available at www.businessmonitor.com/bmo/

Caldes, N., D. Coady and John A. Maluccio. 2004. "The Cost of Poverty Alleviation Transfer Programs: A Comparative Analysis of Three Programs in Latin America. Food Consumption and Nutrition", FCND Discussion Paper 172, IFPRI, Washington DC.

Calomiris, Charles W. and Peter J. Wallison. 2008. "Blame Fannie Mae and Congress For the Credit Mess", *Wall Street Journal*, September 23, 2008.

Capistrano, L.O. and M.L.C. Sta. Maria. 2007. "The Impact of International Labor Migration and OFW Remittances on Poverty in the Philippines", Mimeo Paper, School of Economics, University of the Philippines, Quezon City.

Carnegie Endowment for International Peace. 2010. "Happy New Year? The World Economy in 2010", Tuesday January 5, 2010, Washington DC.

Case-Shiller Home Price Index. Available at www.standardandpoors.com/home/en/us

Center for Responsible Lending. 2007. "A Snapshot of the subprime Market", November 28. Available at www.responsiblelending.org/mortgage-lending/tools-resources/snapshot-of-the-subprime-market.pdf

Centre for Science and Environment. 2008. "NREGA: Opportunities and Challenges". http://www.cseindia.org/programme/nrml/pdf/NREGA_Policy_Paper_2008.pdf

Chhibber, A., Jayati Ghosh and Thangavel Palanivel. 2009. *The Global Financial Crisis and the Asia-Pacific Region: A Synthesis Study Incorporating Evidence from Country Case Studies*, UNDP Regional Centre for Asia and the Pacific, UNDP.

Chou Shin-Yi, Jin-Tan Liu, and James K. Hammitt. 2003. "National Health Insurance and Precautionary Saving: Evidence from Taiwan", *Journal of Public Economics*, 87: 1873–94.

Chou Shin-Yi, Jin-Tan Liu, and James K. Hammitt. 2006. "Households' Precautionary Behaviors – the Effects of the Introduction of National Health Insurance in Taiwan", *Review of Economics of the Household*, 4: 395–421.

Chowdhury, Anis and Iyantul Islam. 1993. *The Newly Industrialising Economies of East Asia*, Routledge, London.

Chronic Poverty Research Center (CPRC). 2008. *The Chronic Poverty Report 2008–09*. Chronic Poverty Research Centre, University of Manchester.

CIA Factbook. 2008. Available at https://www.cia.gov/library/publications/the-world-factbook/geos/pk.html

Citibank. 2009. *Asian Economic Outlook and Strategy*, January.

CLSA. 2009. *Eye on Asian Economies*. Available at www.clsa.com

Coady, D., R. Perez and H. Vera-Ilamas. 2005. "Evaluating the Cost of Poverty Alleviation Transfer Programs: An Illustration base on PROGRESA in Mexico". Food Consumption and Nutrition Division, FCND Discussion Paper No. 199, IFPRI, Washington DC.

Congressional Budget Office (CBO). 2009. *January 2009 Budget and Economic Outlook*. Congress of the United States.

Consensus Economics. 2009. Available at http://www.consensuseconomics.com/global_economic_outlook.htm

Dahlberg, E. 2005. "Insights into migration and spending patterns based on a small-scale study of garment workers in Phnom Penh", Working Paper 221, Stockholm School of Economics, December 2005.

Davidson, Adam. 2008. "How AIG fell apart", Reuters, 18 September 2008. Available at http://www.reuters.com/articlePrint?articleId=USMAR85972720080918

Davies, Ken. 2009. "While global FDI falls, China's outward FDI doubles", *Columbia FDI Perspectives* No. 5, May 26, 2009, Vale Columbia Center on Sustainable International Investment.

Devan, J., M. Rowland and J. Woetzel. 2009. "A Consumer Paradigm for China", *McKinsey Quarterly*, Number 4. Available at http://www.mckinseyquarterly.com/A_consumer_paradigm_for_China_2429

Diokno, B. 2009. "Calibrated Boldness?", *BusinessWorld*, 30 April.

Dowling, J.M. 2008. *Future Perspectives on the Economic Development of Asia, Vol 5 in Advanced Research in Asian Economic Studies*, World Scientific Publishing, Singapore.

Dowling, J.M. and Yap Chin Fang. 2009. *Chronic Poverty in Asia: Causes, Consequences and Policies*, World Scientific Publishing Company, Singapore.

Economics Intelligence Unit. 2009. Country Report July.

Economics Intelligence Unit. 2009a. Downloaded from website eiu.com and eiu.bvdep.com

Economics Intelligence Unit. 2010. Country Reports.

The Economist, various issues. Available at www.economist.com

Eichengreen, Barry. 2009. "Out of the Box thoughts about the International Financial Architecture", IMF Working Paper WP/09/116.

Eichengreen, B. and O'Rourke. 2009. "A Tale of Two Depressions: What do the New Data Tell Us?". Available at http://www.voxeu.org/index.php?q=note/3421

Euroframe. 2009. Available at http://www.euroframe.org/

Ewing, Jack. 2010. "European Central Bank's Tough Balancing Act", *The New York Times,* January 13.

Fallon, Peter and Robert Lucas. 2002. "The Impact of Financial Crises on Labor markets, Household Incomes and Poverty: A Review of Evidence", *World Bank Research Observer*, 17(1): 21–45.

Federal Reserve Bank of Minneapolis. 2010. "The Recession and Recovery in Perspective". Available at http://www.minneapolisfed.org/publications_papers/studies/recession_perspective/index.cfm

Federal Reserve Bank of San Francisco. 2009. Economic Letter, February 6, 2009, House Prices and Bank Loan Performance.

Felipe, J. and G.C. Sipin. 2004. "Competitiveness, Income Distribution and Growth in the Philippines: What Does the Long Run Evidence Show?", ERD Working Paper No. 53, Asian Development Bank.

Financial Times. 16 October 2008. "European call for 'Bretton Woods II'".

Francois, Joseph, Pradumna B. Rana and Ganeshan Wignaraja (eds). 2009. *Pan-Asian Integration*, Palgrave Macmillan.

G20 Leaders' Statement, London Summit, 2 April 2009. Available at www.g20.org

G20 Leaders' Statement, Pittsburgh Summit, 24–25 September 2009. Available at www.g20.org

Geithner, Timothy. 2008. Reducing Systemic Risk in a Dynamic Financial System, Federal Reserve Bank of New York, June 2008. Available at http://www.ny.frb.org/newsevents/speeches/2008/tfg080609.html

Ghosh, Atish. 2006. "Capital Account Crises: Lessons for Crisis Prevention". Paper prepared for the High Level Seminar on Crisis Prevention, Singapore, July 10–11, 2006, International Monetary Fund.

Ghosh, A., M. Chamon, C. Crowe, Jun I. Kim and J.D. Ostry. 2009. "Coping with the Crisis: Policy Options for Emerging Market Countries", IMF Staff Position Note, April 23.

Gill, I. and Homi Kharas. 2007. *An East Asian Renaissance: Ideas for Economic Growth*, World Bank, Washington DC.

Goh Chok Tong. 2006. "Towards an East Asian Renaissance". Address at the opening session of the 4th Asia-Pacific Roundtable organized by the Global Foundation, the World Bank and the Institute of Southeast Asian Studies.

Gordon, R.J. 2009. "US Recovery in May? Can Unemployment Claims Predict the End of the Recession?'. Available at www.voxeu.org/index.php?q=mode/2524

Graves, Philip E. 2009. "The WTA-WTP Gap and Welfare Measures for Public Goods", The Selected Works of Philip E Graves. Available at http://works.bepress.com/philip_graves/41

Gunatilaka Ramani, Guanghua Wan and Shiladitya Chatterjee. 2009. *Poverty and Human Development in Sri Lanka*, Asian Development Bank, Manila.

Guo, Kai and Papa N'Diaye. 2009. "Is China's Export-Oriented Growth Sustainable?", IMF Working Paper 172, August.

Hasan, R., M.R. Magsombol and J.S. Cain. 2009. "Poverty Impact of the Economic Slowdown in Developing Asia: Some Scenarios", ADB Economics Working Paper Series 153, Asian Development Bank.

Hedrik-Wong, Yuwa. 2010. Quoted in *The Economist* January 21, 2010. Available at http://www.economist.com/business-finance/economics-focus/displaystory.cfm?story_id=15328875

Hong, K., J-W Lee and H.C. Tang. 2009. "Crises in Asia: Historical Perspectives and Implications", ADB Economics Working Paper 152.

India. Various Years. *Population Census*. New Delhi: Office of the Registrar General.

Institute of International Finance. 2009. Available at http://www.iif.com/

International Food Policy Research Institute (IFPRI). 2008. "Global Hunger Index", Washington DC.

International Labour Organization (ILO). 2009. *Global Employment Trends*, May Update.

International Labour Organization (ILO). 2009a. "Asia in the Global Economic Crisis: Impacts and Responses from a Gender Perspective: Technical Note for Responding to the Economic Crisis – Coherent Policies for Grow, Employment and Decent Work in Asia and the Pacific", Manila, Philippines, 18–20 February 2009.

International Labour Organization (ILO). 2009b. *Global Employment Trends for Women*, March.

International Labour Organization (ILO). 2009c. *Global Employment Trends Report*, Geneva.

International Monetary Fund (IMF). 2005. "United States: Staff Report for 2005 Article IV Consultation", June 30, Washington DC.

International Monetary Fund (IMF). 2006. "United States: Staff Report for 2006 Article IV Consultation", June 30, Washington DC.

International Monetary Fund (IMF). 2007. "United States: Staff Report for 2007 Article IV Consultation", July 11, Washington DC.

International Monetary Fund (IMF). 2008. *World Economic Outlook*, October.

International Monetary Fund (IMF). 2008a. *World Economic Outlook,* Update November.

International Monetary Fund (IMF). 2009. *World Economic Outlook*, April.

International Monetary Fund (IMF). 2009a. *World Economic Outlook* Update, July 8.

International Monetary Fund (IMF). 2009b. *World Economic Outlook*, October.

International Monetary Fund (IMF). 2009c. *Regional Economic Outlook,* Asia and Pacific, May.

International Monetary Fund (IMF). 2009d. *World Economic Outlook*, October.

International Monetary Fund (IMF). 2009e. *Global Development Finance*, Chapter 3.

International Monetary Fund (IMF). 2009f. Country Report 09/263 Republic of Korea: Selected Issues, Washington DC.

International Monetary Fund Independent Evaluation Office. 2003. "The IMF and Recent Capital Account Crisis: Indonesia, Korea and Brazil". International Monetary Fund, Washington DC.

James, W.E., Donghyun Park, Shikha Jha, Juthathip Jongwanich, Akiko Terada-Hagiwara and Lea Sumulong. 2008. "The US Financial Crisis, Global Financial Turmoil, and Developing Asia: Is the Era of High Growth at an End?", ADB Economics Working Paper Series No. 139, December.

Kashyap, A., R. Rajan, and J. Stein. 2008. "Re-thinking Capital Regulation", paper presented at Jackson Hole Symposium of the Kansas City Fed.

Kawai, M. 2010. "Reform of the International Financial Architecture: An Asian Perspective", *Singapore Economic Review*, 55(1): 207–242.

Kawai, Masahiro and Ganeshan Wignaraja. 2007. "ASEAN+3 or ASEAN+6: Which Way Forward?", Asian Development Bank Institute Discussion Paper 77, Tokyo.

Kawai, Masahiro and Ganeshan Wignaraja. 2009. "Asian FTAs: Trends and Challenges". ADBI Discussion Working paper Series No. 144.

Kawai, M. and M. Pomerleano. 2009. "Bolstering Financial Stability Regulation", Ft.com/economistsforum, 28 August.

Kawai, M. and Pradumna B. Rana. 2009. "The Asian Financial Crisis Revisited: Lessons, Responses, and New Challenges", in Richard Carney (ed.) *Lessons from the Asian Financial Crisis*, Routledge, New York. pp. 155–197.

Klein, L.R. and R.F. Kosobud. 1961. "Some Econometrics of Growth: Great Ratios of Economics", *Quarterly Journal of Economics*, 75: 173–198.

Knight, Frank. 2009. "Global Housing Price Index – Quarter 1 2009". Available at http://www.zawya.com/story.cfm/sidZAWYA20090528053252

Krugman, Paul. 2010. Chinese New Year, January 1, 2010 *New York Times*.

Krugman, Paul. 2009. *The Return of Depression Economics and the Crisis of 2008*, WW Norton and Co., New York.

Krugman, Paul. 2009a. 'That '30s Show", *The New York Times*, Thursday, July 3.

Krugman, Paul. 2009b. "Age of Diminished Expectations", *The New York Times*, December 28.

Krugman, Paul. 2009c. "The Incomparable Economist", *The New York Times*, December 15.

Krugman, P. and M. Obsfeld. 2009. *International Economics: Theory and Policy*, Pearson Education.

Kumar, Rajiv and Pankaj Vashisht. 2009. "The Global Economic Crisis: Impact on India and Policy Responses", ADBI Working Paper Series No. 164, November 2009, Asian Development Bank Institute.

Labonte, M. and G. Makinen. 2002. "The Current Economic Recession: How Long, How Deep and How Different from the Past", Congressional Research Service, Library of Congress, Washington DC.

Leonhardt, D. 2009. "As Economy Turns, Washington Looks Better", *The New York Times*, August 8.

Lipton, M. 1988. "Rural Development and the Retention of the Rural Population in the Countryside of Developing Countries", in J. Havet (ed.) *Staying On: Retention and Migration in Peasant Societies*. Ottawa University Press, Ottawa, Ontario.

Lokshin, M., M. Bontch-Osmolovski and E. Glinskaya. 2007. "Work-related Migration and Poverty Reduction in Nepal". World Bank Policy Research working Paper No 4231, World Bank, Washington DC.

Mahbubani, K. 2008. "The New Asian Hemisphere: The Irresistible Shift of Global Power to the East", Public Affairs.

Mahmood, M. and G. Aryah. 2001. "The Labor Market and Labor Policy in a Macroeconomic Context: Growth, Crisis and Competitiveness in Thailand", in G. Betcherman and R. Islam (eds) *East Asian Labor Markets and the Economic Crisis. Impacts, Responses and Lessons*, Washington DC, ILO and World Bank.

Malaysian Institute of Economic Research (MIER). 2009. Available at www.mier.org.my

Market Oracle. 2009. Available at http://www.marketoracle.co.uk

Mathieu, J., Ashok J. Gadgil, Kristin Kowolik and Susan E.A. Addy. 2008. "Removing Arsenic from Contaminated Drinking Water in Rural Bangladesh: Recent Fieldwork Results and Policy Implications", paper presented at 2008 UNC Environmental Symposium on Safe and Sustainable Drinking Water in developing and Developed Countries: Where Science Meets Policy, Chapel Hill, NC, November 5–6.

McKinsey Global Institute. 2010. *Debt and Deleveraging: The Global Credit Crisis and its Economic Consequences*, McKinsey and Company.

Menzie Chinn. 2009, May 29. "More Thoughts on Potential GDP and Output Gap", in Global Macro EconoMonitor. Available at http://www.rgemonitor.com.global-macro-monitor/256934/more_thoughts_on_potential_gdp_and_the_output_gap

Milkin Institute. 2009. "Mortgage Crisis Overview". Available at http://www.scribd.com/doc/6371820/Milken-Insitute-Mortgage-Crisis-Overview

Mody, Ashoka and Franziska Ohnsorge. 2010. "After the Crisis: Lower Consumption Growth but Narrower Global Imbalances?", IMF Working Paper WP/10/11.

Monetary Authority of Singapore (MAS). 2007. *Asian Financial and Monetary Integration: Challenges and Prospects*, Singapore.

The New York Times. February 6, 2010.

Niimi, Yoko and Barry Reilly. 2008. "Gender Differences in Remittance Behavior: Evidence from Viet Nam", ADB Economics Working Paper Series No. 135, November.

Nishimura, K. 2008. "A Proposal for Public Capital Insurance", unpublished manuscript, Bank of Japan.

Nomura Securities. 2009. *Global Outlook*, Tokyo, Japan.

OECD Composite Leading Indicators. 2009. Downloaded August 8, OECD web site http://stats.oecd.org/Index.asoz?datasetcode=MEI_CLI

OECD. 2009. *Economic Outlook*, Interim Report, May, OECD Paris.

OECD. 2009a. *Economic Outlook*, May, OECD Paris.

OECD. 2009b. *Economic Outlook*, November, OECD Paris.

OECD. 2009c. *International Migration Outlook*, June, OECD Paris.

OECD. 2009d. OECD Database.

Oxford Economics. 2009. "Emerging Asian Fiscal Policy: A Limited Boost but China Could Yet Do More". *Emerging Market Weekly*.

Panagariya, A. 2006. "India and China: Trade and Foreign Investment", paper presented at the Pan Asia Conference on Challenges of Economic Policy Reform in Asia.

Panagariya, A. 2009. "India's Financial Secret Weapon", Brooking Institute. Available at http://www.brookings.edu/articles/2009/01_india_financial_crisis_panagariya.aspx

Park, Y.C. 2009. "The Global Economic Crisis and Rebalancing Growth in East Asia", ADBI Research Policy Brief 31, Asian Development Bank Institute, Tokyo.

Peopleandplanet.net. 2010. Available at http://www.peopleandplanet.net/graphs/Megacities.PNG

Pernia, E.M. 2007. "Migration, Remittances, Poverty and Inequality: the Philippines", mimeo.

Pholphirul, Piriya. 2005. "Competitiveness, Income Distribution, and Growth in Thailand: What Does the Long-run Evidence Show?", *Thailand Development Research Institute*, Bangkok, Thailand.

Phelps, E.S. 1961. "The Golden Rule of Capital Accumulation", *American Economic Review*, 51: 638–643.

Prasad, E.S. 2009. "Rebalancing Growth in Asia", Working Paper 15169, National Bureau of Economic Research. Available at http://www.nber.org/papers/w15169

Prasad, E.S. and E. Sorkin. 2009. "Assessing the G-20 Stimulus Plans: A Deeper Look", Brookings Institution, March.

Prasad, Eswar and Raghuram Rajan. 2006. "Modernizing China's Growth Paradigm", *American Economic Review*, 96(2): 331–336.

Rana, Pradumna B. 2007. "Economic Integration and Synchronization of Business Cycles in East Asia", *Journal of Asian Economics*, 18 (October): 711–725.

Rana, Pradumna B. 2008. "Trade Intensity and Business Cycle Synchronization: The Case of East Asian Countries", *Singapore Economic Review*, 53(2): 279–292.

Rana, Pradumna B. 2009. "Integration and 'Re-centering' of Asia – Historical and Contemporary Perspectives", Institute of South Asian Studies Working Paper 86, 2009.

Rana, Pradumna B. and J.M. Dowling. 2009. *South Asia – Rising to the Challenge of Globalization*, World Scientific, Singapore.

Rana, Pradumna B., T. Chen and W.M. Chia. 2009. "Trade Intensity and Business Cycle Synchronization: Europe versus East Asia", (unpublished).

Ravallon, Martin. 2009. "A Comparative Perspective on Poverty Reduction in Brazil, China and India", Policy Research Working Paper 5080, World Bank, Washington DC.

Ravallion, M. and M. Chen. 1997. "What Can New Survey Data Tell Us about Recent Changes in Distribution and Poverty?", *The World Bank Economic Review*, 11: 357–382.

Reinhart, C. and K. Rogoff. 2008. "Is the US Sub-Prime Financial Crisis So Different? An International Comparison", NBER Working Paper 13761, NBER Massachusetts.

Save the Children website. 2006. Available at http://www.savethechildren.org/
Singapore Department of Statistics. 1998. *Income Components of GDP: Trends and Analysis*, Singapore.
Streitfeld, David. 2009. "The House Trap", *New York Times*, September 8th.
Swinkels, R. and C. Turk. 2006. "Explaining Ethnic Minority Poverty in Vietnam: A Summary of Recent Trends and Current Challenges". Draft Background paper for CEM/MPI meeting on Ethnic Minority Poverty, Hanoi, 28 September.
Taiwan, Council for International Economic Cooperation and Development, Executive Yuan. 2008. *Taiwan Statistical Data Book*. Taipei.
te Velde, D.W., I. Massa and M. Cali. 2009. *The Global Financial Crisis and Developing Countries: Synthesis of the Findings of 10 Country Case Studies*, Working Paper 306, ODI, London.
Tell, Gillian and Paul J. Davies. 2007. "Out of the Shadows: How Banking's Secrecy System Broke Down", *Financial Times*, December 16, 2007.
Thaler, R.H. and C.R. Sunstein. 2009. *Nudge*, Penguin, New York.
UNCTAD. 2009. *World Investment Prospects Survey 2009–2011*, United Nations, Geneva.
UNDP. 2008. *Human Development Index*, United Nations, Geneva.
UNESCAP. 2004. *Economic and Social Survey of Asia and the Pacific*, United Nations ESCAP, Bangkok, Thailand.
UNESCAP. 2009. *Economic and Social Survey of Asia and the Pacific*, United Nations ESCAP, Bangkok, Thailand.
UNICEF. 2009. "Impact of the Economic Crisis on Children", Conference Report, 6–7 January, Singapore.
United Nations. 2008. *Report of the Secretary-General on the Indicators for Monitoring the Millennium Development Goals*. E/CN.3/2008/29, New York.
United Nations. 2009. *World Economic Situation and Prospects*, United Nations, New York.
United Nations. 2009a. "Report of the Commission of Experts of the President of the UN General Assembly on Reforms of the International Monetary and Financial System", New York, 12 September (Stiglitz Commission Report).
United Nations. 2009b. World Food Programme. Internal release 26 May 2009, "Bangladesh Effects of the Financial Crisis on Vulnerable Households".
United Nations. 2009c. Department of Economic and Social Affairs. Expert Group Meeting on the World Economy (Project LINK) 26–28 October 2009, Bangkok, Thailand.
US Bureau of Labor Statistics. 2010. Available at www.bls.gov
US Department of Energy. 2010. United States Energy Information Administration, Gasoline and Diesel fuel update.
Vietnam Academy of Social Sciences (VASS). 2007. *Vietnam Poverty Update Report: Poverty and Poverty Reduction in Vietnam 1993–2004*, Vietnam Academy of Social Sciences, Hanoi.
Wassener, Bettina. 2009. "Finance Jobs Hint at Recovery in Asia", *The New York Times*. September.
Weerakoon, Dushni. 2008. "SAFTA: Current Status and Prospects", Institute of Policy Studies of Sri Lanka, Colombo.
Weller, C. and J. Lynch. 2009. "Household Wealth in Freefall", Center for American Progress. Available at http://www.americanprogress.org/issues/2009/04/household_wealth.html
Wolf, Martin. 2010. "The World Has No Easy Way Out of the Mire", *Financial Times* February 23.

Wood, J. 2009. "A Social Protection Index for Asia". Paper for presentation in the Association for Public Policy Analysis and Management Conference on Asian Social Protection in Comparative Perspective, 7–9 January, 2009, National University of Singapore, Singapore.

Woodward, Susan. 2007. "A Study of Closing Costs for FHA Mortgages", US Department of Housing and Urban Development, Office of Policy Development and Research.

World Bank. 2000. *World Development Report*, Oxford University Press, New York.

World Bank. 2004. *Trade Policies in South Asia: An Overview*, Report No. 29929, Washington DC.

World Bank. 2006. *South Asia: The End of Poverty*, Washington DC. Available at http://go.worldbank.org/DZVHB0C0P0

World Bank. 2007. *Sri Lanka Poverty Assessment – Engendering Growth with Equity: Opportunities and Challenges*, World Bank, Washington DC.

World Bank. 2009. "Key Development Data and Statistics", World Bank. Available at http://data.worldbank.org/data-catalogue.

World Bank. 2009a. *Global Development Finance*, World Bank, Washington DC.

World Bank. 2009b. *Global Monitoring Report*, World Bank, Washington DC.

World Bank. 2009c. *The Global Economic Crisis: Assessing Vulnerability with a Poverty Lens*. Available at http://siteresources.worldbank.org/NEWS/Resources/WBGVulnerability CountriesBrief.pdf

World Bank. 2009d. *Impact of the Financial Crisis on Women, Children and Vulnerability*, Washington DC. Available at http://www.worldbank.org/html/extdr/financialcrisis/pdf/Women-Children-Vulnerability-March09.pdf.

World Bank. 2009e. *Transforming the Rebound into Recovery*, East Asia and Pacific Update, November, World Bank, Washington DC.

World Bank. 2009f. *Philippines: Country Brief July*. Available at http://go.worldbank.org/146KPP1UA0

World Bank. 2009g. *Thailand: Economic Monitor*, November, World Bank, Washington DC.

World Bank. 2009h. *China Quarterly*, October 2009, World Bank, Washington DC.

World Bank. 2009i. *Nepal Country Overview*, World Bank, Washington DC.

World Bank. 2010. *World Development Indicators Online*. World Bank, Washington DC.

World Bank. 2010a. *Global Economic Prospects: Crisis, Finance and Growth*. World Bank, Washington DC.

Xu, Gao. 2010. State-owned Enterprises in China: How Big are They? Available at http://blogs.worldbank.org/eastasiapacific/state-owned-enterprises-in-china-how-big-are-they

Zandi, Mark. 2009. *Financial Shock. Global Panic and Government Bailouts – How We Got Here and What Must be Done to Fix It*, FT Press, Upper Saddle River, New Jersey.

Zhou, X. 2009. "Reform of the International Monetary System", People's Bank of China.

Website

http://www.bihartimes.com/poverty/anup.html

Index